Ethnic Cleansing in the Balkans

This book looks at the phenomenon of ethnic cleansing in the Balkans over the last two hundred years. It argues that the events of the last two centuries can be demystified, that the South East of Europe was not destined to become violent and that construction of the Balkans as endemically violent misses an important political point and historical point.

Ethnic Cleansing in the Balkans argues that ethnic cleansing is a problem that is linked to nationalism rather than being a Balkan phenomenon *per se*. As nationalism spread from Central Europe to the Ottoman regions of Europe, national ideologies replaced the older religious and political affiliations. Muslims came to be regarded as potentially disloyal minorities in Bosnia and elsewhere. In addition, national divisions harking back to the Middle Ages divided the other ethnic groups, who became increasingly mutually antagonistic, eventually leading to minorities being persecuted and driven out, with many victims mistreated and murdered in a demonstrably cruel fashion. Although the acts were often carried out in 'traditional' ways (and have sometimes been described as archaic and primitive), the force behind these acts was a very modern one. At the beginning of the twenty-first century, there are very few multiethnic regions left in South Eastern Europe and large diaspora communities of ethnically cleansed peoples.

Carmichael provides an account of ethnic cleansing in the Balkans as a single historical phenomenon and brings together a vast array of primary and secondary sources to produce a concise and accessible argument. This book will be of interest to students and researchers of European studies, history and comparative politics.

Cathie Carmichael teaches at the University of East Anglia, where she is Lecturer of European History. She studied International History at the London School of Economics, Ethnology at the University of Ljubljana and European Studies at the University of Bradford. For the spring semester of 2002, she was Mildred Miller Fort Visiting Scholar in European Studies at Columbus State University, Georgia. She has written a number of articles on popular culture in South Eastern Europe and is co-author of *Slovenia and the Slovenes* and co-editor of *Language and Nationalism in Europe*.

Routledge Advances in European Politics

Ethnic Cleansing in the Balkans

Nationalism and the destruction of tradition

Cathie Carmichael

Routledge
Taylor & Francis Group

LONDON AND NEW YORK

First published 2002
by Routledge
2 Park Square, Milton Park, Abingdon, Oxon, OX14 4RN

Simultaneously published in the USA and Canada
by Routledge
270 Madison Ave, New York NY 10016

Routledge is an imprint of the Taylor & Francis Group

Transferred to Digital Printing 2009

© 2002 Cathie Carmichael

Typeset in Baskerville by M Rules

British Library Cataloguing in Publication Data
A catalogue record for this book is available from the British Library

Library of Congress Cataloging in Publication Data
Carmichael, Cathie, 1964–
    Ethnic cleansing in the Balkans: nationalism and the destruction of
tradition / Cathie carmichael.
      p.   cm.
    Published simultaneously in the USA and Canada.
    Includes bibliographical references and index.
    1. Nationalism – Balkan Pensinsula – History.   2. Balkan
Peninsula – Ethnic relations – History.   3. Population transfers.
   4. Ethnic relations – Religious aspects.   I. Title.
    DR38.2 .C37 2002
    305.8'09496 – dc 21   2002069881

ISBN 0-415-27416-8

Contents

Plates

Acknowledgements

I was prompted to write this book after discussions with MA Nationalism, Society and Culture students at Middlesex University. I would also like to acknowledge the support of my colleagues in the School of Humanities and Cultural Studies for giving me research leave to write it. The administrative team at Middlesex has been consistently marvellous and helped the last two academic years go by a little more smoothly. I am grateful to all offered suggestions and/or encouragement along the way. Special thanks go to Cathy Derow, Branko Franolić, Stephanie Schwandner-Sievers, Gabrielle Parker, Brian Williams, Kelly Boyd, Martine Morris, Clive Fleay, Sean Kelsey, Nebojša Čagorović, Igor Biljan, Wendy Bracewell, Alex Drace-Francis, Keith Brown, Milena Mihalski, James Gow, Norah Carlin, Tunç Aybak, Chris Szejnmann, Rada Daniell, Saša Pajević, Divna Malbaša, Tracey Gardner, Anna Davin, Sarah Newman, Peter Vodopivec, Keith McClelland, Pat O'Shea, Vivien Miller, Hakim Adi, Melanie Stockford, Norah Carlin, Linda Wild, Sanja Thompson, Divna Malbaša, Ranka Malbaša, Patrick Rechner, Andy Wood, John Hope Mason, Stephen Barbour, Francine Friedman, Patrick Carmichael and Hunt Tooley. I exchanged ideas and books with my neighbour Mark Thompson. Without his help it would have been a lot harder to write this book. Florian Bieber read the text, offered incisive comments and allowed me to use some of his personal photographs of Bosnia, for which I am grateful. Božidar Jezernik, Bojan Baskar, Rajko Muršič, Jonathan Schwartz, Marko Živkovič, Dejan Djokić, Glenda Sluga, John Allcock and Mehmet Ali Dikerdem all read parts of the book and offered useful suggestions. Djordje Stefanović read much of the penultimate version of the text and offered poignant comments, for which I extend thanks. I would also like to thank the Csontvary Museum, Pecs, Hungary for permission to reproduce 'View of Mostar' and 'Bridge at Mostar over the Neretva' both by Csontvary Kosztka Tivadar. My biggest debt of gratitude is – as always – to my family, particularly David, Win and Christina. Una and John have given me every imaginable kind of support: educational, moral and domestic.

Cathie Carmichael
Oxford
December 2001

Plate 1 View of Mostar (Hercegovina) by Csontvary Kosztka Tivadar, 1903, reproduced with kind permission of the Csontvary Museum, Pecs, Hungary.

The Balkans: Topographical

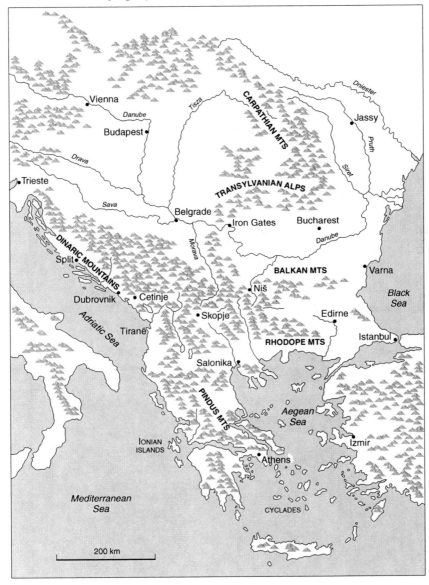

The Balkans in 1878

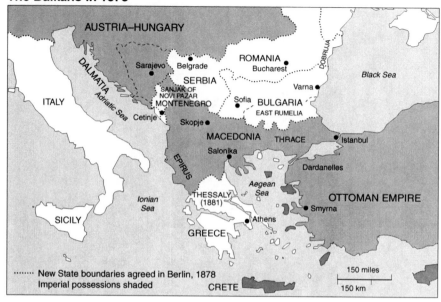

.... New State boundaries agreed in Berlin, 1878
Imperial possessions shaded

150 miles
150 km

The Balkans in 1923

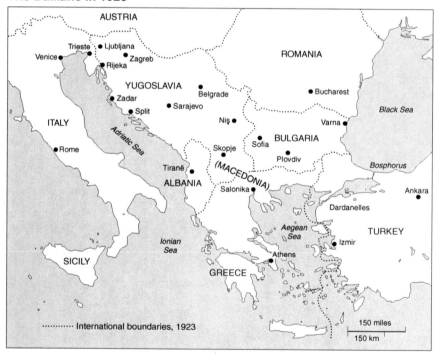

.... International boundaries, 1923

150 miles
150 km

The Balkans in 1942

THIRD REICH

Budapest ●

HUNGARY

Rijeka ●
● Zagreb

HDZ

● Jasenovac

ROMANIA

Belgrade ●

Bucharest ●

Black Sea

Sarajevo ●
Split

SERBIA

ITALY

Adriatic Sea

Dubrovnik
MONTENEGRO
● Cetinje

KOSOVO

Sofia ●

BULGARIA

● Plovdiv

ALBANIA

● Skopje

Edirne ●

Bosphorus
● Istanbul

Tiranë ●

MACEDONIA

Bitola ●

Dardanelles

CORFU

Ionian
Sea

Aegean
Sea

TURKEY

● Izmir

SICILY

● Athens

GREECE

150 miles

········· International boundaries, November 1942

CRETE

150 km

The Balkans in 1945

Vienna ●

AUSTRIA

Budapest ●

HUNGARY

Odessa ●

SLOVENIA
Ljubljana
Venice ●
Trieste

● Zagreb

CROATIA

ROMANIA

Rijeka ●

VOJVODINA

YUGOSLAVIA

Zadar ●

BOSNIA-
HERCEGOVINA
Sarajevo ●

Belgrade ●

SERBIA

Bucharest ●

Black Sea

ITALY

Adriatic Sea

MONTENEGRO
Cetinje ●

KOSOVO

Sofia ● BULGARIA

● Rome

Lezhë ●
Skopje ●

Bosphorus
Istanbul

Tiranë ●
ALBANIA

MACEDONIA

Edirne ●

Dardanelles

Ionian
Sea

GREECE

Aegean
Sea

TURKEY

● Izmir

SICILY

● Athens

········· International boundaries, 1947
– – – Boundaries of republics and
autonomous regions in Yugoslavia

150 miles

CRETE

150 km

The Balkan Peninsula in 2000

- DENMARK
- SWEDEN
  - Copenhagen
- Baltic Sea
- LATVIA
- LITHUANIA
  - Vilnius
- RUSSIA
- RUSSIA
  - Minsk
- BELARUS
- Berlin
- POLAND
  - Warsaw
- GERMANY
- Kiev
- UKRAINE
- Prague
- CZECH REPUBLIC
- SLOVAKIA
  - Bratislava
- Vienna
- MOLDOVA
  - Chişinău
- AUSTRIA
  - Budapest
- HUNGARY
- SLOVENIA
  - Ljubljana
  - Zagreb
- CROATIA
- ROMANIA
  - Belgrade
  - Bucharest
- BOSNIA-HERCEGOVINA
  - Sarajevo
- SERBIA
- ITALY
- Adriatic Sea
- Black Sea
- MONTENEGRO
  - Cetinje
- KOSOVO
- BULGARIA
  - Sofia
- Rome
- Tiranë
  - Skopje
- MACEDONIA
- Salonika
- Istanbul
- ALBANIA
- Tyrrhenian Sea
- GREECE
- TURKEY
- Ionian Sea
- SICILY
  - Athens
- Mediterranean Sea

·············· International boundaries

200 miles

1 Nationalism, violence and the destruction of tradition

Defining and interpreting ethnic cleansing

During the 1990s and the Yugoslavian Wars of Dissolution, fought primarily in Kosovo, Bosnia and Croatia, the term 'ethnic cleansing' was used in the world media to describe the killing and forcible movement of populations deemed to be different on the grounds of their ethnicity, religion or language. It soon entered the standard vocabulary of the English and other languages, but its usage often appears to be both euphemistic and imprecise. This book is an attempt to define what this term might actually mean and to place the events surrounding the practice of ethnic cleansing in a wider geographical and historical context.

In attempting to define ethnic cleansing what is presented here is a study of the impact of nationalism,[1] the formation of new states and the destruction of existing cultures and communities in the region of Europe[2] often referred to as the Balkans.[3] If we accept this term 'Balkans'[4] as being 'tantamount to the Ottoman legacy'[5] in Europe then this geographical term would cover the regions of contemporary Albania, Macedonia, Greece, the Krajina region of Croatia,[6] Serbia, Bulgaria, European Turkey, Montenegro, Bosnia-Hercegovina and Kosovo (and some elements in the historical legacies of Austria, Hungary, Romania and Slovenia). Here we explore some of the reasons why these regions experienced such violent and destructive fratricidal struggles over the last two hundred years and question as to why people deemed to be alien within the new states have been murdered or expelled from the regions they have inhabited for centuries. Throughout the text, the Balkans has been defined as a single historical region and instances of ethnic cleansing as a series of related historical events. This is largely because I have interpreted the origins of the practice of ethnic cleansing as almost entirely ideological. It is not my intention to detract from studies that have focused on single regions or instances of ethnic cleansing or even theses that present these as unrelated phenomena. This study can only be a contribution to an important scholarly and ethical debate that may never be resolved with a single answer, because ultimately what we are dealing with here is the lives of many millions of people, whose own responses to circumstances may be qualitatively different. What the historian can legitimately try to do, however, is to discern if patterns of behaviour have developed over time, while still recognizing the role of the individual. Every case of ethnically inspired murder is unlike any other in important ways, but what interests me here primarily is how and why these events might be deemed to constitute a single phenomenon.

During the last few hundred years, many parts of Europe (and indeed, regions of the globe other colonized by Europeans) have experienced ethnically inspired violence in the wake of state formation which has destroyed, unsettled or damaged older cultures. As a phenomenon it is certainly not restricted to the South East of Europe, nor indeed, as argued in the following chapters, did the ideas that triggered outbreaks of violence even originate there. The extermination of over 90 per cent of Poland's Jews in the early 1940s; the Highland clearances in Scotland in the eighteenth century; the expulsion of ethnic Germans from postwar Czechoslovakia; the transportation of the Crimean Tartars in 1941; the slaughter of Izmir's Greeks and Armenians in the early 1920s; and the exodus of Muslims from the Balkans after the mid-nineteenth century are only a few of the numerous instances of this kind of violence.

Ethnic cleansing has become a broad term,[7] which covers all forms of ethnically inspired violence from murder, rape and torture to forceful removal of populations. In 1993, a United Nations Commission of experts reported to the Security Council that ethnic cleansing involved 'the planned deliberate removal from a specific territory, persons of a particular ethnic group, by force or intimidation, in order to render that area ethnically homogeneous'.[8] As Norman Naimark has stated 'ethnic cleansing bleeds into genocide', suggesting a continuum between the phenomena, and at the present time ethnic cleansing is taking on 'a juridical meaning through the war crimes courts in the Hague, just as genocide was defined by Article II of the United Nations Convention on the Prevention and Punishment of the Crime of Genocide of December 9, 1948'.[9] As Ahmed Akbar has remarked, it has become a 'metaphor for our time'[10] and 'ethnic cleansing' or similar constructions such as the 'cleansing of terrain' was certainly used in the former Yugoslavia in the 1980s and 1990s, drawing on older similar terms by nationalist writers and ideologues. At the Hague Tribunal, Paul Garde described ethnic cleansing as

> a practice which means you act in such a way that, in a given territory, the members of a given ethnic group are eliminated, with the aim that the territory be 'ethnically pure', in other words that it would contain only members of the ethnic group that took the initiative of cleansing the territory.[11]

The perpetrators of such violence are usually clear about their objectives, characteristically constructing the nation in unambiguous terms and anxious to exclude 'non-nationals' and potentially disloyal 'minorities'. The removal of existing populations has clear material benefits for some of those who carry it out: supporters of the regime in postwar Yugoslavia moved into comfortable Slavonian and Istrian homes of the Germans and Italians that they had driven out, creating a 'web of complicity'[12] between themselves and the Communists. This process of appropriation of property occurs continually throughout the period under consideration. Sometimes exchanges have been carried out with a kind of dreadful 'symmetry': in

1995, displaced Croats from Banja Luka in Republika Srpska moved into newly vacated homes in Knin in Croatia previously inhabited by Serbs.

Despite the material advantages to be had from seizing the property of others, the roots of the practice of ethnic cleansing, it is argued here, are more closely tied to ideology. If ethnic cleansing was primarily about greed or a kind of class hatred for those in the community that have better homes or more goods, it is unlikely that it would manifest itself as violence against an ethnic group *per se*. This kind of violence, directed against ethnic communities during times of crisis, has both religious and nationalist origins in European thought and political practice. Christian intolerance of other religions (and of Christians of other denominations in the world of Orthodox/Catholic schism) dates back to before the Middle Ages and was manifested in the Crusades, the persecution of Jews, of Muslims and of religious radicals and heretics, such as Cathars and Anabaptists.[13] From the eighteenth century onwards, consciousness of biological 'race', notions of linguistic fraternity, state-orientated loyalties – the elements that combined to create the ideology generally referred to as nationalism – combined with older prejudices to create the conditions which led to an almost perpetual intolerance of cultural and ethnic diversity and polytaxis (multiple taxonomy or self-identification) in the minds of many Europeans.

Ethnically inspired violence is certainly an integral element of European culture, yet at the same time Europe has also been a home to tolerant cultures, where ethnocentrism is confined to the very edges of society, even if it is not fully eliminated. The zest of ethnic mix in towns like Trieste, Vienna, London, Dublin, Salonika, Paris, Sarajevo or Amsterdam has produced great human achievements and demonstrated that diversity or polytaxis are plausible alternatives to ethnic monoliths. Roy Gutman believes that the old 'Sarajevo with its skyline of minarets, church steeples and synagogues was a testimony to centuries of civilized multiethnic coexistence. It was a place of learning and of commerce: . . . a European jewel.'[14] Although multiethnicity is frequently constructed as a source of structural weakness in the case of the Balkans, it is rarely seen as a weakness when examining contemporary Switzerland or Great Britain.

The interpretation of texts

This book has been written as a form of *histoire-problème*, in the sense that the term was used by the French *Annales* school of historians.[15] In effect, adopting this approach has meant examining ethnic cleansing in the Balkans as a single historical phenomenon or series of phenomena related first and foremost to the spread of nationalist ideas and the collapse of the hegemony of the Ottomans and then subsequently the Habsburgs in this region and the competitions of various state projects that competed to replace this hegemony in the region. As Lucien Febvre once said 'to pose a problem is precisely the beginning and the end of all history. No problems, no history.'[16] The 'problem' that we encounter here is that nationalism as an ideology effectively destroyed alternatives. In the following chapters, I explore some of the reasons why the adherence to the idea of the single nation as opposed to other forms of collectivity was so powerful and in intellectual terms so paradigmatic from the end of the eighteenth century. Its advocates eventually destroyed all the alternatives to nation states: the Ottoman Empire, the Habsburg Monarchy, Royalist Yugoslavia[17] and then in the 1990s the Federal Republic of Yugoslavia. While some of the contemporary Balkan states claim to be Ethno-Federations, at the beginning of the twenty-first century they are certainly far less ethnically mixed than they would have been had population movement and ethnic cleansing not taken place.

Initially, I assumed that the actions of individuals during times of war and ethnic cleansing could be interpreted hermeneutically and that by studying first hand accounts of ethnic cleansing and the atrocities that went with them a great deal about the phenomenon itself would be revealed. Thus, the closer[18] that one could get to the original event, the nearer one would be to understanding what actually took place and why. This approach reveals not only the influence of the French historical school, but of the cultural anthropology of Clifford Geertz, which has proved very influential among historians attempting to decode and interpret past events. Geertz examined single 'events' or 'texts' (most famously cock fighting in Bali) in order to try and discover how certain actions, symbols and signs might convey meaning about the culture that he was describing.[19] The approach of Geertz has been highly influential among historians of popular culture in Europe, including Robert Darnton and Natalie Zemon Davis particularly when examining and decoding pre-modern cultures.

The historical sources pertaining to ethnic cleansing do present us with numerous events (often distressing and horrific) that might require 'decoding' in order to understand the process better. At a military court in Niš in the Federal Republic of Yugoslavia in November 2000, Nebojša Dimitrijević a reservist in the Yugoslavian Army was asked why he had written in his diary entry in late March 1999: 'two persons cleaned up'. What had happened is that two elderly and infirm Albanians, Rukije and Ferez Krasniqi, had refused to leave their homes in the village of Gornja Susica in Kosovo in 1999 and had been shot. The 'cleaning up' referred to the fact that the reservists had then burnt the bodies.[20] In this case, it is almost as if those that have been constructed as disloyal to the Yugoslavian state, in this case the Albanians, were removed in a way that suggests a strong ritualistic element. Given that the Krasniqi were probably Albanianized Serbs (the original surname was probably Krasnić), their 'betrayal' is all the more poignant.

Other events concerning the killing of individuals who have come to represent minorities have a strong symbolic content.[21] A British cleric, Robert Walsh, witnessed attacks against Greeks in Istanbul in the 1820s: a young man was

> forced to his knees by two Turks pressing on his shoulders, and in that position a third came behind him with his kinshal . . . With a single horizontal stroke he severed his head from his neck; his body was thrown into a puddle in the middle of the street for passengers to trample on and his head was laid contemptuously between his thighs.[22]

In this account it appears that the death of the victim (in this case a Greek in Istanbul, who had been identified and equated with the rebel Greeks in the Ottoman Empire) is not the sole point. The act of execution is also highly symbolic with the additional intention of humiliating the essence of the man even after death has actually occurred, on the grounds of his alterity. Decapitation is perhaps one of the most vivid and extreme forms of murder. The Croatian fascist Ustaša persecuted Orthodox priests during the Second World War, especially in the Krajina region, sometimes decapitating their victims.[23] More recently, in 1993 Serb soldiers in Bosnia found the heads of their comrades who had been decapitated by Muslim extremists.[24] When these photographs were published in the Belgrade journal *Vreme*, this must have reminded the readers of the tower of skulls (Čele-kula) that was erected in Niš by the Turks to punish the rebel Serbs in 1809 and tapped into their conscious or unconscious fears of Islamic extremism in whatever form.

Symbolic elements within traditional cultures may be stronger and more 'consistent' as Mary Douglas argued than the 'fragmented' symbolism of more modern societies.[25] Certainly many of the events that are examined in the following pages show evidence of the profound importance of a unitary and consistent symbolism. Even events, which seem to transcend interpretation, such as the horrific torture and murder of the Croat Slavko Ećimović in Prijedor in Bosnia in June 1992, may possibly be examined as part of an analysis of what actually happened, although it would be hard to adequately describe the final moments of a man who must have suffered a great deal before he eventually died. Before he 'disappeared', Slavko's mutilated face in which the eyes had been ripped from the sockets was displayed to the other prisoners. He had also been badly beaten. The sadism of the act was not completely 'random' as he had been an outspoken critic of the local Serb nationalists before his death.[26] His punishment was a very individual and specific one somewhat similar to the treatment of traitors elsewhere.[27] According to Vladimir Dedijer, writing in the Communist newspaper *Borba* in 1941, partisans selected for death by the Četnik Filip Ajdačić were killed in an almost identical fashion.[28] In both cases, this appears to have been a punishment for 'political crimes' and was as brutal as could be imagined. Since Dedijer's diaries were published in the early 1950s and widely available in the former Yugoslavia[29] and other similar material was used by the Communist regime to discredit their former political opponents during the Second World War, it may even be the case that recitations of the events of the 1940s provided a grisly *Urtext* for the 1990s and Ajdačić a model for future 'Četnik' behaviour.[30] When Croatian policemen were murdered in Borovo Selo in May 1991, their bodies were mutilated in the same way as Slavko Ećimović and the victims of Filip Ajdačić. The Croatian public were relayed the information graphically in the newspapers and the 'Serb "enemy within" was now demonized beyond all reason' and referred to openly as 'Chetniks'.[31] In Belgrade, the man who clearly wanted to be seen as the heir to the Četnici, Vojislav Šešelj, boasted that it was his men who had carried out the killings.[32] Later when he was interviewed on Serbian television, Šešelj said that they would use 'rusty shoehorns' to remove the eyeballs of Croats, although he later admitted that this was 'black humour'.[33] But by this time the Croatian public were terrified and begun to pour into Zagreb from the rural regions.

Dedijer and the other writers described the actions of their enemies during the war in the hope that these events would not be repeated and not to create a prototype for acts that would lead to the violent disintegration of Yugoslavia. Nevertheless, texts are powerful things and the circulation of rumours about atrocities served a clear purpose for both sides in the Serb-Croat war of 1991. An actress from Zagreb who performed on the stage in Belgrade was driven out of Croatia by the end of 1991 after receiving threats. 'The people who called her on the phone did not "merely" threaten: they called her a "Chetnik whore", they graphically described in detail how they would torture her to death, which parts of the body they would cut off.'[34]

Symbolic acts of cruelty seem to be a recurrent theme in the ethnic cleansing of the Balkans. In a sense, atrocities might be seen as a general human response to crisis and similar acts of mutilation occurred elsewhere in the last century.[35] But the nature of the atrocity itself may be more culturally specific or at least mean something to the people it is intended to terrify. John Allcock recalled an interview with a Croatian politician who wanted to travel to Borovo Selo in 1991 'in order to acquaint himself directly with the nature of the mutilations alleged to have been inflicted on the Croat victims of the ambush there',[36] suggesting that what had occurred could be interpreted in some way by a non-participant in the event. Christian Giordano has juxtaposed the concepts of 'honour' and 'dignity' and sees these concepts as historically grounded, writing that 'in these (Balkan) societies honour has slowly become less and less important so that it has become an "archaic moment" i.e. an island of tradition, albeit great and important, in a sea of modernity'.[37] One of the primary reasons why these atrocities have been committed in particular ways is that these 'islands of tradition' are still relatively strong in the Balkan context, whereas in more Europeanized societies, they are more fragmented. This is not to say that the state and individuals in the latter countries have jettisoned force, violence and cruelty and banished them to the realms of the past, but it may mean that the importance of the symbolic and the preservation of honour is less and less important if we historicize this problem.

In addition to a hermeneutic interpretation, which has been influenced by the anthropology of Clifford Geertz, the Marxist idea of the 'truth' of the revolutionary crisis, famously used by Leon Trotsky when describing the events of 1905 in the Russian Empire might also have some explanatory value in interpreting the occurrences in question here. Trotsky, an eyewitness, participant and later chronicler of the events surrounding the formation of the first soviets (as well as one of the most important sources on the Balkan Wars in his role as war correspondent), found that the chaos of the revolutionary situation revealed a great deal about the tensions of life before:

> (r)evolution raises the 'normal' insanity of social contradictions to the highest possible tension . . . And yet the entire modern development condenses, strains and accentuates the contradictions and makes them unbearable, consequently preparing the state of mind when the great majority 'goes mad'.[38]

Like revolution, war and crisis also appear to raise 'the normal insanity of social contradictions' and sometimes lead to almost Bakhtinian carnivalesque rites,[39] which either parody the structures and routines of everyday life or are integrated into social events.[40] Sometimes individuals have been killed or violated in an almost 'festive' manner by the perpetrators, who have mocked them and their suffering. A young woman from Liplje in Bosnia reported that she was raped in front of her father by Četnici, one of them shouted to him that he was going to marry her.[11] In such cases, there must surely be some link between incidents of rape and notions of patrimony. In the inverted and terrible world of war and crisis, the father is mocked as his daughter is taken from him by force, but his importance and his presence in the 'transaction' are still acknowledged. In Bosnia in 1992 a dummy, reminiscent perhaps of a scarecrow, was set up at a checkpoint to look like a mutilated corpse.[12] The message again is unambiguous, those manning the checkpoint indicating a willingness to perpetrate such mutilation and torture on the bodies of prisoners. Its display is clearly a deterrent, but is also a symbol of power and ruthlessness, and can be interpreted as an assertion of territorial control, the dummy serving as a warning to transgressors.

When we examine and compare patterns of behaviour during war and crisis elsewhere, it appears that they do tell us a great deal, not only about the human psyche and popular culture, but also about tensions or antagonisms (in the Marxist sense of the word) that are suppressed during peacetime. Joanna Bourke has looked at military culture during the twentieth century in the English-speaking world. Patterns of behaviour among ordinary soldiers indicated that, during fighting, patterns of racial hatred and misogyny emerged – manifested both in their actions against their victims and their attitudes towards each other.[13] These seem to follow clear and predetermined cultural patterns, which might allow us to try to construct a 'method in madness'.[14] In more modernized or Europeanized societies these cultures may be more marginal and fragmented, but nevertheless survive in some manner.

Throughout the initial stages of writing the book, my point of departure was that if patterns of behaviour during the crises of war and ethnic cleansing were examined, they would reveal some 'truths' about societies and cultures in which they occurred. According to this methodological approach, every instance where a Muslim crucified a Christian or vice versa would thus reveal depths of loathing that had been suppressed during peacetime. Every example of theft of property would thus represent long-standing covetousness and every hate text would crystallize rather than simply codify established beliefs and every rape of one neighbour by another would represent unfulfilled fantasies of power over the other that had been sublimated. Such a view is supported by analysis of the pronouncements of those who foment and organize genocide and ethnic cleansing, even if it is not made explicit by its perpetrators. Philip Gourevitch describes how, in the midst of genocide in Rwanda, announcers on *Radio Télévision de Mille Collines* reminded *genocidaires* what awaited them in each Tutsi household they attacked: '. . . the radio, the couch, the goat, the opportunity to rape a young girl'.[15] At the same time, the perpetrators, even after the event, often justified their actions in terms of 'defending the . . . [Hutu] tribe against the Tutsi'.[46] Dubravka Ugrešić projects a similar picture of war in Yugoslavia in the early 1990s being promoted – in the short term at least – as 'an attractive male adventure' comprising 'shooting and shagging, screwing and killing'.[47]

From reading many first-hand accounts of ethnic cleansing, a rather different perspective has emerged that has led me to question some earlier assumptions. If I began with an indexical or diagnostic approach where details spoke to an entire story, then later I found another set of stories that began to change this process of interpretation. Rather than revealing a society or more accurately a number of cultures and societies at their worst, many of these materials seem to indicate that war is experienced as unnatural by the perpetrators of violence as well as the victims. War has destroyed very complex cultures, replacing them with empty social shells. Attempting to inject symbolic value into their actions often reveals, not depths of hatred, but the very shallowness of that emotion. Artificial constructions of hate and alterity need to be continually repeated. If they are not, people will soon return to their old patterns of behaviour.

It is often stated that many of the perpetrators of ethnic crimes in the recent wars in the former Yugoslavia were very ordinary people: it was the crisis that made them into murderers. Sakib Ahmić, a Muslim villager (from Bosnia) 'testified that he had watched the Croat Kupreskić brothers "grow up into decent people" until the fighting began in their village. They broke into his home and murdered his son Naser and daughter-in-law Zehrudina, as well as their children . . .'.[48] Little in their behaviour before the war had indicated that they had even as much as hated their Muslim neighbours, let alone feel so strongly about them that they would murder them. Duško Tadić, a Bosnian Serb who was found guilty of killing his Muslim neighbours, including his former best friend, at the Hague Tribunal clearly had a nationalist worldview before the war started,[49] but his sadism may only have been ignited by propaganda in the preceding months and years and the actions of very few individuals show prejudices before the crisis erupted. The Tribunal recorded the 'violent and cruel way' the murders had been committed and one of the judges remarked: 'You committed these crimes with intention and sadistic brutality.'[50] He was the first person to be convicted of war crimes in Europe since the Second World War, but prior to the Bosnian war, Tadić had been a very ordinary person who owned a bar and was noted for his enthusiasm for sport. The people he killed had frequently drunk in his bar and almost all considered themselves his friends. This crime was a series of murders that would not have happened without the manipulation of anti-Islamic feelings and the moment of crisis in 1992. Many others had not been prepared in any meaningful sense for their role in ethnic cleansing. A Croat from Kostajnica told the writer Slavenka Drakulić 'the war made a murderer out of me, because there was nothing else to do but to fight back'. Drakulić added, 'the last part of the sentence he (said) so softly I (could) hardly hear him'.[51] One JNA soldier from Belgrade told a journalist in 1992 'Vukovar was more of a slaughter than a battle. Many women and children were killed . . . I deserted after that. (It) continues to haunt me. Every night I imagine that the war has reached my home and that my own children are being butchered.'[52]

These differing interpretations of the available texts have not been fully reconciled in the book and could probably never be, as patterns of behaviour certainly vary enormously between individuals. It would be perilous to attempt to create a single grid for cultural responses to ethnic cleansing (although some clear patterns of behaviour do emerge), even though the ideological *origins* of crises may be very similar. By assuming a historical approach to the phenomenon of ethnic cleansing and seeing it as having a single ideological origin without actually arguing that it is a single cultural practice, I risk being accused of committing the error of relativism, of constructing an 'artificial'[53] or 'false'[54] symmetry between all national and ethnic groups. Having stated that nationalisms are similar at the level of ideology, it would be morally banal to level all the *dramatis personae* involved in the politics of the Balkans, as if they were all equally guilty for what has happened.

In practice there is a qualitative difference between those who use violence and force and who create, manipulate and take advantage of crises as part of their political repertoire, and those who do not. And, while it is sometimes possible to ameliorate the situation of ethnic groups who are suffering from low levels of discrimination, it is not possible to 'give people back' their lives, to restore full health to the injured or to return complete mental health to those who have been violated. While we may argue about the various motives and methods of the organizers and perpetrators of ethnic cleansing, their victims are united in their misery and, in death, cease to enjoy whatever privileges – real or imagined – their ethnic background provided. 'Serbs', 'Croats' and 'Muslims' killed during the shelling of Sarajevo are all equally dead. A person may be killed on the grounds of their national identity but – despite the claims of nationalists – this ceases to have any function thereafter and their body cannot be reclaimed for the nation: it is gone forever.

When presenting their cases to the outside world, many nationalists have attempted to portray their circumstances as unique. Dubravka Ugrešić was informed by her plumber Jura in Croatia in 1993: 'We are an internationally recognised victim . . . And there is no way that any victim can ever be . . . normal.'[55] In January 2001, 5 per cent of the population of Croatia demonstrated against the planned extradition of General Mirko Norac to the Hague Tribunal to face accusations for war crimes.[56] After years of relentless propaganda that had presented the violent acts of Croats as patriotism and the behaviour of their Serb and Muslim neighbours as aggression, it is hardly surprising that so many ordinary citizens in Croatia see the behaviour of generals as acceptable within the rules of war. Given that convicted war criminal General Tihomir Blaskić was publicly honoured by Franjo Tudjman before he was delivered to the Hague as the HDZ's sacrificial lamb, the nature of the Croatian response is understandable. In any crisis the *balance of responsibility* may rest with nationalists from one particular ethnic group – in 1991 in the Serb-dominated regions of Croatia – the impetus for the aggression clearly initially came from Serb nationalists who were encouraged by unscrupulous nationalists in Belgrade, who then utterly abandoned them to their fate in 1995. But in many senses they were provoked, not only by their own leaders, but also by a government in Croatia, which was determined to reincorporate the fascist period of history into the mainstream of political life (for example, by renaming streets after Ustaša ministers) and then to disingenuously deny that they were threatening Serb culture in the Krajina in any sense. Wherever the balance of responsibility does lie in any particular case in South Eastern Europe (and these should be examined individually), historically there has been no ethnic group that has been *unaffected* by ethnic cleansing.

For the purposes of this book, the Ottoman world before 1800 and its legacy up to the present day is defined as 'traditional'[57] (although the term premodern might also be used problematically) and the rejection and destruction of that tradition as 'nationalism', although the two concepts are not always diametrically opposed, as a kind of 'millet identity' (in which religion is the primary definition of identity) and some of the collective mentalities of Balkan Muslims survived until the twentieth century and affected the way they were constructed by Christian nationalists.[58] Here Maria Todorova seems to have made an extremely important point when she states:

> the Balkans [have become] . . . European by shedding the last residue of an imperial legacy, widely considered an anomaly at the time and by assuming and emulating the homogeneous European nation-state as the normative form of social organization. It may well be that what we are witnessing today, wrongly attributed to some Balkan essence, is the ultimate Europeanization of the Balkans.[59]

But we might also define the Ottoman Balkan world as 'traditional' because popular culture was relatively autonomous from or at least separated from literate culture and the state relatively distant from the lives of the people. In every society, as Robert Redfield noted, 'great tradition and little tradition have long affected each other and continue to do so . . . [they are] . . . two currents of thought and action, distinguishable, yet ever flowing into and out of each other'.[60] Balkan pastoralists and peasants were never 'primitive isolates'. Even in Montenegro, an island of non-Ottoman government in the Balkans, the society was reliant on a supply of gunpowder from the outside world for its continued existence.[61] Nevertheless, illiteracy rates throughout the Balkans before the twentieth century were much higher than in Western Europe, often as high as 95 per cent.[62] In these circumstances, 'little' or popular tradition at a local level was much richer, less standardized[63] and less well informed by literate or 'great' traditions, although it can be seen from the widespread survival of songs of the *guslari* or other folksingers that there was strong communication between regions. Rom orchestras, some travelling, some foreign adopted diverse styles in the performances of music for weddings and other ritual events.

The arrival of Europeanized ideologies destroyed much of the tradition or changed it in some quite profound ways. In the nineteenth century, the songs of the *guslari* became the basis for the reconceptualization of the Kosovo story amongst Serbs.[64] The deeds of ancient Greeks became the standard by which modern Greeks (and indeed other Christian peoples in the Balkans) constructed their identity as 'civilized' and non-Muslim, although the culture they were celebrating was pagan and putatively violent, at least if we are to judge any culture by its literary remains, such as the *Odyssey*.[65]

By the late eighteenth century, as a result of the variety of different cultures and practices, the Balkans, which had been preserved long after similar practices had died out in Western and Central Europe, became what Maria Todorova has referred to as the '*Volksmuseum* of Europe'.[66] Writers from outside the region often took a great deal of vicarious interest in these societies. Part of the allure for travellers, journalists and other writers was perceived difference from their own milieus. Mary Edith Durham, an English writer and early anthropologist, spent a great deal of time recording tattoos and hairstyles of the northern Albanians.[67] The French writer, Vialla de Sommières described Montenegro in almost purely Homeric terms in the early 1800s[68] (although some have questioned whether he actually went there[69]). Frequently, Western writers became passionate advocates of one national group in the Balkans and championed its cause. George Gordon, Lord Byron died in the struggle for Greek Independence in 1824, although admittedly of illness and not in battle. Since the mental world he inhabited was populated by heroes from classical Greek mythology, it was perhaps a fitting end to an epic life. The distinguished Irish writer Joyce Cary fought in Montenegro during the Balkan wars as his own contribution to the final demise of the Ottomans.[70] During the Balkan wars and the First World War, nurses and voluntary workers from across Europe came to the aid of their beleaguered neighbours in South-East Europe.[71]

Despite a fascination with variety and larger than life Homeric types and cultural variety, many of those who wrote about Balkans cultures had a desire to homogenize and simplify what they saw in order to 'Europeanize' the region. The historian Robert W. Seton-Watson described Macedonia as a problem of racial intermixture 'defying all possible unraveling'[72] as if it were wholly desirable to untie this apparent knot. Western writers wanted Balkan cultures to be codified in their own terms, so they 'reduced' 'tamed' and 'familiarized' these cultures for their often avid audiences creating a 'learning of appropriation'.[73] Commenting on Eastern Roumelia, Robert Hamilton Lang felt that '[w]ith the exception of an insignificant number of Mussulmans and Greeks, her population is Bulgarian in race, language and sympathy indeed so thoroughly Bulgarian that a stranger can scarcely perceive any difference between the two peoples'.[74] Fanny Copeland, a passionate advocate of the 'Yugoslav idea' who was active at the Paris Peace Conference in 1918 announced that

> [f]rom the ordeal of war, pestilence, famine and persecution, the Yugo-Slavs [sic] have emerged again as one people, as homogenous as they were when they first descended from the Carpathians. Yugo-Slavs all, they cherish the old individual names, mementoes of past triumphs and tragedies.[75]

She saw these people as a single unit because it fitted with her own political taste and orientation. She and many another of a romanticist or nationalist bent then had to witness the outcome of this grand homogenizing idea. Very little of this

Western scholarship on the Balkans during the last two hundred years was genuinely 'original' or contributed to extending actual knowledge about the region. Leopold von Ranke's celebrated *History of Servia*, was largely informed by listening to Vuk Karadžić.[76] However, without doubt the actual collection of data by enthusiasts from Western Europe created an actual empirical basis for subsequent ethnology and preserved texts and recorded practices that might otherwise have been lost.

Enter nationalism, exit tradition

le moment est arrivé de soulever et vaincre.[77]

Nationalism and the creation of nation states was an ideological model that ran counter to complex traditions and daily realities for most Balkan peoples. Ethnic cleansing accompanied the spread of nationalism and state formation in the Balkans after the Ottoman Empire and its mentalities began to lose their grip in the eighteenth century. As Arnold Toynbee put it, '[t]he introduction of the Western formula (of the principle of nationalism) among these people has resulted in massacre . . . Such massacres are only the extreme form of a national struggle between mutually indispensable neighbours, instigated by this fatal Western idea.'[78] If we were to compare the ethnic composition of the regions under consideration in this book in 1800 and in 2000, very great changes in population would be evident. In Greek Macedonia by 2000 the non-Greeks numbered only a few thousand. Turks, Slav Muslims, Christian Slavs and Jews once populated this region and in many places outnumbered the Greeks. In Western Anatolia, towns with majority populations of Greeks or Armenians such as Izmir had their populations driven out in 1922. The Krajina region of Croatia lost it majority Serb population in 1995, after four years of war that wiped out many Croatian villages and claimed the lives of thousands. In 1941, Krajina's Serbs suffered at the hands of a fascist regime that killed many thousands of Serbs in this region and in Bosnia. In Vojvodina and Slavonia, Jews, Germans and more recently Croats and Serbs have been pushed out. Thousands died in Kosovo in 1944 and again in 1999 when vicious interethnic rivalry between Serbs and Albanians resulted in murder and mass exodus. In Sandžak in Serbia, in Macedonia and in Montenegro, Slav Muslims have been pressurized to assimilate or leave. Bosnia lost hundreds of thousands of its people to ethnic cleansing during the Second World War and the 1990s. These regions have not only lost 'minorities', they have had their overwhelming constituency changed. Although it may be somewhat problematic to equate 'tradition' with multiethnicity, polytaxis and diversity, there is barely a single region, which remains multiethnic in the Balkans or that has escaped the ravages of ethnic cleansing. Serbs and Hungarians still cohabit peacefully in Vojvodina. Macedonia may not become another Bosnia, but peaceful coexistence in that country looks increasingly unlikely after the interethnic fighting in 2001.

The first nationalist ideas arrived in the Balkans from Western and Central Europe generally in the form of histories and ethnographies published by 'native scholars' of their own peoples. Herderian cultural nationalism, which emphasized the innate and by inference, political bonds between speakers of the same language was transmitted by a number of important intellectuals at the end of the eighteenth century and the beginning of the nineteenth century. Through the work of the Habsburg imperial librarian Jernej Kopitar[79] and the collector of folk poetry Vuk Karadžić, the reading public of Europe became familiar with epic poetry (for which there was also something of vogue). But the process of the codification of popular knowledge became intricately linked with the 'invention' or reforging of national identities for the people in the Balkans. Amongst Serbs, recognizably modern national ideas were produced in Novi Sad by intellectuals who created an entrepôt of central European-orientated culture, where histories and studies of Serb culture were sold (after publication in Vienna). In order to create a Serbian entity from the disparate groups of Orthodox peoples who spoke variants of Serbian, the unifying factor of the medieval Serbian state was stressed over the recent past and present.[80] This vogue for the privileging of a 'golden age' of the ancient over the contemporary was shared by intellectuals of a Romantic bent from Scotland to Cyprus.[81] It was enthusiastically transmitted through literature, travel accounts and what might be coyly described as ethnography without any 'obligation towards the social and material reality'[82] of the present.

Greek self-identification was encouraged by Greeks of the diaspora and Philhellenes, whose main point of reference was the literary world of the classical Greeks.[83] The Ottoman Greeks, many of whom had been highly influential in the running of the state, were even more diverse in their character than the Serbs and their communities were scattered across Asia Minor and the Aegean. In 1893 the state census indicated that of 3.1 million people living in Istanbul, only 1.4 million were actually Muslims, many of the remainder being Greeks.[84] The creation of a modern Greek nation was a severe disruption of the history of this people and it led to the severance of the Greek presence in modern Turkey after 1923 and the Treaty of Lausanne.[85] Other Balkan groups, such as the Bulgarians and Albanians discovered their medieval or other origins from the eighteenth century onwards and began to organize themselves primarily on national rather than regional or dynastic grounds, or in the case of Croatia in a juridical definition of a '1,000 year old state' which introduces the constitution of 1991.[86] Turning back to a 'golden age' in the past for the various ethnic groups of the Balkans had implications for neighbouring peoples. For both the Greeks and the Serbs, Macedonia was the object of their historical projections. To some extent the idea of a 'Greater Greece' (*Megali Idea*) rested on the restitution of the Byzantine Empire and the possessions of Alexander of Macedon. For the Serbs, Macedonian territory was part of the medieval legacy from the Empire of Tsar Dušan. Both these national groups undermined and militarily opposed the autonomy of Macedonia and together with Bulgaria parcelled up the Ottoman *vilayet* in 1913.[87]

In this region of Europe, the reception of nationalism was complicated by the fact that people who spoke the same language (in functional terms) and were therefore of the same 'race' (in the pseudo-biological terminology of nationalism), but had different religions. Croats, Bosnian Muslims, Serbs, Montenegrins all spoke a language which was once codified as Serbo-Croat, but in religious or national terms that did not necessarily make them a single entity. Pomaks and Bulgarian Christians were divided by religion and united by language. Slavonic rivalry and reciprocity is an important motif within Balkans nationalism and accounts for much of the intolerance between ethnic groups. Other national frontiers, although apparently easier to discern were also fluid or porous. Montenegrin and Albanian clans exchanged brides. Some Albanians in Kosovo were possibly Albanianized Serbs.

One of the reasons why nationalism has been so successful, all but eclipsing other ideologies is that it mimics an essence.[88] Quite clearly, there are very few boundaries between what Georg Elwert has referred to as 'we-groups'[89] (i.e. groups of individuals that see themselves as constituting a collectivity) that are not recent and culturally formed and which might therefore constitute an 'essence'. Many individuals cannot easily be corralled into one ethnic group or another, even if they are the most passionate advocates of the 'cause' of that nation. Accusations that his family were in fact Catholic and Croat have dogged the career of the Serb nationalist Vojislav Šešelj.[90] In 1994, Mirjana Marković attacked claims that he was 'not a son of the Serbian nation spiritually . . . he is an alien, a primitive and aggressive alien'.[91] Given that religious boundaries were often quite fluid in some Balkan regions until recently, many individuals would find themselves in the same position as Šešelj. In Croatia in the 1990s, some individuals even went as far as to change their names to make them seem more definitively 'Croat'.[92]

Because it instrumentalizes the language of hearth, home, blood, brotherhood and soil as well as emphasizing the importance of heroism, justice for the ethnic community and sacrifice, modern nationalism successfully merges patriotic emotion and *Heimatliebe* with primordial (and often quite crude) ideas of difference. Politicians who use the rhetoric of nationalism often appear to gain popular support because they seem to be defending those pre-existing homely values.[93] When Slobodan Milošević visited Kosovo in April 1987 the speech he delivered to pacify the distressed Serbs was a combination of populism[94] and a reworking of the Serbian Academy Memorandum about the 'three tortured questions' facing the Serb people.[95] Two separate ideological skeins became entangled at this crucial point.

Nationalism, particularly in its Central European version, with the notion that a single people or *Volk/Narod* should inhabit a state, affected the sections of the Balkan Christian populations as leaven effects dough,[96] and it became thoroughly paradigmatic in Balkan terms of self-reference and self-construction, often eclipsing other older identities. Nationalism was translated into a doctrine of liberation from foreign oppression: initially this meant liberation from the Ottomans, but subsequently the Habsburgs after the 1870s and the Italians and Germans during the First and Second World Wars. The formation of individual states was also seen as part of the manifest destiny of a particular people and this implied that defence of the nation was a patriotic duty. At Gazimestan, near Kosovo Polje, at the site where the Serbs who perished on the field were buried on St Vitus' day in June 1389, Slobodan Milošević interpreted the significance of the anniversary of the medieval Battle of Kosovo polje with reference to the position of Serbs in the Federal Republic of Yugoslavia: 'Six centuries later, today again we are at war and waiting for the battle to come.'[97]

Nationalism was also successful in becoming the ideology that replaced Ottoman culture, ultimately proving more durable than communism, fascism or the peasant politics of the interwar years. Often the actions of committed individuals or of pivotal organizations have proved crucial, and contemporary organizations and entities are keen to claim lineage from political precursors: one hundred years after the foundation of the Macedonian Revolutionary Organization (VMRO) in Salonika, Macedonia was admitted to the UN.[98]

This nationalism, whatever its aspirations for the future shape of states and whoever it included within the nation thoroughly negated the preceding centuries of Ottoman civilization. In the late eighteenth century, most of the Southeast of Europe was under the dominion of the Porte in Istanbul and had been so since the high Middle Ages. Although it was a cruel and despotic regime in many respects, the Ottoman Empire did far less to try to change the character of their subject peoples than Christian rulers might have. They allowed a form of religious self-government, known as the millet system for Jews and Christians and left much of the day-to-day running of the regions to local governors who were often corrupt, but rarely made much effort to reform society in a Prussian sense. Although until the eighteenth century the state stole away many young men from the Christian Balkans to train them as government officials or janissaries, it did not force populations to homogenize on a grand scale, to speak Arabic or Turkish or adopt Turkish manners (although many did so by dint of the advantages that this gave them). The Ottoman state did not usually force conversion to Islam, although there were a number of instances of *jihad* (struggle) to combat internal rebellion. Whatever the overall reality of daily existence for Balkan peoples in the Ottoman Empire was (and this is a controversial historical subject which has been somewhat prone to mystification on all sides), the past was vividly constructed as an aberration; a dark age of collective suffering, imprisonment and martyrdom imposed on Balkan Christians by the 'Infidel'. Centuries of cohabitation and relative tolerance were generally ignored. In his notorious doctoral thesis Nobel laureate Ivo Andrić opined that 'Bosnia was conquered by an Asian warrior people whose social institutions and customs negated all Christian culture and whose faith . . . interrupted the spiritual life of our country, twisted it and created out of that something totally different.'[99] Because nothing good could be gleaned from the more recent past, nationalists frequently took recourse in arguing about ancient and medieval pre-Ottoman polities,[100] attempting to create appropriate models for the present from historical fantasies. As a result they frequently became involved and subsequently become involved in arguments about population and settlement in previous centuries or even millennia. For instance the presence of Orthodox people in Krajina was delegitimized by reference to the medieval kingdoms of Tomislav and Zvonimir.[101] Even rivers such as the Sava and Drina had enormous power as emotional geographical reference points. This privileging of the past over the present was to have a catastrophic effect in many regions. In Krajina, the majority

Serb population was constructed as alien by Croat nationalists and their removal the 'solution to Croatia's centuries-old problem',[102] just as the majority Albanian population in Kosovo were also seen as a historical 'squatters' by Serbian nationalists.[103]

The Balkans in international affairs

Aside from anthropological, literary and other curiosity, the Balkans has also been the focus of concerted international interest at a diplomatic and political level over the past 200 years. In the nineteenth century the solution to the decline of the 'sick man of Europe', namely Turkey, was seen as imperative by almost all concerned, even if they did not agree what should replace it.[104] This became the foundation for what was referred to as the 'Eastern Question'. Antipathy to the Ottomans from the European public and the geopolitical designs of the British, French, Habsburgs and Romanovs in this region turned local revolutionary nationalists into expert practitioners of brinkmanship and the holders of the moral conscience of Europe. A letter sent from 'Orschowa in Servia' to the 'August Council of Sovereigns' at the Congress of Vienna in 1815 reminded the European diplomats of the

> groans of an unfortunate nation, whom the Turks are exterminating . . . not more than four days journey from Vienna . . . The ferocious Mussulmans massacre, impale them, violate their women and children, impel them to abjure the religion of their fathers and convert, with insatiable barbarity, all that flourishing country into one vast and gloomy tomb.[105]

The plight of the Balkan Christians became a familiar theme in European newspapers during the remains of the nineteenth and early twentieth centuries as political leaders sought recognition as their liberators. Tsar Alexander announced in 1877: 'Christians of Bulgaria . . . you are passing through a memorable period. The hour of deliverance from Mussulman depotism has at length struck . . . gather closely under the safety of the Russian flag . . . therein lies your strength and your safety.'[106] By 1878 and the Congress of Berlin the independence of Montenegro, Serbia and Bulgaria was recognized and the administration of Bosnia and Hercegovina increased the power and hegemony of the Habsburg monarchy in this region. After the Balkan Wars of 1912–13, which finally saw the end of the Turkish 'yoke' and heralded the disintegration of the *vilayet* of Macedonia, the Balkan states took on recognizably modern national forms. Albania was recognized as an independent state in 1912. At the Treaty of Versailles in 1918, a Kingdom of Serbs, Croats and Slovenes (later known as Yugoslavia) was created. In the interwar period, these new states became increasingly unstable, all succumbing to dictatorship by 1929. In the 1930s further fragmentation took place until all the 'Wilsonian states' (i.e. those created or recreated at Versailles under the influence of US President Woodrow Wilson) collapsed in 1941 or were kept alive by Axis alliances. During the period 1941–5, the Germans and Italians recreated the map of

Southeastern Europe almost from scratch, indulging the whims of paramilitary groups in exile such as the Croatian fascist Ustaša and relying on puppet regimes elsewhere. Gradually after 1943, Axis power collapsed and the Balkan countries found themselves divided between the 'spheres of influence' of the Soviets, British and Americans in 1945. Since the Soviet sphere was deemed to be almost the entire region except Greece, where there was a bitter Civil War until 1948, which had some ethnic dimensions, the Stalinist model of the 'national question' became the dominant paradigm for the postwar Communist regimes.

Stalinist nationality policies (codified in the Yugoslavian Constitution in 1946 and in almost identical constitutions in the other communist states) brought a level of peace to the region, but this peace was derived from the barrel of a gun. However, it also ossified certain pressing questions such as the status of Kosovo,[107] and failed to provide adequate solutions in areas with large minorities, such as Krajina. The end of communism brought with it an end to the totalitarian solution to the legacy of multiethnicity. The Communists themselves turned into fully-fledged nationalists. In Bulgaria, in the 1980s, in an attempt to bolster his flagging regime the Bulgarian Communist leader Todor Zhivkov tried to force ethnic Turks to adopt Bulgarian names and many left for Turkey, returning very slowly in the following years. In comparative terms, the period between 1945 and 1985 was one of the most peaceful in the region of the last two hundred years.

The transition from communism to nationalism had a disastrous outcome in Yugoslavia as the former republics competed over the shape of borders and the status of ethnic minorities. Had Tito been able to find a viable successor then the preservation of a Yugoslavian identity might have been possible. It seems quite paradoxical in some respects that Yugoslavism did not eclipse the dominant nationalist paradigms among Serbs, Croats and even Slovenes. If we are to regard modern nations as 'imagined communities' as Benedict Anderson has argued,[108] then it does indeed seem curious that this identity failed to survive the communist period. It may, of course, yet reappear as an Internet phantom or a device for expansionism from one of the existing states. No doubt there will be many intellectuals who having done their best to trash a united Yugoslavia and Yugoslavism in the 1980s will try to rekindle their lost youth with what is known in Croatia as 'Yugo-nostalgia'. For whatever reason, Yugoslavism did not survive long enough to become the equivalent of a 'British' or 'American' identity to unite different peoples with a common historical experience.

The 1990s brought a new dimension to the 'Eastern Question' with the war in Yugoslavia. In the years between 1991 and 1999, war and ethnic cleansing changed the human map in Croatia, Serbia, Bosnia and Kosovo. The overarching cause of these wars was the discontent, which emanated from Serbian communities in all three regions about the implications of the disintegration of the Communist state and the loss of their 'protection' from Belgrade. These perhaps legitimate fears of Serb communities were utilized by Slobodan Milošević, who ruthlessly exploited nationalist discontent, first to gain power by mobilizing agitated Serbs from Kosovo in 1987 and then using the wars and general lawlessness in Croatia and Bosnia from 1991–5 to create a police state in which paramilitaries and criminals lived like minor kings, exploiting revenues from smuggling tobacco, drugs, armaments or motor vehicles.

Initially the international community appeared to actively support Milošević, believing naively that he would restore strong government in Yugoslavia and apparently caring very little that this might mean abuses of human rights and a disregarding of the clear democratic wishes of the populations in Croatia and Slovenia for independence in 1991 and subsequently in Macedonia and Bosnia in 1992. United States Secretary of State James Baker visited Belgrade in May 1991 and gave Milošević the green light to bring the rebel republics of Slovenia and Croatia into line. In the next year a strong impression was created that they and their allies would do little to actively support these new states (the governments of Britain, the United States and France in particular). As a result very little was done to stop the attacks on civilian populations by paramilitaries and remnants of the former Yugoslav People's army (JNA) that began in Croatia in 1991 and then were carried through to Bosnia with such devastating effect until 1995. During the wars in Yugoslavia the international community was handicapped by its insistence on equating those who used force as part of their political repertoire and those who did not. Mark Wheeler described this attitude as 'the albatross of bowing and scraping to warlords'[109] and this attitude certainly prolonged the agony of the Yugoslavian wars in the 1990s as did the attitude that suggested that all parties were equally responsible for the fighting. The embargo on armaments imposed by the United Nations in 1992 meant that the government of Bosnia-Hercegovina was unable to buy military hardware to protect itself from both internal and external aggression.

Humanitarian intervention, in the form of the United Nations Protection Force in Croatia and Bosnia, helped to alert the public outside the region to the atrocities being committed and some valuable humanitarian aid was delivered by UN forces and by international agencies such as the Red Cross and numerous private individuals across the world. The role that the media played in highlighting the human tragedies of the wars was also undoubtedly important. Nevertheless, the extent of the problem and the extent to which representatives of the 'warring factions' would disingenuously lie during international negotiations and then carry on with their previous military strategies added to a general 'lack of will' on the part of the international community to identify in Churchillian terms 'who was doing the most killing', and this led to a series of policy blunders. In 1995, the United Nations virtually supervised the ethnic cleansing of its own nominated 'safe havens' in Eastern Bosnia in the summer of that year. The Dayton Peace Accords were signed by all the so-called 'warring factions' at the end of 1995 after the collapse of the Bosnian Serb army at Bihać and the loss of Krajina.

At Dayton, the issue of Kosovo, with its largely Albanian speaking population was left unresolved and became a major issue in international affairs when the Kosovo Liberation Army (KLA) began to organize armed resistance to the regime of Milošević in 1998. Failure to resolve this issue in a series of international meetings culminating in Rambouillet in France in 1999, led to air strikes by the North Atlantic Treaty Organization (NATO) in March of the same year. Having made an equation between all sides fighting in the war in Bosnia, the international community then clearly began to see President Milošević as the chief villain of the piece in the former Yugoslavia. Milošević sensed that he had been handed personal responsibility for the entire crisis, stating that 'Rambouillet was not a negotiation . . . It was a Clinton administration diktat . . . it was a recipe for the independence of Kosovo, which clearly we could not accept.'[110] In the early 1990s, the USA had seen the Serbian regime as a potential gendarme for the region and a necessary participant in the Dayton accords. By 1999, the Serbian President had been indicted as a war criminal. After the capitulation of the Belgrade government in June 1999, NATO and United Nations forces (KFOR and UNMIK respectively) moved into Kosovo to attempt to rebuild a community shattered by war and ethnic cleansing. In 2001 the United Nations and NATO were embroiled in a dispute between the Albanian community and the government in Macedonia, which flared up seriously in the spring of 2001.

In February 1993, the International War Crimes Tribunal was approved by the United Nations Security Council and mandated to prosecute the accused on every side of the war in the former Yugoslavia for war crimes and crimes against humanity. By the beginning of 2001, the Hague Tribunal had indicted less than fifty Serbs out of possible hundreds who took part in atrocities in Croatia, Bosnia and Kosovo in the 1990s. The number of prosecuted from other ethnic groups and nationals was even lower. Its costs had soared to many million dollars by 2001 and it is expected to be in existence for at least until 2004.[111] The Hague Tribunal may only ever deal with a tiny percentage of the real criminals who were responsible for ethnic cleansing in the former Yugoslavia. Some have already died of natural causes, others are ordinary men or women who may hope to live out their lives as obscure citizens and escape prosecution. Others might live the life of unrepentant exiles in Argentina or elsewhere, like the Ustaša escapee from the Second World War Dinko Sakić, who was eventually brought to trial and sentenced to a maximum of twenty years in jail in 1999 in a court in Zagreb after having been found personally responsible for the death of 2,000 individuals at the deathcamp of Jasenovac in 1941–5.[112]

Given the enormity of the crimes committed and the level of infrastructural damage in the region, it is likely that it will remain the focus of international affairs for some years to come. Catching the biggest fish of all for the Hague tribunal, namely Milošević, in the early summer of 2001, may have tremendous symbolic and even cathartic value, but the prevention of such conflicts should ultimately be a far higher priority for the international community than the limited 'justice' that can be meted out after the event.

Themes and motifs

The following chapters examine the destruction of tradition and the phenomenon of ethnic cleansing from a number of different thematic angles, including the ideologies of instrumentalization (nationalism, anti-Islam, fascism and communism), the destruction of community and *Heimat*, symbolic violence, gender-associated violence, the Balkan bandit tradition and the 'use' of ethno-psychology. The weight of the narrative leans towards Yugoslavia, the contemporary period and the wars in that country in the 1990s. Nevertheless, the themes have been selected because they represent some of the main cultural *Leitmotive* for interpreting the events of the past two hundred years. In abandoning a more conservative narrative account of serial events with a preference for a thematic approach, it is argued that a chrono-logical narrative *per se* will not necessarily explain what has taken place in the Balkans. Annales historian Fernand Braudel was acutely aware of the problems associated with *l'histoire evénémentielle* (the history of events):

> though by its nature the most exciting and richest in human interest of histo-ries, it is also the most elusive. We must beware of that history which still simmers with the passions of the contemporaries who felt it, described it, lived it, to the rhythm of their brief lives, lives as brief as our own. It has the dimensions of their anger, dreams, and their illusions.[113]

Indeed a recitation of chronological facts can only serve quantitative purposes and may even lead to gratuitous conclusions about the cyclical nature of violence in this region. It is highly likely that the South East of Europe will now be relatively peaceful for many years to come, with the probable exception of Macedonia. The concluding remarks in Chapter 8 reiterate the importance of countering destruc-tive ideologies by suggesting that radical pluralism and multiethnic societies cannot expect to survive unless they are defended through education and other forms of active ideological support.

2 Mountain wreaths

Anti-Islam in Balkan Slavonic discourses

The end of the Ottoman Empire

Physical destruction of the Islamic communities of the Balkans is a process that has taken place over the last two hundred years or so as the Ottoman Empire began to fragment. During the period from 1821 to 1922 alone, Justin McCarthy estimates that the ethnic cleansing of Ottoman Muslims led to the death of several million individuals and the expulsion of a similar number.[1] Hundreds of thousands of Muslims were also killed, primarily on the grounds of ethnicity, during the Second World War and the Yugoslavian Wars of Dissolution. Ideological marginalization of Islamic communities accompanied the decline and fall of the Ottoman Empire, but as an ideology or a series of related ideas, it draws upon far older prejudices going back to the Middle Ages against the 'Turk' and the religion of Islam in pan-European discourses, which have been used as a justification to persecute Muslims alongside Jews.[2] As the Ottoman Empire weakened and rival European powers encouraged the development of nationalist ideologies among the subject peoples, the Muslims in the Balkans sometimes became viewed as a kind of ethnic 'fifth column',[3] leftover from a previous era, who could never be integrated successfully into the planned future national states. The end of the Ottoman presence has parallels elsewhere with the 'unmixing of peoples' that accompanied the post-Imperial age and in itself was not unique to the Balkans (and nor either were hostile discourses towards such populations).[4] Sometimes Muslims left the mainland Balkans without the actual use of force, but because they experienced such inconvenience staying in their homes.[5] On other occasions, Muslims from the Balkans simply left because they did not want to 'live as slave where the Turk was previously the master'.[6] Individuals whose families had left the Balkans often grew up with this sense of loss. Şevket Aydemir, who was born in Edirne, former Adrianople, in 1897, remembered: 'ours was a refugee neighbourhood. The flotsam of torrents of refugees torn by war and massacres from the Crimea, Dobruja and the banks of the Danube . . . the returning remnants of the conquering armies.'[7]

Jovan Cvijić stated Slav Muslims were traditionally seen by Orthodox Serbs as 'neither Serbs, nor Turks, neither water nor wine, but odious renegades'.[8] The struggle to rid themselves of the Ottomans became an important part of self-identification for the Balkan Christians. It characterized both the culture of the liberation movements of the nineteenth and early twentieth centuries and older popular culture. In Senj the sixteenth-century heraldic images in the churches included a mace, a winged lion holding in its paws a sword and a severed Turk's head.[9] In Macedonia in the village church in Zlatari, which is dedicated to St Demetrius, 'the warrior saint, mounted on horseback, is sparing a fallen heathen. The artist in the Zlatari fresco has made no mistake in representing the heathen's identity. It is clearly a Turkish-looking soldier who is being stabbed by the saint's spear.'[10] In the Morea region of Greece in 1821, there was a popular revolutionary song with the chorus, 'the Turk shall live no longer, neither in the Morea, nor in the whole earth'.[11]

Much of the hostility towards Muslims at the level of popular culture has been distilled and then used in the repertoires of extreme nationalists to create an artificially extreme distrust of the Muslims who continued to live in the Balkan region. As Ivan Čolović has argued, what starts out as taunts and literary constructions of hate, can end up as actual practices.[12] Extreme nationalist ideas are especially pervasive because they are based on very crude notions of difference. Similar patterns of behavior *in extremis* and attitudes towards Muslims on the grounds of difference are discernable across the period under consideration.

Anti-Islam in the Balkans was initially encouraged and reified by the Western European public who were generally very pro-Christian and represented the Greeks during the war of independence as heirs of the classical epoch in a literal sense. The 'Bulgarian atrocities' of the 1870s, as Vesna Goldsworthy points out, set off a very agitated public debate in Britain about the role of the Ottomans, which polarized the Liberal and Tory Parties under Gladstone and Disraeli respectively. The anger was fuelled as 'reports of mutilation, rape, torture and murder covered the front pages of the British daily papers'.[13] In 1876, Thomas Carlyle wrote to *The Times* calling for 'the immediate and summary expulsion of the Turk from Europe'. He continued, . . . 'the peaceful Mongol inhabitants would . . . be left in peace and treated with perfect equity . . . but the governing Turk with all his Pasha and Bashi Bazouks (from the Turkish *başi-bözök*), should be ordered to disappear from Europe and never to return'.[14] Like the legendary appearance of Atatürk with his troops at Nif on the outskirts of Izmir in 1922, the uprisings of Balkan Christians against the Ottoman overlords were interpreted as a quintessential combat between cultures, as a 'clash of civilizations' to borrow Samuel Huntington's contentious term.[15]

Anti-Islam in Serbian and Montenegrin discourses

Because the Serbs were the first people to take up the challenge of driving out the Ottomans and because also much of the literature analysing the wars in Yugoslavia in the 1990s has looked at the roots of anti-Islamic sentiments, it may be instructive here to look at the Serbian case in more detail. Early Serbian nationalism and the production of a national idea depended very largely on a small number of individuals in the late eighteenth and early nineteenth centuries such the Vuk Karadžić and the ruler of Montenegro, the *Vladika* (Bishop) Petar II Petrović Njegoš. Many of the early Serb intellectuals received their training and developed their ideas under the aegis of the Habsburg Monarchy, so their ideas can be very directly linked to the growth of Romantic nationalism in Central Europe with its emphasis on the national spirit and the authenticity of the common people. However, although the Romantic notion of the *srpski narod* (the Serb nation) should have included all South Slavs speaking the language which was referred to as Serbo-Croat from 1850s until 1990s by many commentators and linguists,[16] nationalist ideas which developed in the nineteenth century tended to exclude Muslims from the nation, because by adopting Islam they were perceived to have become de facto Ottomans (and were sometimes referred to indiscriminately as 'Turks').[17] Like many of his contemporaries, Karadžić had historical, linguistic and racial views as to what constituted a nation[18]. He stated that there were five million people who spoke the same language (*štokavski*), but they were divided by religious confession. He added, 'only the three million Orthodox consider themselves as Serbs . . . [Muslims] think that they are true Turks and call themselves that, despite the fact less than one in a hundred of them knows Turkish.'[19] His view of Serbdom combined notions of primordial ethnicity with Herderian linguistic consciousness. To his mind all five million were Serbs, whether they knew it or not, and what had happened in the medieval Empire of Dušan was as important as the intervening centuries, although he specifically did want to take out Turkish loan words from the Serbian language.[20] He was, however, one of the first writers to use the word 'cleanse' (*očistiti*), with all its Christian overtones of the redemptive powers of baptism, to describe the killing of Muslims in Belgrade in 1806.[21]

Karadžić, who spent many years as a protégée of the Slovene linguist and Imperial librarian Jernej Kopitar in Vienna in the early nineteenth century, was one of the scholars responsible for codifying and thus elevating the scattered ballads of the guslars (players of a stringed instrument, the *gusle*) into a national literary canon.[22] One of the most important themes of these epic poems was the struggle against Ottoman domination and many had ancient motives, which can be traced back to the Middle Ages. Interest in South Slav epic poetry, which was exceptionally well-preserved at the turn of the nineteenth century, was found all over Europe at the time.[23] Walter Scott translated the ballad of *Hasanaginica* into English and Jacob Grimm read and favourably reviewed Karadžić' work.[24] The appeal of epic poetry was not just cultural. To some extent Serb anti-Ottoman sentiment and activity suited the geopolitical interests of both Habsburgs and the Romanovs at that time. As a cultural artefact it has left a long-lasting mark on Serb and Montenegrin national consciousness.

An important text, and arguably the most important single text to encourage the idea of a historical betrayal by Slavs who had converted to Islam was the poem *Gorski Vijenac* (The Mountain Wreath) published in 1847 by Petar II Petrović Njegoš, who was the Prince-Bishop of Montenegro from 1830 until his early death in 1851. The main theme of the poem is the supposed dilemma faced by his predecessor *Vladika* Danilo (1700–35) about what to do with Montenegrins who had become Muslim. The poem contains many references to smiting Slav Muslims, including the threat of Vojvoda Batrić that: 'we will burn down Turkish homes so that no trace of the dwellings of our home-grown faithless devils could be known'.[25] Vladeta Popović described Njegoš' poem as revealing the 'essence and substance of a race that has had to go through many tribulations and fight against many difficulties'[26] thereby giving it the status of a genuine historical account rather than the poetic vision of an educated man who had read Ossian as well as Ivanhoe and the Greek classics.[27] *Gorski Vijenac* was read by subsequent generations of Montenegrins and other South Slavs, achieving canonical status very rapidly. It has been called a 'true breviary of interethnic hatred'.[28] It is probably the chief textual link between the discourse about Islam and everyday life for the people themselves. For Milica Bakić Hayden, '[Njegoš'] depictions of the converts as traitors whose weakness and opportunism deprived them of the religious and cultural identity bequeathed to them by their forefathers in Kosovo are reflected in popular – if tacit – perception of Muslims among Serbs and Montenegrins'.[29] For Nobel prize winning novelist Ivo Andrić, Njegoš was 'the complete expression of our basic, deepest collective sentiment, for this motto (let be what cannot be!) deliberately or not, led all our struggles for freedom until modern times'.[30] The youthful members of *Mlada Bosna* who competed for the privilege to assassinate Archduke France Ferdinand in Sarajevo in 1914 had all memorized *Gorski Vijenac*[31] and believed it was their manifest destiny as good Serbs to drive out foreign rulers, be they Turks or Habsburgs.[32] Whether Njegoš' work represents a kind of *Urtext* for popular sentiment or whether he was largely informed by popular culture is a moot point. Jovan Cvijić mentions an eighteenth-century case of a Montenegrin of the Ozrinić tribe who dreamt that he was to rid himself of his Muslim neighbours, which he then did and similar things may have occurred elsewhere in the form of a nocturnal culture in waiting.[33] Therefore it is not completely fair to isolate a single text from the context in which it was written, that is Montenegrin, which was almost an island of non-Ottoman government in the Balkans. However it is probable that Montenegro's identity, particularly its quintessentially non-Islamic character, was manipulated by its intellectuals and other nineteenth-century writers of pan-Serbian sympathies.

Research by the anthropologist Zorka Milich, carried out in 1990, indicates that many stereotypes in Montenegro have part of their origin in the nineteenth century and thus form a direct link to the nationalism of Njegoš, rather than some older tribal culture. Milich herself is not entirely uncritical about Montenegrin culture as it has been traditionally constructed, stating 'though the uninitiated might find many of the tribal practices of Montenegro primitive and distressing, it is essential that they be viewed in the context of a traditional warrior society – original and unpolluted'.[34] Nevertheless, her research represents a tremendous repository of popular beliefs and reflections on custom. She questioned a number of centegenarian women in Montenegro and uncovered a wide range of beliefs about and prejudices against Muslims. Some of them exhibited mistrust and dislike of 'Turks', others only a mild awareness of difference. Jovana, aged 102, stated that '[t]he Turks were evil. When they saw a good Serb, they did everything in their power to kill him.'[35] She remarked that the custom allowing a widow to marry her husband's brother was 'disgusting' and the use of cosmetics by the women made them 'stink'. She also felt that the wearing of a veil was a 'strange custom', prefacing this remark with 'who knows why?'.[36] Another informant, Ljubica aged 112, when asked her opinion of *poturice* (Christian converts to Islam) replied: '[M]ost of the Turks round here are our people . . . They should be ashamed of themselves. Their religion is not better than ours.'[37]

An ambivalence towards Muslims, from Karadžić onwards is an important aspect of Serbian and Montenegrin national consciousness. Although some were clearly of an eliminationalist mindset (and here Njegoš is clearly of this orientation), others believed that Muslims were redeemable for the nation. This problematic remains central, even amongst the most extreme Četnici. In Foča in Bosnia during the Second World War they were about to kill a Muslim who pleaded with them that he had been a patriotic Serb. They replied, 'Inasmuch as you were a Serb, you sullied the Serb name, because you are a Turk. And since you helped us, we shall not torture you.' Instead the man was shot.[38]

Certainly anti-Islam was not confined to Serbs and Montenegrins: after the Second World War, it was also commonplace in the popular culture of the other republics of Yugoslavia and was not a problem that the Communists ever dealt with forcefully, despite a commitment to brotherhood and unity. *Gorski Vijenac* was read as a school textbook in Communist Yugoslavia in every republic and available in Slovene and Macedonian translations. That is not to say that every person who read these texts were 'contaminated' by their poetical content: Tim Judah discusses a conversation between Aleksa Djilas and his cousin.

> 'How did the Muslims in your class react when they had to read *The Mountain Wreath* and learn parts of it by heart?' His cousin was dumbstruck. 'It had never crossed his mind to ask his Muslim classmates such a question – even though some were his close friends. Clearly he did not connect them with the Muslims against whom Njegoš wrote.'[39]

Most canons of national literature contain elements that are not in keeping with a contemporary emphasis on what Richard Rorty has called 'sentimental education'.[40] The plays of William Shakespeare could quite easily be used to construct contemporary Francophobe or anti-Semitic stereotypes. An acquaintance of mine claimed that a relative of his had insisted on using the term 'blackamoor' to refer to North Africans, a term she had 'reinvented' by reading *Othello*. Most adult speakers of the English language consciously and sub-consciously use Shakespearian phrases in everyday language.[41] As Anthony Smith has pointed out John of Gaunt's eulogy of England in *Richard II* still has considerably evocative power.[42] During the Second World War a Montenegrin priest amongst the Partisans, who was reading *Gorski Vijenac* aloud was asked to remain silent by a hodža: 'Please don't say that bit about the Turks. It won't go down well with the Muslims.'[43] After the war, despite the goodwill and/or naivety of certain individuals it is sometimes clear that the educational system of the Communists failed to tackle the problem of discrimination in literature. One Muslim from the Bosnian village of Dolina who was born in 1953 told Tone Bringa during some of the lessons he and his classmates had been portrayed as the losers throughout twentieth-century Yugoslav history. Furthermore, particularly Muslim cultural characteristics (such as modes of dress and speech) were branded old-fashioned. So the message inherent in the socialist progressive Yugoslav education system was that '"muslimness" belonged to the past'.[44] In the 1980s in Bosnia, Muslim habits were frequently seen as rustic 'old-fashioned' and 'village-like'.[45] In that sense the elimination of Muslim communities, as envisaged by extremists, was a war on tradition and the past. This had already begun to happen in the nineteenth century with the destruction of intricate town planning and clumsy introduction of more Western styles in town planning.[46] In Bulgaria in the mid-1980s, the Communist militia would 'go from house to house and anything that resembled a Turkish garment they would seize, tear up and trample in the mud'.[47] As Radoslav Radenkov remarked '[a]ncient folk costumes that had been passed down . . . were taken from old wooden chests and thrown onto heaps outside. To this pile would be added all books found in Turkish [including] . . . the Koran.'[48] In the year 1989 when Bulgarian Turks were free to leave for Turkey, some 370,000 left, although 155,000 returned within a year.[49]

Mistrust of Muslims, both Slav Muslims and Kosovars, existed alongside tolerance at an unofficial level in Yugoslavia, but it needed to be awakened by nationalist intellectuals after 1974 to have a significant political impact. Moreover, the ineffective response of the Communist authorities to the national question, only belatedly allowing Muslims to define themselves 'in the ethnic sense' after 1971 and allowing them forms of ethnic individuation such as the wearing of traditional dress and the building of new mosques was too little too late to prevent the drift into rival extreme nationalisms. After the death of Tito, many lost their inhibitions about openly nationalist politics.[50] During the mobilization of Serbian nationalism in the late 1980s by Slobodan Milošević, his supporters (particularly in Montenegro) would turn up to rallies with placards with provocative anti-Islamic slogans: 'Oh Muslims, you black crows,[51] Tito is not around to protect you,' or 'I'll be the first, who will be the second to drink some Turkish blood?'.[52] The main themes of the rallies were traditional Serb nationalism, and relations with the Kosovo Albanians were more prominent than incipient threats towards Slav Muslims. Nevertheless, the forces that Milošević unleashed cannot be regarded as insignificant when viewing the subsequent events of the 1990s.[53]

In invoking the influence of *Gorski Vijenac* or any folkloric text, it would be as well to be careful to avoid essentialization about the nature of Serb or Montenegrin culture and national consciousness. Folklore and the analysis of other texts from popular culture are very often used in the literature on the Balkans to make rather sweeping assertions about national character. Ivo Rendić-Miočević characterizes the Dinaric Serbs as suffering from 'projection', 'narcissism' and 'paranoia', which he dubs the 'Prince Marko syndrome'[54] with its obvious idea of the continuity of folk traditions from the epic songs of the guslari to the present day. Branimir Anzulović is also undeterred about making pronouncements about the link between popular culture and violence.

In Balkan highland culture, violence is often taken for granted, without any sense of guilt or sorrow for the victims . . . A high level of violence and the condoning of the most vicious cruelty as just punishment can be observed in the Serbian folk song 'Grujo's Wife's Treachery'.[55]

If we were to try and create other personality types on this basis, we could state that the Americans had a morbid fascination with drowning because they sing 'Clementine' or that the English had a fixation with decapitation because they sing 'Oranges and Lemons'. Recent critics of the political use of folklore in the 1990s have pointed to ways in which folklore has been misused by the Croatian and Serbian governments.[56] A realization of the part that governments, nationalist ideologues and the media have played should deter scholars from making unguarded comments about popular culture.

The many foreign writers who have visited the Balkans since the early nineteenth century also helped to circulate and replicate the singular notion[57] of Ottoman oppression versus Serb or Montenegrin heroism and were often moved by the idea of the perpetual struggle against the Turks, (although many expressed their horror at brutal spectacles such as the dozens of severed and desiccated Turks' heads surrounding the *Vladika* residence in Cetinje).[58] In his poem 'Montenegro', Tennyson sought to encapsulate many of the contemporary European images of a perpetual and valorous struggle between Orthodox and Muslim communities:

> They kept their faith, their freedom, on the height.
> Chaste, frugal, savage, arm'ed by day and night
> Against the Turk; . . .
> O smallest among peoples! rough rock-throne
> Of Freedom! warriors beating back the swarm
> Of Turkish Islam for five hundred years, . . .[59]

For many of these foreign writers, the Ottomans, their culture and the lands that they ruled for centuries were constructed within a literary trope, which has been described by Edward Said as 'Orientalism',[60] which was set up as opposite and inferior to the supposed values of Europe or the Occident. As part of a general rejection of the past, South Slav writers began to use the same tropes to describe the Ottomans as other European writers (although it is also fair to state that for many foreign writers Southeastern Europe still had many 'oriental' characteristics or more particularly Balkan features, which set them apart from Europe.[61]) Ryan Gingeras has studied anti-Ottoman sentiment press coverage in Britain during the Illinden Uprising in Macedonia, which depicted Islam as being essentially violent in its nature and the Turk as 'savage', 'barbarian' or 'fanatical'. He quotes from the *Manchester Guardian* when it commented that 'slaughter of children, outrage against women, devastation, mark the path of these Turkish savages in 1903, just as seven centuries ago they marked the path of Ghenghiz Khan'.[62] Serb and Montenegrin rejection of their own Islamic heritage was part of a European-wide *Zeitgeist*.

It would be unfair to state that all 'memory' of Turkish persecution was para-noid in its character: it is 'based on more than mere emotional and political conjecture'.[63] Writing in the seventeenth century the Croat Juraj Križanić consid-ered that

> All nations curse foreign rule and consider it the worst shame, misfortune and humiliation . . . the disgrace is less if a nation has been conquered by arms than if it has allowed itself to be fooled by alluring words and accepted the yoke of foreign will of its own free will. Arms can only conquer the body, while the mind remains free . . . that is why our people along the Danube, Croats, Serbs and Bulgarians, bear their misfortune more easily. For they, militarily defeated, are forced to carry a German or Turkish yoke.[64]

As Vera Mutafchieva reminds us the hegemonic practices of the Ottomans in the Balkans were accompanied by many individual and collective cruelties, such as forced conversion to Islam, the Janissary system and discrimination in taxation.[65] After the rebellions of the 1590s, the Serbs were punished by the removal of the bones of a canonized thirteenth-century archbishop, Sveti Sava, which were then incinerated in Belgrade.[66] The Ottomans then ordered a *jihad* against the cult of Sava.[67] In 1804, the revolt against the Ottomans had a specific cause linked to the atrocities committed by the Dahis, and other Balkan populations had similar griev-ances at this time. In 1815, the Ottomans took fearful revenge on their rebellious subjects. A priest from Nikolja, Athanasius was impaled along with twenty others. On 26 January in that year Tartar regiments were sent to punish the inhabitants of Belgrade. As *The Times* reported

> 131 Servians, who had been detained, were beheaded or impaled . . . In var-ious parts of Bosnia, the *tekal* (the crier during the war) proclaimed for three successive days war against the infidels[68] . . . In this violent crisis no hope remains unless their deplorable situation excite the compassion of other powers, who can save these wretched Christians from utter destruction.[69]

Had Ottoman rule ever been acceptable to the Balkan populations many more would have converted to Islam and it is unlikely that traditions of banditry would have developed along the extensive border areas or that uprisings would have occurred in the way that they did.[70]

However, it is also possible to deconstruct many of the tenets of anti-Turkish mythologies: Božidar Jezernik has examined the case of the representations of eyes gauged out of holy murals in Orthodox churches in the Balkans and argued that many of the claims of nationalists were fraudulent.[71] One could argue that there was a great deal of synthesis and peaceful cohabitation between Serb and Ottoman culture over many centuries. Use of aromatics and spices in cuisine, the rituals surrounding the drinking of coffee and the recreational use of tobacco as well as the melodies of folk tunes and the wearing of amulets and talismans have all been linked to the Turkish legacy. Jovan Cvijić even argued that Dinaric fatalism was linked to Turkish notions of *ksmet* (destiny).[72] However, since anti-Islam is an ideology, any deconstruction of myth has the mere status of a historical opinion. Perhaps it also misses the main point, namely that historical myths represent one truth about the past, abandoning attempts to tell the whole truth in the way that Picasso, during his blue period, abandoned attempts to tell the whole truth about colour.[73] Ivan Čolović employs a phrase taken from the work of the ethnographer Veselin Čajkanović, *klicanje predaka* (the cheer of ancestral voices) to illustrate how the dead are summoned up to serve the political purposes of the living.[74] Ottoman oppression was certainly one fact about the Serb and Montenegrin experience of the past, but not the only one and it was open to conscious or unconscious manipulation by nationalists. As a metaphor for oppression, it was often invoked and remained active within the repertoire of nationalists. In Banja Luka, Roy Gutman recorded an interview with Major Milovan Milutinović, which he described as 'the most bizarre I ever heard from a military man. What raised my eyebrows was the reference to janissaries . . . 'Which century are you talking about?' I asked. He replied, 'It is a new and recent phenomenon.'[75] When the Republic of Serbia's power was deemed to be threatened by the granting of autonomous region status to Kosovo and Vojvodina after 1974, Dobrica Ćosić stated: 'The Republic of Serbia has been reduced to a pashalik of Belgrade, given up (inféodée) to the begs of Priština and the archdukes (voïvodes) of Novi Sad,'[76] invoking very emotive political terms from the past.

Another 'truth' about relations between Christians and Muslims throughout the Balkans is that they often had much closer and certainly more complex relations than nationalist myths might lead us to believe. Miloš Obrenović, 'the prince who successfully pushed the Ottoman landlords out of Serbia in the 1820s, slept on rugs and shelves in the Turkish manner, dressed with a turban, ruled with the brutal irresponsibility of an Ottoman Pasha, and was called only half-jokingly by his subjects "the Sultan"'.[77] Elsewhere the dress of Christians remained highly Turkish in style and once rejected they had to individuate themselves in rather inconvenient ways. An officer in the Bulgarian army reported that

> we entered Lozengrad without a fight . . . everywhere on the doors of Christians' homes a cross had been drawn, sometimes in a very vivid paint that leapt to the eye. It was obvious that they were still very frightened. Many Christians had previously worn the fez, but now they threw their fezes away, and as they had no caps, they went around bareheaded.[78]

The names of many well known Serbs and Montenegrins are etymologically partly Turkish (Karadžić, Asanović, etc.). Albanian surnames have obvious Islamic roots, but so too do the names of many Greeks, Croats and Bulgarians. We cannot preclude other forms of interpersonal relations. In 1815, the rebel Obrenović 'first conducted his Muslim blood-brother, Ashin Bey, to safety and then proclaimed the opening of a new "war against the Turks". Messages were sent round the country that the inhabitants should kill anyone they encountered wearing green clothes – the sign of a Muslim.'[79] In Macedonia in the 1990s the anthropologist Jonathan

Schwartz was told to 'take a small piece of firewood from each side of (a) donkey and throw them both onto a small pile by the church gate. He said, "It's a present." I answered, "But you are a Muslim." "I know, but we all do it here. It's a sacrifice."'[80] More recently, on the Hungarian border with Vojvodina in a camp housing Bosnian refugees, there were two nearby cafes frequented by Serbs and Muslims respectively. As a woman from Zvornik explained: 'When they get drunk, since the places are very close to each other, they sing in the dark together and laugh and cry.'[81] After dark, people were only identifiable by common language and inebriation and ceased to care about other forms of alterity. In Macedonia in 1939, a traveller asked men and women why they did not dance the kolo together and was told, 'It has always been like this in these parts. Perhaps the Turks taught them the dance.'[82] These stories illustrate that there were complex and ambivalent reactions to Muslims and Islam at the level of popular culture, which was never so definitively anti-Muslim as Njegoš 'imagined'.

Misha Glenny has argued that the very closeness between religious communities in Bosnia was an important factor in explaining patterns of ethnic violence:

> the Bosnian Serbs, Croats and Muslims have been adorned with many different cultural uniforms over the centuries, by which they identify one another as the enemy when the conflict breaks out. Despite this, underneath the dress they can see themselves reflected . . . The only way that fighters can deal with this realisation is to exterminate the opposite community. How else does one explain the tradition of facial mutilation in this region?[83]

John Allcock has argued concerning the former Yugoslavia that 'traditional codes of morality require that individuals be ready to kill their neighbours, with whom they might be "in blood"'.[84] During times of peace interethnic tensions were difficult to discern even in parts of Kosovo where ethnic division may have been more fixed. In 1999, a massacre of ethnic Albanians in the town of Suva Reka was apparently instigated by a local man Zoran Petković, a 'Serb who was friendly with the Albanians . . . even as relations deteriorated between the two ethnic groups.'[85] A local policeman Islam Yashlari, when asked of his opinion of Petković after the massacre, replied: 'I don't know what happened to him. He was just a guy who didn't like to work too much, then when the war started he changed. He wanted to be somebody.'[86] The survivors were able to recount their story because they were sheltered by a local Serb family. It is also probable that during the wars in Bosnia and Kosovo young Serb men were forced on pain of death to kill their neighbours in a cynical act of spreading guilt and responsibility for ethnic crimes by nationalist extremists, which really has nothing whatsoever to do with either traditional morality or consciousness of ethnicity.[87]

Serbian and/or Montenegrin popular culture is therefore not *per se* anti-Islamic although elements of mistrust between religious communities may have primordial characteristics. *Gorski Vijenac* is of its era and belongs more to modern discourses about nationalism rather than to popular culture, despite it quasi-epic format. Nevertheless, by 1878 and the Congress of Berlin, which recognized the sovereignty of Serbia and Montenegro, a putative hatred of 'Turks', which by inference could also include Slav Muslims was seen by nationalist writers as a defining Serb trait. The lack of chronological coherence to this myth can be seen by the comment attributed to a Serb bishop Duchitch (Dučić) by the American John Reed in 1915: 'In Serbia, we do not trust too much to God. We prayed to God for five centuries to free us from the Turks and finally we took guns and did it ourselves.'[88]

Another aspect of the rejection of the 'Turkish yoke' and Islam is the invocation of the idea of a 'Turkish taint' (the shame of having cohabited with an 'oriental' culture for many centuries and its legacy in popular culture and mentalities). Marko Živković illustrates this idea with the example of a televised session of the Serbian parliament in 1994, when a member of the opposition group DEPOS played a tape-recording of Iranian pop music alongside turbofolk.[89] When he had proved that the melodies were very similar, he quoted Vladimir Dedijer: 'We Serbs sometimes behave as if we were made (i.e. begotten) by drunken Turks.'[90] Živković describes this as 'deep self-recrimination . . . couched in the idiom of self-Orientalization'.[91] It is as if the Turkishness that has been so forcefully repudiated can never really go away and continues to define the mentalities and culture of the Serbs, despite themselves. In 1876, a British reporter for the *Illustrated London News* recorded that 'with their fezzes and loose robes, these people of Belgrade have a wonderfully Turkish look about them. But how they hate the Turks.'[92] An example of the cynical use of self-orientalization can be found in the conversation between Stojan Protić (who wrote under the pseudonym Balcanicus) and Ante Trumbić of the Yugoslav Committee in 1917, reported by Ivan Meštrović in his memoirs. Protić is quoted as saying that

> When our army crosses the Drina, it will give the Turks twenty four or even forty eight hours to return to the faith of their ancestors. Those who are unwilling will be struck down (*posjeći*) as we have done on other occasions in Serbia.[93]

Trumbić was silent, but Meštrović could see that his hands were trembling. Then he asked Protić if he was serious, who replied, 'Very serious, Mr Trumbić. In Bosnia with the Turks one cannot use European methods, but must use ours (*po naški*).' Rastko Močnik's argument about the construction of such categories of self has some pertinence here: 'what may appear as a discourse of self-degradation, actually operates as a discourse of domination.'[94] In these terms, Protić' argument serves the position of nationalists very well, but remains essentially a highly cynical construction or self-constitution. As Močnik continues

> contrary to Orientalism, where the logic of domination is imposed by colonial rule, in Balkanism, it is the immanent logic of self constitution that generates the incapacity to conceive of oneself in other terms than from the point of view of the dominating other.[95]

During the twentieth century anti-Islam continued to be an essential *Leitmotiv* within Serbian and Montenegrin nationalist discourse. To some nationalists, it remained the unsolved problem of Yugoslavian politics. In 1933, the President of the Council of Ministers, Milan Srškić stated, 'I cannot stand to see minarets in Bosnia; they must disappear.'[96] The notorious lecture given by Vasa Čubrilović in 1937 to the *Srpski kulturni klub* about the ethnic cleansing of Albanians from Kosovo[97] contains a distillation of his anti-Islamic prejudices and self-orientalization. Kosovo and Bosnia were the sites of particularly vicious interethnic fighting in the period from 1941 to 1945. Elsewhere in Yugoslavia during the Second World War, Muslims were targeted on the grounds of their faith and ethnicity.[98] It is estimated between 86,000 and 103,000 Slav Muslims were killed in Bosnia and Sandžak. Many perished at the hands of Serb nationalist Četnici. In the 1920s some Četnik extremists supported the 'uniting of Slav Muslims with Kemal-Pasha (i.e. Atatürk)'.[99] In the 1930s the newspaper *Vidovdan* continued to publish inflammatory anti-Muslim opinions.[100] Similarly there were some, including Government minister Kosta Krstić who wanted to send the Albanians of Kosovo on a 'one way ticket' (*bezpovratno*) to 'Asia'.[101] During the Second World War, the Četnik ideologue Stevan Moljević, who advocated 'cleansing the land of all non-Serb elements', believed that the government in exile in London 'should resolve the issue (of emigration) with Turkey',[102] although with the Communist ascent to power and the defamation of the Četnik movement, the plan remained a theory, seemingly relegated to the past. However, Moljević' ideas didn't entirely disappear in the wake of relatively good interethnic relations after the Second World War. They were resurrected in 1991 by the self-styled heir of the Četnici, Vojislav Šešelj, who had been jailed for his nationalist views in the mid-1980s, when he told the German newspaper *Der Spiegel*, that Muslims were islamicized Serbs, whom he would drive out of Bosnia to Anatolia, if they opposed any attempt to take away their status as a nation.[103]

In the postwar era, the Communist regime in Yugoslavia attempted a fine balancing act between the nationalities within its borders with various levels of success. In the 1980s, after the death of Tito, Yugoslavia's Muslims were again remarginalized by certain Serb nationalists such as Miroljub Jevtić, who attempted to link the rise of Islamic 'fundamentalism' in the wider world but particularly Iran to the Muslims in his own country.[104] In Belgrade in 1989, a journalist informed Sabrina Ramet that, 'they [i.e. Bosnian and Kosovo Muslims] have big families in order to swamp Serbia and Yugoslavia with Muslims and turn Yugoslavia into a Muslim republic. They want to see Khomeni in charge here.'[105] According to Norman Cigar, Serbian scholars specializing in Oriental Studies (including Jevtić), 'contributed considerably to making hostility towards the Muslim community intellectually respectable among the broad strata of the Serbian population'.[106] Some priests in the Orthodox Church played a significant role in this process of radicalization[107] but as a whole the Church remained ambivalent in its support of anti-Muslim activities in the 1990s. Amfilohije Radović made extremely anti-Islamic and anti-Croat statements, while others, such as Patriarch Pavle, frequently made pleas against violence and war crimes. A tense situation was inflamed by the trial of Alija Izetbegović for 'nationalism' after the circulation of his anti-Communist 'Islamic Declaration' in 1970.[108] Other Yugoslavs thought that he was advocating a state based on Islamic religious law (*sharia*).[109]

Elsewhere the denial of a Bosnian spirit of mutual respect between religious communities by Šešelj,[110] who echoed with his characteristic lack of originality some of the negative sentiments of about Islam and the cultural life of Bosnia's Muslims propagated by the writer Ivo Andrić,[111] was a flagrant manipulation of history and a genuine tradition of peaceful coexistence in that republic. It was also during this period that interethnic relations deteriorated considerably in Kosovo,[112] although the Albanians there were not considered to be traitors to the Serbs in the way that Slavonic speaking Muslims were.[113] The novelist Vuk Drašković, whose own political attitude towards the Muslims has been marked by inconsistency, also broke 'the mould shaped by Tito'[114] with the publication of *Nož* (The Knife) in 1982,[115] which has notable anti-Islamic sentiments in its depiction of interethnic violence during the Second World War in Hercegovina.

From rhetoric to ethnic cleansing

The link between the propaganda of the 1980s and the fighting of the 1990s has been well documented. After the breakdown of Communist authority between 1987 and 1990, official media in Serbia, Kosovo, Montenegro and Croatia became filled with 'hate-filled panic-mongering rhetoric',[116] which clearly prepared the populations of certain regions and republics for interethnic strife. Prior to the Bosnian elections of 1992, the Serbian Democratic Party (SDS Srpska Demokratska Stranka) told voters that

> if Bosnia became independent they would once again be subjected to the laws of the Muslim landlords, agas, begs and pashas, and that independence represented a rollback of everything Serbs had died for since 1804, if not 1389 . . . [Serbs] were told that for hundreds of years they had been Bosnia's single largest community and that in the last twenty-five years the Muslims had suddenly 'outbred' them.[117]

In April 1992, a Serb soldier Miloš fighting in the siege of Sarajevo told journalist Ed Vulliamy:

> Their [Muslim] women are bitches and whores. They breed like animals, more than ten per woman . . . Down there they are fighting for a single land that will stretch from here to Tehran, where our women will wear shawls, where there is bigamy . . .[118]

Prior to the massacre at Srebrenica in Bosnia, in which thousands of Muslim men were executed and dumped in the surrounding killing fields, Ratko Mladić appeared on Bosnian Serb television on 11 July 1995, telling viewers that the moment for revenge against the 'Turks' had finally come. He announced that

Srebrenica was now 'Serbian' and that it was his gift to the 'Serb nation'.[119] His speech was the final part of a drama that had opened in the Bosnian Parliament on 15 October 1991, when Radovan Karadžić told the Muslims that they had chosen a path to their own annihilation by seeking independence.[120] In such rarified circumstances, it appears that certain numbers of people simply abandoned their experience and sense, becoming motivated by carefully constructed and whipped up 'instinct' to destroy the other, however chimerical these notions might have been in practice. Homi Bhabha is probably right when he states that 'rumour and panic are, in moments of social crisis, double sites of enunciation that weave their stories around the disjunctive "present" or the "not-there" of discourse'.[121] Negative stereotypes outlived the war and dislocation of the Muslim population. Some 400 Serbs asked to characterize Muslims in a questionnaire in 1997 in Belgrade described them as 'primitive', 'mendacious', 'hostile to other nations', 'dirty', 'uncultivated', 'squabbling', 'stupid', 'cowardly' and 'lazy'.[122] In the same year Mitar Debelonogić published a series of short stories in Republika Srpska entitled *Balije* (Muslims), relating to the dehumanization of Muslims and the self-image of the Bosnian Serb soldiers.[123]

The mythology of the destruction of the Islamic communities is in sharp contrast with reality of rubbish, rubble and destruction of community. On driving through Kozarac in Bosnia, a town that had a population that was 90 per cent Muslim before 1992, Margaret Vandiver was shocked by the destruction she saw:

> The mosque was in ruins and its minarets lay broken in the weeds. In the Serb part of town, on the other hand, a football game was underway, meat roasted on spits and people met in coffee houses and bars, while a block away, the ruined homes of their former neighbours stood as testimony to the terrible crimes committed.[124]

Although she felt that the fact that life was going on amongst the Serbs in Kozarac was a testimony to their indifference to the plight of their former neighbours, the fact that the old buildings had been left in ruins may represent what Stanley Cohen has characterized as a 'state of denial', especially as the destruction of Muslim heritage was comprehensive in some places, with concrete covering the sites of religious buildings and denials that Islamic communities had ever existed.[125] Cohen argues that '[d]enial is understood as an unconscious defence mechanism for coping with guilt, anxiety, and other disturbing emotions aroused by reality. The psyche blocks off information that is literally unthinkable or unbearable' and as a result, as Cohen says 'the unconscious sets up a barrier, which prevents the thought from reaching conscious knowledge. Information and memories slip into an inaccessible region of the mind.'[126] One of the accused soldiers in the military trial in Niš in 2000, Dragiša Petrović, stated that he remembered the events in Gornja Susica in Kosovo, in which elderly Albanians were murdered, as if 'through a fog'. This may be cynical obfuscation, but may also be the psychological mechanism by which he denied his own participation in (and responsibility for) the events.[127]

The practice of ethnic cleansing does not organically erupt from within a society. It is a planned affair, announced in advance, its practice intimately linked to a small number of individuals who see it as either a desirable or unavoidable part of their wider political concerns. Hate texts feed into a low level awareness of difference, which exists at the level of popular culture, but would never come to widespread violence if individuals with power did not provoke it. To state that there is a link between nationalist propaganda and popular culture can in no way diminish the responsibility of the individual. Ideologies are like ajar doors, which any individual more or less chooses to walk through. Nevertheless, an individual surrounded by carefully constructed hate images will tap into existing prejudices, perhaps lodged at the back of the mind, such as an adolescent reading of Njegoš and could in extreme circumstances be overtaken by the crisis of the moment.

Orientalism and its discontents

Attitudes towards Muslims in Croatian nationalist discourses are also marked by ambivalences. On the one hand, the Croats have inherited a kind of orientalist discourse about Islam, its adherents and their culture, which is reminiscent of the ideas put forward by Serb, Greek and Bulgarian nationalists. On the other hand many Croatian nationalists have regarded the Muslims of Bosnia as unredeemed Croats, whose religious affiliation has not altered their basic genetic 'Croathood'. Sometimes this orientalist attitude was used to condemn Serbs by association. Ante Trumbić to Henri Pozzi in Zagreb in 1935:

> You are not going to compare, I hope, the Croats, the Slovenes, the Dalmatians whom centuries of artistic, moral and intellectual communion with Austria, Italy and Hungary have made pure occidentals with these half-civilized Serbs, the Balkan hybrids of Slavs and Turks. They are barbarians, even their chiefs, whose occidentalism goes no further than their phraseology and the cut of their clothes.[128]

The Croat gusle singer Mile Krajina lamented that the introduction of a Turkish language course at the University of Zagreb in 2000 was a return to the forced learning of the language during the Ottoman times.[129] Given that the Ottomans rarely forced Balkan populations to learn Turkish, this prejudice shows the power of ideas over experience. The late Croatian Defence Minister Gojko Sušak claimed that 110,000 Bosnian Muslims (some 5 per cent of the entire population!) were studying fundamentalism in Egypt, thus echoing the Serbian orientalists of the 1980s.[130] Many Bosnian Muslims did not feel any less threatened by the nationalism of Croats than by that of Serbs. President Alija Izetbegović once wryly remarked that choosing between Franjo Tudjman and Slobodan Milošević was like choosing between a brain tumour and leukaemia.[131]

Orientalist themes were also present in the arts. One of the classics of Croatian literature, *Smrt Smail-age Čengijića* (The Death of the Aga Ismail Ćengijić) by the poet Ivan Mazuranić, explores the theme of Slavic Christian resistance to Turkish oppression in Hercegovina.[132] The moderate and philosophical Stjepan Radić initially referred to the Bosnian Muslims as 'Muslim Croats', but after his travels in that region in 1910, he decided that they were neither Croats nor Serbs, whose national definition along religious lines and rivalry had sidelined Islamic speakers of the same language.[133] Paradoxically Croat fascists enthusiastically embraced the incorporation of Muslims into their ethnos. The fascists took on board Ante Starčević' belief that the Muslim Slavs 'are of Croatian stock, the most able (*najstanje*) and purest nobility that Europe has'.[134] In 1941, the Uštasa Mile Budak in a speech at Križevci declared that 'we Croats are happy and proud of our (Christian) faith but we must be conscious of the fact that our Muslim brothers are the purest of Croats just as our blessed late teacher Ante Starčević told us . . . This is something we must build up, as we build up the *Nezavisna Država Hrvatska* (Independent State of Croatia).'[135] The Ustaša *poglavnik*, Ante Pavelić, was even pictured wearing a ceremonial fez.[136] For some Croats, Bosnia represented their own unredeemed lands. In 1990, a Canadian Croat Josef Zorek told Misha Glenny: 'Croatia and Bosnia and Hercegovina together form a bio-geographic, historic, ethnic whole as an indivisible unit of the Croatian nation. Their future is bound together, and through organization it will become a sovereign Croatian state.'[137] Franjo Tudjman believed that the 'majority of the Muslims is in its ethnic character and speech incontrovertibly of Croatian national origin'.[138] This particular quirk of Croat fascists did not prevent the destruction of Muslim material culture or the ethnic cleansing of Muslims in Hercegovina in 1993 by Croat extremists and paramilitaries, particularly in the Lasva valley. The village of Ahmići was razed to the ground and some of its inhabitants burnt alive.[139] In the nearby camp of Kaonik, Muslims were rounded up and forced to do backbreaking labour. Some of the female inmates were raped.[140]

In 1991, Croatian nationalist Anto Valenta published a study entitled *Podjela Bosne i Borba za Cjelovitost* (The Division of Bosnia and the Struggle for Unity) in which he advocated a Lausanne style exchange of population, creating Croat, Serb and Muslim 'regions' (*regije*) from the former Socialist Yugoslavian Republic, whose borders had been decided upon historical grounds in 1945. According to his calculations 194,000 Serbs would leave the central Muslim regions, to be replaced by the same number of Muslims who would leave the Serbian entity. Similarly, 170,000 Croats would leave the central part of Bosnia to be exchanged for 170,000 Muslims coming in from the Croat region. He also advocated the exchange of some 95,000 Serbs and Croats respectively from their regions.[141] This pre-war theory was put into horrific practice by Croatian paramilitaries in May 1993. Mario Cerkez, the commander of the HVO Vitez brigade took advice from Valenta about military tactics and the ethnic cleansing of Muslims.[142]

Many writers and some Muslims have claimed that a sense of moral superiority prevailed amongst Muslims in the Balkans to the extent that they did not always recognize the dangers they were facing. It is true that many subsequent victims of ethnic cleansing find it hard to accept that their society will deteriorate and that atrocities will be perpetrated: Muslims are not alone in this. A woman refugee from Sarajevo explained this feeling particularly well. She went to Subotica and was living there, but could not be reconciled with the treatment she sometimes received: She recalled that 'a woman came up to me in the middle of lunch and spat at me in front of fifty other people'. She was then called a '*balija*' (a derogatory term for Muslim in Serbian and Croatian). The woman continued: 'Many nights, I used to wonder what I did wrong to make people behave toward me in such a way. I knew that my depression came from the fact that I was not capable of getting used to it. I had lived so long in a city of love with the greatest possible mixing of ethnicities.'[143]

In 1991, 'many Sarajevan Muslims held fast to the belief that, although Serbs and Croats may fight, Muslims were too civilized and would remain calm in the face of all'.[144] . An American writer was told by a survivor of the Bosnian wars:

> [O]ur attitude . . . [w]e called it merhamet – that you felt sorry for someone who has bad luck. Philanthropy. You like all people. You want to support everyone. If you can help, you help. You can even forgive bad things. You can find good in all religions. You will be good and decent to everyone . . . Only Bosnians believed in brotherhood and unity and agreed with that idea . . . When Tito gave speeches, he'd say, 'You must uphold brotherhood and unity . . . And I think that only Muslims and Macedonians tried to avoid any kind of conflict in the former Yugoslavia . . . "For all" that is one of the main sayings of merhamet.'[145]

There is little evidence, however, to suggest that Muslims have adopted superior patterns of behaviour to Christians in the Balkans, although the balance of responsibility for the violence and ethnic cleansing of Muslims clearly comes from within nationalist and nominally Christian discourses.[146] A missionary Julius Richter, who witnessed a pogrom against Armenians in Turkey in the 1890s recorded that the

> massacre was heralded by the blowing of trumpets and concluded by a procession. Accompanied by the prayers of the mollahs [sic] and muezzins, who from the minarets implored the blessings of Allah, the slaughter was accomplished in admirable order according to a well arranged plan. The crowd, supplied with arms by the authorities, joined most amicably with the soldiers and the Kurdish *Hamidieh* on these festive occasions. The Turkish women stimulated their heroes by raising a gutteral shriek of their war cry, the *Zilghit* and deafening the hopeless despair of their victims by singing their nuptial songs. A kind of wild cannibal humour seized the crowd . . . the savage crew did not even spare the children.[147]

The account suggests a widespread participation in the ethnic cleansing of Armenians by Turkish (and Kurdish) Muslims and all the symbolic elements of alienation that occurred in Bosnia and elsewhere in the Balkans. During the reprisals for the Ilinden Uprising in Macedonia in 1903, according to Bulgarian sources, 9,830 houses burnt down by the Turks and 60,953 people left homeless.[148] In Bulgaria in 1912 in the village of Karaj-Chiflik local people were slaughtered as they sought sanctuary in the church. One eyewitness, Vladmir Nemirovich-Danchenko, who had witnessed the atrocities in 1877–8, recalled 'the church . . . completely blackened by fire. On the path dead children, little girls with split skulls and legs spread apart . . . once my eyes get used to the dark, I see the pile of burnt bodies of people desperate to break down the doors.'[149] The behaviour of Muslim government troops also became brutal during the recent war and they committed atrocities against Serbs and Croats.[150] No culturally specific patterns of cruelty can be deduced from reading the narrative of the decline of Muslim populations, but similarities between cultures are striking and parallels between these events and others outside the Balkans can and should be made.

By the beginning of the twenty-first century, Muslim communities are more fragmented than ever before, with the possible exception of Albanians in Kosovo and Albania. The marginalization and weakening of these communities may have been inevitable after the collapse of the Ottoman Empire and the introduction of the European principal of nationality into the Balkans, but it was certainly aided and abetted by a discursive radicalization that began to construct these Muslim communities as aliens and outsiders, whose existence could never be reconciled with the nation states of Montenegrins, Serbs, Croats, Greeks, Bulgarians and latterly even Macedonians.

3   Bandits and paramilitaries

The area once known as Yugoslavia is a jumble of steep hills, dusty plateaus and impenetrable valleys – a terrible place to fight, but a wonderful place for guerilla warfare.[1]

Bandit traditions

The tradition of banditry and liminal existence on the margins of the Ottoman Empire was a fact of life from the fifteenth to the early twentieth centuries.[2] Those men, who for whatever reason could not continue to live under either corrupt local governors or the Ottoman state with its laws that discriminated against non-Muslims, found themselves on the 'ramparts of Christianity', but also all too often on the edges of the Habsburg lands and until 1815, the Venetian Empire. The idea of the bandit became an integral part of Balkan tradition at the level of popular culture and they were known variously as četnici or hajduci across the region from Bulgaria to Dalmatia. In the late sixteenth century peasants between Niš and Sofia sang rebel songs on their way back from the fields in the evening, which glorified the bandits living on those margins.[3] For the peasants, the bandits represented in some sense their 'hope for justice and fascination with violence', becoming a 'vehicle for the discussion of social values, regardless of the realities of bandit actions'.[4] Sometimes the life of a bandit seemed an exciting alternative to daily life, even for children. Somewhat later, as a Muslim refugee in Edirne at the turn of the twentieth century, Şevket Aydemir remembered that as a child 'our most popular game was to play at bands (*çete*) and committees (*komite*) . . . Those who took part in the game would turn back the edges of their fezes to make them look like the hats worn by Greek and Bulgarian bandits.'[5]

By the time of the first uprising in Serbia in 1804, the Balkans 'had a floating population of soldiers, deserters, bandits – men who had lost land, home or kin as Ottoman rule retreated or retaliated'.[6] Kristo Punoshevitch told George Sava in the summer of 1939 that the leaders of the 1804 rebellion against the Ottomans were 'hayduks, robbers, riff-raff, just like me . . . it was people like us who fought the first battle for Serbian liberty'.[7] Over the years, bandits had been a considerable menace to Ottoman authority. Back in the early seventeenth century, the intrepid

Scottish traveller, William Lithgow described the bandits known as Uscoks or Skoks who lived in the Senj area of the Adriatic : 'They are marvellous swift on foote and dayly annoy by land their neighbouring Turkes with inroads, fetching away great spoyles and booties, of cornes, cattell and horses.'[8] David Urquhart, writing in the 1830s, believed that banditry was so extensive in the Ottoman domains because of the widespread abuses of local despots, the pasha and agas, rather than a more general and systemic problem coming from the Porte. He described the Greek mountain bandits, the Kléphtai thus:

> The peasant, chained down by family attachments . . . endures labour, pay; but ventures neither to remonstrate nor complain, until some crowning indignity bursts all these bonds at once; he flies to the mountains . . . and with Albanian kirtle, pistol in his belt and musket over his shoulder, he presents the veriest contrast to what he has been. The tame, submissive beast of burden becomes the wolf of the plain and vulture of the mountain.[9]

Generally Balkan bandits have held a deep commitment to being a kind of army in waiting in the mountains, ready for when they are needed by the Christian populations (for bandits were rarely Muslim, except for some of the Albanian kaçaks). Traian Stoianovich has argued that non-Muslims in the Balkans who anticipated liberation from the Ottomans had a 'millenarian outlook' and that they possessed a 'concept of the dead as a participant age cohort', somewhat similar to the Celtic Arthurian legends.[10] Thus, in times of need the dead would return to fight for justice. Some believed that Kraljević Marko, a Turkish vassal who played an important role in South Slav and Serb folklore as a symbol of rebellion, was biding his time before he awoke and 'drove the Turks across the blue sea'.[11] During the Ilinden Uprising in Macedonia in 1903, the čete had made their plans to drive out the Turks. 'Hundreds of men began digging, uncovering the buried weapons which had been lying hidden for months and years in anticipation of the event.'[12] In the 1990s, the idea of summoning up an army to rid Bosnia of the remaining Muslim populations was used by their opponents. In 1991, Radovan Karadžić warned that 'we could mobilize and arm up to half a million soldiers in BiH . . . such a war would be bloody and tough . . . it would settle many things'.[13] He often repeated the idea that the war in Bosnia was a kind of final showdown between Serbs and Muslims. (These comments must be seen as largely rhetorical given the widespread problem of desertion amongst Serbs and Montenegrins fighting outside their republics in the early 1990s[14] and the fact the draft call in the Federal Republic of Yugoslavia in 1991/2 was such a patent disaster in numerical terms.)[15]

The genius of the first rebels against the Ottomans was to link these traditions to a more general political struggle against a foreign overlord and eventually to constructions of national identity. This also meant that a certain kind of political roughness and violence became a central rather than peripheral[16] part of post-Ottoman Balkan political life from the beginning of the nineteenth century.[17] The first uprising against the Ottomans was led by Karadjordje ('Black George' whom *The Times* referred to by his Serb name of 'Czerni George') who had been a one time hajduk as well as an Austrian army auxiliary.[18] Karadjordje became a model for Albanian kaçaks, who thought that if he and his 'rayas could win a piece of land from a mighty empire, why could they not do the same'.[19] In Greece the bandits were also mobilized in the struggle for independence from the Ottomans. C.M. Woodhouse commented of the Kléphtai that their 'rough leaders in the Peloponnese . . . early acquired a craftier understanding of the political issues of the revolution [of 1821]'.[20] Their existence became a definitive part of national identity: the Četnici, Kléphtai, Kaçaks and Macedonian revolutionary VMRO had some of their roots in the hajduk or bandit tradition.

During the course of the nineteenth century, bandit traditions came to represent single national traditions. The process of mobilizing bandits as anti-Ottoman forces became equally important in the struggle for 'national liberation'. In 1912, Trotsky compared the Macedonian Četnici to Italian Carbonari, who had fought a guerilla war for the unification of Italy in the mid-nineteenth century, dubbing them 'national revolutionaries'.[21] After the outbreak of the war the Montenegrin Punoshevitch wrote to Sava informing him of his new status:

> I am the leader of the Chetniks. We are an old organization. We are outlaws. Yet no government has been able to suppress us. None has dared, nor I think has any ever thought it wise to make the attempt. We came into being to fight the Turks. We have our own uniforms and our own code of laws. We have fought in every Balkan War. We are the natural guerillas of our country.[22]

Even after the fall of the Ottoman Empire, bandits in border or contested areas even served to destabilize the new states. Albanian kaçaks operated in Kosovo for years after that region was incorporated into Serbia[23] and kaçak bands in Macedonia started cattle rustling. In 1918, an estimated 10,000 animals were stolen in the Debur region.[24] One Serb described their activities as 'not plain criminal, political or social brigands as such, but a particular type of Albanian outlaw . . . nowadays assuming a new nationalist . . . form'.[25] In some sense these extensive traditions of bandit violence and liminality are linked to the origins of the political movement that was responsible for paramilitary fighting and much of the ethnic cleansing[26] and it is quite clear that modern nationalists have utilized bandit mythologies quite extensively.

Četnici, invented tradition and murderous gangs

After the breakdown of authority in Yugoslavia in 1941 and the rapid Nazi partition of the country, the first sign of revolt from the citizens came from within Serbia and more significantly from former army officers led by Draža Mihailović. These Serbian monarchists, or Četnici as they became universally known, were conscious of the past and again like their predecessor linked their own political movement with older struggles. The strength of this partly oral tradition can be in seen during the Second World War. The organization into četas by distraught Serbs in the fascist Independent Croatia (*Nezavisna Država Hrvatska*) after the first

Ustaša atrocities in April 1941 was often on a rapid, 'spontaneous and local basis',[27] preempting the formal leadership of either Mihailović or the Partisans, although they initially referred to themselves as *ustanici* (rebels) not as Četnici.

Although they were formed primarily to oppose the German occupation and partition of royal Yugoslavia, Četnici spent more energy ethnically cleansing regions of Bosnia of Muslims and Catholics and eventually collaborated with the Germans, (although it is fair to add that the Partisans entered into a brief agreement on non-confrontation with the German troops after the Neretva battle and used that time to strike a decisive blow at the Četnici). They were conscious that their knowledge of territory could give them the upper hand, utilizing traditions of guerilla fighting. An anti-Partisan pamphlet found in Gračac in 1942 commented that the Communists had 'treacherously opened our free mountains, for centuries the asylum of the Serbian people, to the greatest enemies of the Serbian people, the wild Ustaše and the Turks'.[28] Local knowledge was also used elsewhere to give the fighters the upper hand. In Greece during the Second World War, the guerillas known as Andartes used the *limeria* or lairs used by the Kléphtai in earlier generations.[29] The Serbian Ozren unit founded in September 1991 and named after the mountain in Bosnia sought to uphold the 'best' traditions of their predecessors.[30] Mirko from the village of Ljeskovac in the Romanija mountain region of Bosnia told a journalist in 1997 that it would be impossible to catch Bosnian Serb General Ratko Mladić to take him to the Hague because foreign troops did not understand the terrain fully:

> How could they (SFOR) approach him? They will be pierced by the pine trees if they jump with a parachute, and we are here to track them down in the forest. This would be worse for them than Vietnam. If they take the road to get him, we will finish them off with anti-tank shoulder launchers. There are as many people here as you like, both us and the soldiers.[31]

During the Yugoslavian wars of dissolution some of the bandit tradition was effectively mobilized[32] and much of the fighting was undertaken by paramilitaries as opposed to regular soldiers in the JNA (Yugoslav People's Army, – that effectively disintegrated between 1991 and 1992), although it is fair to say that without the tacit and sometimes active support of the JNA, the paramilitaries would probably have been a lot less confident in their tactics. In the 1991–2 period, it appears that the relationship between the paramilitaries and the JNA evolved. By the time of the final struggle for Vukovar in November 1991, they were very closely cooperating. Paramilitaries were often used as infantry and for the explicit purpose of ethnic cleansing. The Serb paramilitary fighters in Croatia and Bosnia often referred to themselves and were referred to by others directly as Četnici and drew some of their inspiration from fighters in the Balkan Wars and the Second World War. The strength of this myth of the Četnik fighter was of inestimable importance during these military campaigns. Mladen Vuksanović, who was based in the Bosnian Serb Army headquarters in Pale in 1992, described how his nationalist colleague Miodrag Tarana had threatened him for his lack of commitment to the Serbian cause. As Vuksanović explained:

His rage at me and the 'Turks' who must be exterminated swells with every glass . . . [he] keeps saying that he is a 'real chetnik', and there are thousands of 'Serb militia' up on Jahorina along with Arkan's men, just waiting for the word to sweep down on Sarajevo.[33]

During the twentieth-century wars, Četnici even dressed in traditional fashion. In the nineteenth century, they were supposed to wear traditional high trousers and *opanke* (bark sandals).[34] The Serbian home guard during the Balkan Wars wore the same peasant dress with *opanke* and lamb skin caps, as its government attempted to draft even the elderly in a desperate attempt to survive against a formidable enemy.[35] To take on the appearance of primitive rebels by harsh necessity rather amused the partisan fighter Vladimir Dedijer as he remarked that 'with our laden horses and rifles, we looked like hayduks . . . in the theater'.[36] The Četnik leader during the Second World War, Draža Mihailović quickly lost the formal appearance of a Yugoslavian officer and wore a heavy beard for most of the war. His colleague Dragoslav Račić 'was something of a model Balkan revolutionary . . . wearing a large beard and the local peasant dress'.[37] In the 1990s beards quickly reappeared amongst the extreme national fringes as a badge of warriorhood in Serbia itself and amongst Bosnians and Montenegrins.

By the late 1980s, young people in the former Yugoslavia had been toying with nationalist imagery on the fringes of established culture for some years, most notably in the Republic of Slovenia where the rock group *Laibach* regularly dressed up in Nazi uniforms in their concerts or poked fun at the more kitsch end of the art of the Tito era.[38] However harmless the Slovene rock scene might have been, the revival of far right imagery amongst Serbian youths had more obvious active purposes, although it is likely that this kind of playful and creative irony found in Slovenia was somewhat insidious given the role of chauvinism and antipathy towards 'Southerners' in that republic's politics in the late 1980s. This form of 'irony' was not so popular in Bosnia, even among young people.[39] In 1991, Misha Glenny described the scene on the Belgrade street Knez Mihailova with 'young men with long hair, beards and denim jackets all selling bile of Chenikdom: t-shirts with the words "Freedom or death" curled around a skull and crossbones or proclaiming "Ravna Gora . . . the camp of Serbia's heroes", not to mention the endless streams of Chetnik and nationalist songs on tape'.[40] Not content with selling their 'bile', these young men would join up with the various brands of Serb paramilitary groups that were recruiting at this time, with the tacit and sometimes active acceptance of the regime. Sometimes little boys of five or six wearing fatigues and 'carrying plastic replicas of assault weapons'[41] would accompany their parents on the streets of Belgrade. In Zagreb, there were obvious signs of militarization of society by the outbreak of war in the early 1990s.[42] The neo-fascist Dobroslav Paraga leader of the *Hrvatske Obrambene Snage* (HOS – Croatian Defence Forces), set himself up in the faded grandeur of the Hotel Esplanade 'complete with crewcut paramilitaries in black camouflage strutting round outside the door'.[43] Croat children were acculturated early into military ways. In the Lašva valley in the spring of 1992, a witness at the Hague

Tribunal remembered that 'even small children had camouflaged uniforms made for them by their mothers'.[44]

In 1991 and thereafter until 1999, Slobodan Milošević and Franjo Tudjman used right-wing radicals, sometimes playing one group off against another both 'so that they could appear the more moderate and stabilizing factor to the international community and to undercut other nationalist parties in their opposition'.[45] They also were able to disassociate themselves from the worst fighting in the theatres of war, because it was difficult to link either of them directly to the fighters, although undoubtedly chains of command (*vojne linije*) stretching to Belgrade and Zagreb did exist and will be established more definitely in the trial of Slobodan Milošević in the Hague Tribunal.[46] Vojislav Šešelj claimed that the ethnic cleansing of the Bosnian town of Zvornik 'was organized in Belgrade'. Moreover he stated that:

> The army (JNA) engaged itself to a small degree – it gave artillery support where it was needed. The operation had been prepared for a long time. It wasn't carried out in any kind of nervous fashion. Everything was well-organized and implemented.[47]

Elsewhere in Bosnia, there were clearly some links between the Milošević regime and paramilitary actors. One former Red Beret (a unit of the Serbian Ministry of Internal Affairs), a group led by Franko Simatović, described the actions of his brigade in Mostar:

> They took about a hundred Muslim and Croat civilians – men and women – from a shelter and lined them up on the banks of the Neretva river. Standing on the other side, I watched as five of the Red Berets executed them all. Some were shot, others they knifed or bludgeoned with rifle butts as they screamed for mercy. Eventually, an excavator came to bury the bodies.[48]

In the 1990s, the actions of the HOS and the Četnici drew heavily on imagination and 'invented tradition'.[49] The black uniforms of HOS and their Ustaša paraphernalia were obvious reinventions of the uniforms of the Second World War. For some people the reappearance of old historical symbols was in itself quite bizarre and frightening. One Bosnian who was driven out of his home town commenting in 1992, remembered that 'they looked to me like real Chetniks, which I had seen before only in films about World War Two.[50] Another Bosnian from Bijeljina remembered how in 1992 as she attempted to cross the border her bus was stopped: 'In front of the bus a drunk man with a long beard and a strange cap, red eyes and a knife stained with blood stood saying, "Is there a balija I have to kill?". As my blood froze in my veins, I remembered the movies about Partisans and Chetniks and I realized that he looked exactly like a Chetnik from the movies.'[51] Sometimes victims of ethnic cleansing could only make sense of their experiences by recourse to the events of 1940s (and it is clear that those who donned historical costumes knew that after years of anti-fascist propaganda, the mere sight of such uniforms ensured that many poeple vacated their homes very quickly. Zlata Filipović recorded that the convoys leaving Sarajevo in 1992, reminded her 'of the movies I saw about Jews in the Second World War'.[52]

Intellectuals such as Vojislav Šešelj, who refounded the Serbian Četnik Movement in June 1990,[53] very consciously drew on reinvented tradition. He crowned himself as heir to Stevan Moljević and was promoted to the highest Četnik rank of 'vojvoda' (duke) by Momcilo Djujić, a leading Četnik from the Second World War and elderly émigré, living in exile in the United States.[54] In the way that Nicolo Machiavelli is reported to have dressed himself up in a toga before addressing an imaginary Roman senate in his study,[55] he clothed himself in imaginary costumes from the Second World War. In 1991, Šešelj was photographed in Croatia wearing a Četnik fur hat (*šubara*) and carrying a gun.[56] His ideology was book-learnt (or rather map-learnt) since he has had rather a creative gaze when looking at the maps of neighbouring countries. He planned to cut down Croatia to a tiny size[57] and in 1992 he spoke in favour of a partition of Macedonia between the Former Republic of Yugoslavia (FRY), Bulgaria and a small portion going to Albania.[58] He also decided to jettison support for the London based Crown Prince Alexander Karadjordjević on the grounds that he was too anglicized, switching his support to Aleksie Dolgorukii Nemanjić Romanov who claimed to be a descendant of the medieval Nemanja dynasty (and no doubt a few other royal families if his surname is anything to go by).[59] Šešelj certainly tapped into a current in Serbian nationalist discontent. After his arrest for 'anti-party activities' in 1984, he even attracted international attention from Human Rights campaigners such as Amnesty International.[60] Without its artificial revival in the 1980s, traditions of fascism, bandit fighting and *četništvo* would have died from lack of fresh air and new blood. But the behaviour of the Četnici in the later part of the twentieth century was never that of freemen struggling against an alien oppressor: the enemies were essentially internal. Its central defining core was the creation and/or preservation of a state for all Serbs to live in with no toleration towards ethnic or religious minorities.

Četnici traditionally took no prisoners. Matija Ban's *Pravila o četničkoj vojni* (Regulations for Četnik Warfare) published in Belgrade in 1848 stated that the main aim of fighting was to kill and that a final kill should always take place.[61] Četnici who were captured expected to be killed and showed themselves to be contemptuous of death[62] or at least they cultivated this reputation. (Amongst regular soldiers in the Croatian campaigns of 1991 and in Kosovo in 1999, they had a reputation for terrorizing civilians, but running from the first signs of battle.) In Borovo Selo in Croatia in July 1991, a young soldier Ivan described the capture of a Serb from Šid:

> He was a reservist, thirty years old, but extreme you could tell straight away. He had a membership card of the Chetnik's party and a photo of Šešelj . . . We called their barracks, we thought that maybe we could work out an exchange of prisoners . . . From the barracks they said: those men of ours who you've captured don't deserve to live if they allowed themselves to fall into the hands of Ustashas. When we capture yours, you know what we do to them. And this reservist he started to laugh, he was proud of it . . .[63]

Paramilitaries used a reputation for their cruelty and ruthlessness to frighten their enemies. During the Balkan Wars, Macedonian Komitadji floated the bodies of headless Albanians under the Vardar bridge in Skopje.[64] The Bulgarian hajduk was described as a man who lived beyond the law and without the sympathy of the peasantry 'without friends except for his comrades . . . he rarely limits himself to simply robbery, but murders with a pure lust for bloodshed'.[65] Četnik terror during the Second World War is well documented. Jozo Tomasevich has argued that Četnici, like the Ustasa,[66] followed the 'cult of the knife'. The tradition of using metal weapons when they had guns available is somewhat puzzling, but seems to confirm that the ritual of killing and having been seen to have killed was as important as the outcome (i.e. ethnic cleansing). The Gurkhas in the British Army also retain some of these beliefs. The so-called 'black troikas' of the Četnici would use knives during their terror campaigns, earning them the Partisan nickname of '*koljači*' (cut-throats).[67] Elsewhere knives were used, when other more modern weapons would have been more 'efficient'. In Pale in 1997, a journalist was told: 'there is a kind of knife, we call it *krvokolj* (blood-knife), that is what one should use against SFOR'.[68] During the Balkan Wars, Macedonians would shout '*na Nozh!*' (i.e. go in with the bayonets!) before battle.[69] Trotsky as war correspondent and witness to many events of the Balkan Wars comments on the high morale of the Bulgarian soldiers who put flowers in their caps marching to the front. He felt that the 'war offered the masses of the Bulgarian people the prospect of finishing at last with the Turkish past and the Turkish present',[70] but he also noted that morale was low among the Turks who did not always use bayonets,[71] perhaps confirming Joanna Bourke's thesis about the importance of direct and 'intimate' killing in modern warfare and the importance of the bayonet.[72] Moreover as Slavoj Žižek has argued

> soldiers often fantasise about killing the enemy in a face to face confrontation, looking him into [sic] the eyes before stabbing him with a bayonet (in a kind of military version of the sexual False Memory Syndrome, they even often 'remember' such encounters when they never took place).[73]

The use of terror is not an effective long-term strategy for maintenance of power. During the Second World War, the Četnici set up a primitive concentration camp at Kosovo kod Knina, which the local Communists compared to Jasenovac.[74] Their victims included Communists, Muslims, Croats and Montenegrin Greens.[75] It was probably the savagery of the Četnici and their reputation for gratuitous cruelty that 'forfeited whatever chance they might have had of expanding their popular base'.[76] It is also likely that the Bosnian Serbs use of terror tactics was a major structural weakness in the 1990s, allowing as it did an alliance to form in the short term between Croatian nationalists and the Bosnian government. In 1943, the ability of the Partisans to unite all Yugoslavia not only gave them a military edge over the Ustaša and Četnici, but also meant that they were able to exploit their victory in a moral sense for many years, giving them greater political durability, at least while their leader Tito was still alive.

Matija Ban's *Pravila* also stated that it was necessary for Četnici to be abstinent (*trezven*). (In modern Serbian this word is used in a figurative sense, to mean commonsensical, but nevertheless the point is clearly about sobriety and self-discipline.)[77] This is somewhat ironic given that the alcoholic state of Četnici in Bosnian War was frequently commented upon. Misha Glenny also states that a Macedonian JNA officer told him that Croatian paramilitaries took drugs and drunk during the war in Croatia in 1991.[78] Martin Bell describes one of the militiamen on patrol in Bosnia as 'drunk, dangerous and barely coherent'.[79] Ed Vulliamy was also shocked by the state of the fighters:

> At the start of the war, these roadblocks were usually manned by some bog-trotter who would ostensibly remove the safety catch on his Kalashnikov while pointing it at the driver's seat and, summoning his mates, wave you down. . . . It was advisable to extinguish all cigarettes when winding the window down, since the guards' breath, blowing at close range, was usually highly flammable. . . . Many fighters still wear flowing hair and beards strewn with bits of old food.[80]

The Croatian media derided the Knin uprising as the '*Balvan revolucija*' (log revolution) because the local Serbs had used tree trunks to make roadblocks around the Krajina. They also generally depicted the rebels as bearded, primitive drunkards.[81] Četnici were also frequently described as dirty. Rape victims from Brezevo polje in Bosnia had vaginal infections of staphyllococus and other bacteria that originate in dirt and faecal matter, after being raped by Četnici. They reported that the rapists were dirty and smelt bad and in some cases already had blood on their bodies.[82] Here the violation of Muslim habits of cleanliness was intensified by the introduction of 'matter out of place' (blood, filth and stench), as anthropologist Mary Douglas put it, and must have been particularly traumatic for the women bought up surrounded by traditional rituals of purification.[83] Again these violations of women were in direct contradiction of bandit and četa traditions. According to Eric Hobsbawm, there was a potent superstition amongst the Greek Kléphtai that anyone who touched a woman would be tortured and killed by the Turks and this belief was held elsewhere as well.[84] During the 1804 Uprising Karadjordje had his own brother executed for rape.[85]

Given the behaviour of certain fighters, it has been commonplace for their opponents to dehumanize them in some way. Četnici were described by Vladimir Dedijer as 'blood-thirsty animals'.[86] During the war in the 1990s, Serb fighters – often dubbed 'Srbo-Četnici',[87] were relentlessly dehumanized by sympathizers of Bosnian Muslim and Croat victims of the fighting, as well as outside observers. Ed Vulliamy referred to the Bosnian Serbs as 'a neanderthal bunch'.[88] In psychological terms, a dehumanization of the aggressors probably helps the victim to come to terms with what has happened to them, but the use of such terms has very little value beyond the short term catharsis of hate. One victim of ethnic cleansing told Dona Kolar Panov:

Imagine, people working all their lives, and then they come and burn down, destroy everything. Destroy what they can't steal. You remember when we watched the tape that showed us those houses in the village where Serbs had their war headquarters? They (the Serbs) lived like animals. They ate, slept and defecated in the same room. Just like animals.[89]

As Kolar Panov explains, 'She then went on to compare the images of clean-shaven Croatian soldiers seen marching to the music on the video-spot of the song "Croatian Guard" with the bearded, drunken Serbian irregulars devouring lamb on a spit which they stole from the villagers.'[90] According to Vitomir Belaj, very negative essentialist stereotypes of Serbs circulated through the medium of jokes in Croatia in the Autumn of 1991. In the well-known popular saying about Turks, found across the Balkans *'Nit u mora mire, nit u Turaka vire'* ('You cannot measure the sea, you cannot trust a Turk'), *'Turaka'* was simply replaced by *'Srbina'* (Serb).[91] Serbs were said to possess 'Byzantine' characteristics, which became a euphemism for cruelty and undemocratic behaviour. Discussing Croatia in the early 1990s, Dubravka Ugrešić wrote that 'Byzantine is simply another (more refined) word for Serb, which in the same linguistic and ideological system means: sly, dirty, deceitful, in other words whoever is different from us.' She cited a newspaper article published in Croatia as an example of this kind of racism: 'Ordinary Croatian people are not the same as ordinary Serbian people who are aggressive and collectively frustrated by the Serbo-Byzantine philosophy of life – kill, seize, steal, dominate.'[92] The irony of these stereotypes is that before the 1990s, Serbs were frequently constructed in a kind of Piedmontese fashion as being the 'best' Yugoslavs.[93]

Četnici were not the only irregular fighters in the Yugoslavian wars of the 1990s; many others fused invented tradition with bizarre forms of modernity. The *Beli Orlovi* (White Eagles) led by Dragoslav Bokan and *Arkanovci* (Arkanovites) led by 'Arkan' were wanted criminals in other parts of Europe, with links to mafia-style operations.[94] Perhaps most bizarrely of all, Mirko Jović's psychopathic *Vitezovi* (Knights) were hired to play medieval Serbian knights in a film about Kosovo, released on the six hundredth anniversary of the occasion.[95] Many of the KLA volunteers were Albanian Americans who flew in to train during the war in 1999 wearing the star and stripes mixed up with Albanian insignia.[96] Paramilitaries in the Krajina were dubbed *knindje*, which sounds like the word in the American version of the title of the Japanese cartoon 'Teenage mutant Ninja turtles'. In an example of sick humour somewhat widespread during this period, the Croat *Jokeri* (Jokers) unit dressed in black and white and donned Ustaša insignia.[97] In 1993, they sprayed the slogan '48 hours of ashes' on a minaret in the Lašva valley (oddly echoing Stojan Protić' timescale for the ethnic cleansing of Bosnia in 1917)[98] and they 'laughed' at a Muslim woman as they made her jump from a balcony on top of her dead son whom they had just killed.[99] These men wore Joker 'patches'. Other 'accessories' worn by Croat paramilitaries included a leather bag with images of the Ustaša minister of interior Andrija Artuković,[100] knives and religious paraphernalia. Dario Kordić, former Vice President of HVO, wore fatigues and a rosary as he gave the Ustaša salute in Bosnia.[101] Elsewhere in the world in recent years murderous gangs have dressed up in bizarre ways emphasizing perhaps the Bakhtinian nature of their practices. The paramilitaries used by 'Papa' Doc Duvalier in Haiti dressed up in dinner jackets before going out to kill. In Rwanda the paramilitary *Interahamwe* wore distinctive black and yellow suits and most recently in Sierra Leone expensive western sunglasses have been worn as 'military chic'.

It is probable that most of the atrocities associated with ethnic cleansing in the Balkans were carried out by paramilitaries. From the 1870s until the 1910s, Turkish irregulars, the Bashi-Bazuks (başi-bözök), were often reported to be cruel and violent in their treatment of Christian populations. The American reporter John MacGahan, who wrote for the London News reported the atrocities carried out by the Bashi-Bazuks after the Bulgaria Uprising of 1876. In one village he found

> a sight that made us shudder. It was a heap of skulls, intermingled with bones from all parts of the human body, skeletons, nearly entire, rotting, clothing, human hair, and putrid flesh lying there in one putrid heap, around which the grass was growing luxuriously . . . We looked again at the heap of skulls and skeletons before us and we observed that they were all small, and that articles of clothing, intermingled with them and lying about, were all parts of women's clothing. These, then were all women and girls.[102]

In Anatolia in 1921, a group of Greek irregulars *Mavri Mira* ('Black Fate') were chiefly responsible for murdering Turks and ransacking villages.[103] In Kosovo in 1999, a paramilitary group was formed known as *Munja* (lightning). One Serb regular soldier reported that the main interest of this group was 'robbing . . . and raping women. They were a dirty group of men who had no qualms about killing women and children . . . They weren't disciplined like us.'[104] They were reputed for their cruelty and sadism and indeed cultivated this image. Until 1993, the Croatian Defence Force paramilitaries had a reputation for greater 'efficiency' (i.e. ruthlessness and cruelty) than regular Croat soldiers and their public recruitment and advertisements were commonplace in Zagreb.[105] In Macedonia in 2001, a number of paramilitary groups have formed including the Scorpions, Tigers, Wolves and Lions who are said to have 'close though informal links to Macedonia's hardline Minister of the Interior Ljube Boškovski'.[106]

These men, (unlike Vojislav Šešelj's Četnici who were generally bearded, drunk and often middle-aged), were as Noel Malcolm puts it, 'young urban gangsters in expensive sunglasses'[107] more likely to have been inspired by video nasties or Bruce Lee than guslar epics of revenge. As John Allcock has remarked, 'Rambo sweatbands or bandoliers, bizarre haircuts, idiosyncratic "uniforms" and the use of black balaclavas by paramilitaries have been assimilated as components of a style of warfare, the sources of which must be found outside the Balkans.'[108] Like the Second World War and previous conflicts in the Balkans, the wars in Yugoslavia gave many young men and a few women as well a chance 'to indulge their wildest fantasies'[109] and to fuse historical images from books and films with modern and 'stylish' fighting from video games and cartoons.

Indicted war criminal Arkan recruited his fighters from Red Star (*Crvena Zveda*) Belgrade's football[110] team supporters club.[111] Radovan Karadžić had also been involved in football coaching in Sarajevo (although there is little evidence that he actually recruited amongst the players). Arkan formed his paramilitary Tigers from supporters who had been 'prone to uncontrolled outbursts of nationalist shouting'.[112] From this rabble, he formed a much more discipline group. As he later commented, 'You know our fans, they like to drink, to joke about. I stopped all that in one go, I made them cut their hair, shave regularly, not drink.'[113] As Florian Bieber has stated, 'the link between hooligan nationalism and the Yugoslavian wars, lies not only with the popularization of nationalism through symbols and slogans. It also lies in direct links between sports and party functionaries who understood the violent potential of football supporters.'[114] Arkan was a smart if somewhat pompous dresser and people who disliked everything he stood for were struck by his personality. For the journalist Martin Bell, writing in 1996, he was 'a man of great fluency, dynamism and surface charm'.[115] Similarly, Simatović was described on campaign in Bosnia as wearing 'sharp civilian clothes and had longish hair and expensive-looking sunglasses. He said that he came as a representative of the state of Serbia and that we were "Serbian knights", shock troops in a war against Serbia's enemies and that the fate of all Serbs depended on us.'[116]

Another poignant and particularly distressing aspect of the Yugoslavian wars was the way in which 'amateur' fighters took on the role of what has been referred to as 'weekend warriors'. To become this kind of bandit or fighter, an individual needed no papers, no military discipline and could quit and go home whenever they wanted.[117] One former camp prisoner from Bosnia remembered that 'we called them weekend soldiers. They were the worst. They were people who worked in Switzerland, France, Germany. They came to the camp at weekends they killed as much as they wanted and then left.'[118] Similarly in Rwanda in 1994 the paramilitary *Interahamwe* relied on the actions of 'part time' sadists and most of the killing was carried out with *panga* machetes not bullets.[119] A US lawyer Michael Stechow recalls the scene of devastation in a meadow above Lubenic in Kosovo: 'I found it covered with bullet casings and cigarette butts, as well as glass from broken bottles. It seems that the Serbs sat there, drinking, smoking and shooting people for fun.'[120] In 1992, the director Pawel Pawlikowski filmed such a scene on the 'archetypal hajduk mountain'[121] of Romanija,[122] when he captured a shot of the Russian poet Eduard Limonov firing on Sarajevo for 'sport' while in the background, a guslar sang and lambs were roasted on spits.[123] Johan Bos, a Dutch UN sergeant in Bosnia gave the following description of the Serb military police in Bratunac in 1995:

> They bragged about how they had murdered people and raped women. . . I didn't get the feeling they were doing it out of anger or revenge, more for fun . . . Each had an Alsatian dog, a gun, handcuffs and a terrifying-looking knife with a blade about 9 inches long.[124]

From examining the practice of ethnic cleansing across two hundred years in the Balkans, there appears to be a tripartite relationship between ideologists of nationalism who concoct or manipulate discourses of alterity to serve their own political purposes, the victims and the genuine sadists who carry out these acts. On a balmy night in April 1987, the relatively minor politician Slobodan Milošević was propelled to instant celebrity by his apparently spontaneous assurance to the beleaguered Kosovo Serbs with the words, 'From now on no-one will dare to strike you!' As Dubravka Ugrešić has commented on this speech, he 'touched the infantile pulse of his people',[125] but perhaps more basically he tapped into the coward's desire for revenge, however inappropriate that might have been in the circumstances of the Communist Party of Yugoslavia's official policy of 'brotherhood and unity'. Throughout the fighting in the 1990s and most probably in the other instances of ethnic cleansing in the Balkans, ideologues have attempted to harness tradition to legitimize acts of brutality, revenge and cowardice. Giving sadists a script, be that nationalism or some other discourse of alterity is merely a basic recipe for the maintenance of power or of forging a new power base. But any politician or even ideologue ruler who attempts to exploit these forces and tries to gamble with *fortuna*, takes an enormous political risk. Violence ultimately begets violence. Trotsky described the Komitadji in Macedonia in 1912 as a mixture of 'nationalist zealots . . . [and] thugs'.[126] On closer inspection, the bandits who practised ethnic cleansing in the 1990s were not traditional bandits or latter day heroes of any kind: they were simply extremists and murderers who donned historical names and costumes in a perverse, but thoroughly modern form of warfare.

4   Fascism and Communism

The end of the Balkan Jewish and German communities

Fascism developed as an ideology in the Balkans simultaneously with its development in the rest of Europe. In almost every respect it was intellectually dependent on Nazi racial theories and Italian political practices.[1] Native fascist movements in South Eastern Europe included the Zbor movement found by Dimitrije Ljotić in Serbia, the Iron Guard in Romania and the Ustaša in Croatia led by the *poglavnik* (Führer) Ante Pavelić, which became the party of government in 1941, installed by joint agreement between the Third Reich and Mussolini. Without the sponsorship of the Axis powers these groups, who had tiny numbers of supporters in the late 1920s, would have been unable to have serious political impact beyond terrorism,[2] which was itself financed by the fascist governments.

Although fascists were responsible for some of the worst human rights abuses and responsible for the killing of the majority of Jews in the Balkans and peoples of other nationalities such as the Roma and the Serb population of the Dinaric region, its ideological roots are much more specifically located in the period from the late nineteenth and early twentieth centuries than the other ideological forces that led to the practice of ethnic cleansing. Historical anti-Semitism in the Balkans, although it existed in popular culture, was by no means as developed in this region as it was in Central Europe or in the Romanov monarchy.[3]

The destruction of the Balkan Jewry is as terrible as any of the narratives of the Holocaust. Their settlement in this part of Europe goes back many hundreds of years, but a large number of these Jews were Spanish or Ladino speaking Sephardic Jews, who came to the relatively tolerant South East of Europe after their expulsion from Spain by the Inquisition in the fifteenth and sixteenth centuries. Here they rebuilt their lives and worked in professions such as weaving, trade or medicine.[4] Daniel Elazar estimated that the Jewish communities of Turkey, the former Yugoslavia, Bulgaria and Greece numbered over 300,000 individuals in 1900, with the greatest concentrations in cities such as Sarajevo, Dubrovnik, Rutschuk,[5] Istanbul and, above all, Salonika, which had a majority Jewish population in the city itself until its annihilation in the early 1940s. Although Jewish communities had been fragmented and dislocated by the collapse of the Ottoman

Empire, it was during the Second World War that they were systematically destroyed: at least 80 per cent of Yugoslavia's Jews were killed during the Second World War[6] and by the 1980s there were probably fewer that 50,000 Jews across the region as a whole.[7]

In Serbia, under the puppet government of Milan Nedić, Jews were also persecuted. Most of the executions and deportations were carried out by the Gestapo or other Nazis, but they were aided by the local Serbian fascists or Ljotićevci. The genocide in Serbia was carried out with horrific speed and cruelty and within months of the imposition of Nazi government more than 20,000 Jews and Roma had been killed.[8] In Šabac, Jews were shot and left in the street; at dawn, 'the bodies were gathered in the town square. Jewish refugees from the Kladovo transport were brought up from the internment camp . . . The refugees were forced to carry the dead men through the town and then hang their bodies from electricity poles.'[9] Other Jews met their deaths in camps. On the murder of the Jews in Novi Sad, the Serbian writer Alexandar Tišma commented: 'A whole community had its spiritual and physical life here; its customs, its physiognomy were brushed away like so many crumbs of bread.'[10] Some Jews from elsewhere in the Balkans managed to flee to relative safety in Italian occupied Albania, but many were subsequently deported and murdered by the Gestapo in 1944.[11]

In Salonika almost the entire Jewish community, which numbered several tens of thousands, was wiped out during the Nazi occupation of Greece. Initially Jews were made to wear yellow stars with either 'Jude' or 'Evraios' (written in German or Greek respectively) on their clothes.[12] After systematic humiliations, the majority of the Jews of the city were transported to Auschwitz, where they were either gassed immediately or experimented on by the regime.[13] The Jewish library of Salonika, containing over 10,000 volumes, was transported to Frankfurt by a team of 'researchers' working for Alfred Rosenberg.[14]

What little remained of Balkan Jewish heritage was to come under attack during the war in Bosnia fifty years later. When the National Museum in Sarajevo came under fire from the Bosnian Serb army which had encircled the city, many priceless manuscripts in what was perhaps one of the richest cultural repositories in Europe were destroyed. The fourteenth-century Sarajevo Haggadah, a Prayer book used for the Feast of Passover 'with exquisite Hebrew calligraphy and coloured illustrations'[15] which had been hidden by a Muslim curator during the Second World War was once again spirited out of the Museum to safety in 1992.[16] In April 2001, the United Nations Coordinator in Bosnia Jacques Klein announced that the Haggadah would be restored to its original glory by a team of international experts, evoking it as a 'symbol of cultural resistance to ethnic strife'.[17]

In Croatia, in a clear imitation of the racial policies of the Third Reich and Italy since 1938, the Croatian fascists were quick to wage war on their own population. Within two months of the Ustaša installation into power in 1941, Jews lost their right to citizenship. They were 'forbidden to sign business contracts, ordered to wear yellow armbands and compelled to undertake forced labour; and their property was requisitioned'.[18] Jews in the Independent State of Croatia (*Nezavisna Država Hrvatska* NDH) were taken to the Jasenovac camp, where many of them perished in circumstances of extreme cruelty. In 1942, a fascist guide to Croatia, published in Germany, reported that '(T)he Jews who remain in Croatia, particularly those who were put in the Jasenovac camp in Slavonia, were obliged to do productive work as manual labourers.'[19] The reality was far more horrific. Summary execution, starvation and torture were the order of the day with many of the inmates dying very rapidly.[20]

During the period 1941–3, Muslims, Jews and Serbs were the primary victims of ethnically inspired murders, but others were killed on grounds of being communist, in religious orders or for simply helping their neighbours. Between the defeat of Italy in 1943 and the final capitulation of the Third Reich, the Italian and German speakers of the Balkans lost their protectors and became perceived as 'fifth columnists' themselves in the way that Muslims were often regarded as 'aliens'. Some ethnic Germans left for Germany in October 1944 and others were expelled at the end of the war.[21] The Italian communities of the Adriatic littoral were driven north to Trieste or elsewhere in Italy, to become permanent exiles or 'esuli' as they are known in Italian political discourses. Others met a terrible fate when they were pushed down *foibe* or holes in the limestone Karst. After 1943, there was an often fatal conflation, on the part of the Partisans in the Adriatic region, between the notion of 'fascist' and actually being ethnic Italian or German. In Basovizza, a predominantly Slovene village outside Trieste, in May 1945 a priest Don Matalan 'witnessed 250 to 300 civilians and about forty German soldiers being executed'. It was claimed that they were all dead before that were thrown into the limestone ravines or *foibe*.[22]

After the war, the victorious Communists drove the German and Italian speaking populations out of Yugoslavia, although again this action was associated with a particular historical 'moment' and the justice meted out by 'victors', it is likely that without the war, any Yugoslav government would have continued to use assimilatory policies rather than ethnic cleansing to 'deal' with minorities. The ethnic cleansing carried out by Communists at the end of the war cannot be linked definitively to long-term trends or patterns as there was no long-term antipathy for either ethnic group within the Communist or Marxist movement generally. Indeed Tito's partisans wanted to hold on to territorial gains made in Italy and Austria, notably the port of Trieste which they liberated in 1945, and the majority German parts of Carinthia that contained a Slovene minority. The actions of the Communists were motivated by short-term circumstances at the end of the war, although the tendency for local partisans to settle old scores and the ubiquitous role of sadism was probably an important factor in explaining violence against both communities. This is not to say that what occurred was not brutal. Josip Mirnić suggested that 100,000 Germans (about half the total ethnic population) left Vojvodina spontaneously and of their own free will (*dobrovolno*) when the Third Reich collapsed, since their fate was so inextricably linked to that of the occupiers.[23] However, in his memoirs, émigré writer Boris Pekić, remembered how the partisans in his village in Vojvodina indiscriminately murdered ethnic Germans, including the teenage girl who was his first love.[24] Recent research on the fate of the remaining Germans suggests that they were very harshly treated by the Titoist regime, which assumed their collaboration with the occupiers and many were interned in camps as they were elsewhere in Eastern Europe.[25] Those that did not die from hunger or disease left Yugoslavia, ending hundreds of years of German population settlement in Slavonia, Vojvodina and in many major cities.

Croatian nationalism and the Ustaša

The Croatian national question is underpinned by the problem of territorial incompatibility. Like the Serbs, the Croatian have shared the lands thay inhabit with people who neither describe themselves as Croats nor speak Croatian. Croatian national identity developed in its modern form in the eighteenth century. One of its earliest proponents was Pavel Ritter Vitezović who constructed an image of a Croatian state which was far larger than Independent Croatia in the 1990s. In some respects he was a precursor of the Illyrian idea, although with a decidedly Croatian aroma. For later nationalists, the continuity of a thousand years statehood under the Hungarians and subsequently the Habsburgs who preserved the 'State rights' of the early medieval kingdom, rather than religious confession or language was the most important thing that nationalists looked to for defining the parameters of their nation.

But within that state there were also a small number of Hungarians; Italians in the coastal regions, especially in Dalmatian and Istrian towns; a large number of Orthodox Serbs living in the Dinaric Karst; and, until the eighteenth century, a number of Muslims. In Slavonian towns and in Zagreb there were Germans, and in Dubrovnik and Zagreb there were Jews. The Croatian lands were thoroughly multicultural at the beginning of our period of discussion, but by 2000 were predominantly Croatian speaking and nominally Catholic. Within a state's right tradition, a civic Croatian nation state should have been able to embrace non-Croats within its borders. But a strong element within Croatian nationalism regarded individuals from other ethnic groups as essentially undesirable 'aliens'. In 1990, when Franjo Tudjman made the notorious remark that he was glad that his wife was neither a Serb nor a Jew[26] he was strangely echoing (consciously or not) the NDH minister Mile Budak who described Serbs and Jews as 'enemies (*neprijatelji*), . . . who must be moved out whether by force or kindness'.[27]

Ethnic cleansing in Croatia is partly linked to the Balkan Ottoman legacy and the existence of border communities who were neither Catholic nor Croat. Orthodox Slavs living in these border regions, who had been the gendarmes of the Habsburgs in the so-called Vojna krajina or military frontier became the primary focus of Ustaša hate ideologies in exile in Italy. In 1939 with the *Sporazum* ('mutual agreement') brokered between the Croatian Peasant Party led by Maček and the Stojadinović government in Belgrade, Croatian nationalists achieved their precious goal of semi-autonomy within the Yugoslavian kingdom, but division at the centre in the Belgrade government left the state weak and vulnerable to the aggressive foreign policies of the Axis powers. Yugoslavia's enemies were ranged on all sides and the regime remained predominantly pro-British. With the collapse of the state in April 1941, the Axis states quickly installed puppet fascist regimes in the region. The Ustaša led by Ante Pavelić was an existing group in exile, who had been active and vociferous in their hostility to the regime since the late 1920s and who were behind the assassination of King Aleksandar Karadjordjević in 1934. Pavelić, in true fascist style, had made his intentions quite clear before 1941: he announced in an editorial of the newspaper Ustaša that in order to create an ethnically pure Croatia he would use 'all means, even the most terrible'.[28]

The response of Croatia's mainstream politicians to the role of the Ustaša in the spring of 1941 was crucial. On 10 April, Vlado Maček, Yugoslavia's Vice-premier and President of the Croatian Peasant Party (Hrvatska Seljačka Stranka HSS) broadcast to the Croatians telling them to cooperate with the new regime[29] (although it is clear that Maček did not fully realize what to expect from Pavelić). When German troops entered Zagreb (and nearby Maribor) they were greeted enthusiastically by many local people, a fact that the Croats were never allowed to forget after the war, as the painful truth was captured on celluloid.[30]

The campaign of terror which the regime then unleashed against the Serbs as well as the subsequent persecution of Jews and Roma was horrific even by the standards of the early 1940s. In a speech made in Nova Gradiška in June 1941, Milovan Žanić (an NDH minister) declaimed:

> I say this openly, this state, this our homeland must be Croat and nothing else. Therefore those who have moved in must go. The events of centuries, and especially of the past twenty years, show all compromise is impossible. This must be the land of the Croats and no-one else, and there are no methods that we Ustashe [sic] will not use to make this land truly Croatian, and cleanse it of the Serbs who have endangered us for centuries.[31]

Milija Bjelica from Koriška jama in Hercegovina recalled the terrible events of killing Serbs in May 1941. 'Their [Ustaša] behaviour towards us was inhumane. [I]t is likely that they volunteered for this pogrom, firmly convinced that now the Serbian people in the NDH and of course in Hercegovina would be grubbed out like weeds.'[32] The population of the entire village of Glina, save two, were killed in 1941. The writing above the entrance of the Serbian Orthodox church in the village became a striking example of such climate of fear and mistrust: '*Sačuvaj naš Bože kuge i Hrvata!*' (God save us from the plague and from Croats).[33] The fascists also enlisted a number of Catholic priests who supported and legitimized their campaign of ethnic cleansing. Dionizije Juricević, a priest in Pavelić government announced:

> In this country no-one but the Croat can live and anyone who does not accept conversion, we know what to do with him; where to send him. . . . You need not think that I, because I am a priest could not take a machine gun in hand and wipe out everything, right down to a baby, that is opposed to the Ustasha rule and the Ustasha state.[34]

Inspired by orders from Pavelić, sworn Ustaša (somewhat similar to the Nazi Einsatzgruppen who operated in the Ukraine) carried out the ethnic cleansing among Orthodox communities in the NDH so rapidly in the early summer of 1941 that some confused Serbs, who were neither nationalists nor on bad terms with ethnic Croat neighbours, would report the actions of Ustaša to the authorities, largely because they could not believe that these actions could be sanctioned by a legitimate government and must be the work of terrorists.[35] Similarly, Muslims trained by the SS to carry out atrocities against Serbs in Bosnia and Hercegovina in 1943, were equally fanatical. Some 12,000 men volunteered to join the Handžar division of the SS to ethnically cleanse Bosnia.[36] It is often unclear as to why these men became such sworn opponents of Serbian and Jewish citizens of the NDH. Milovan Žanić discussed the threat from Serbs who had 'endangered' them 'and who will endanger us again if they are given the opportunity',[37] which seems a purely rhetorical fantasy in which the term endanger can be interpreted in a number of ways, but one in which nationalists often indulge. According to this discourse one has to be not merely a good citizen but to proactively take part in the destruction of other communities. It is strikingly similar to the proactive behaviour of the Bosnian Serbs in the early 1990s, who claimed to be preventing Islamic fundamentalism from spreading to the Balkans before this had actually happened.

Although it is often stated in the literature on Croatian nationalism that a high proportion of the Ustaša were natives of the Dinaric region, their behaviour in 1941 represents a significant break with the past and cannot be ascribed to the culmination of purely 'local passions' in the Vojna krajina. Dinko Tomašić argued that 'the Ustaša state is conceived as an enlarged family of the patriarchal type in which the whole authority is vested in the hands of the patriarch . . . the leaders and ideologists of the Ustaša state of Croatia themselves come mostly from villages in the Dinaric parts of Croatia, where peasants still live in large families of the old patriarchal kind.'[38] I strongly disagree with the contention that the roots of *ustaštvo* can be found within the traditional practices of this region, and would argue that they are far more closely linked to the limited penetration of literacy and the development of proto-fascist racial theory from nineteenth-century ideologues. The anti-Serb sentiment of the Ustaša was of relatively recent historical vintage, having been initiated by the nineteenth-century Croat writer Starčević, founder of the Croatian Party of Right (Hrvatska Stranka Prava HSP). There is no long-term precedent for antagonistic Serb–Croat relations in the same way that poor Christian–Muslim relations have their origins to some extent in the oppressive practices of the Ottoman state, and little evidence of interethnic rivalry before the twentieth century. It has been argued that Serb gendarmes were used by the Karadjordjević regime to terrorize the local population and had become resented as a result.[39] Communist Party statements written with the all the lack of intellectual and political clarity that allegiance to the Comintern brought, initially 'saluted' the Ustaša rebellions, while still deploring their links with the fascists.[40]

The leader of the Croatian fascists Pavelić once said that, had it not been for Ante Starčević, the Independent State of Croatia (NDH) could not have existed. For Starčević, writing in the later nineteenth century, the Serbs were an 'unclean race'[41] bound together only by a servile nature and should be forced to submit to Croatian political hegemony. Along with his colleague and co-founder of the Party of Right (*Stranka prava*), Eugen Kvaternik, he believed that 'there could be no Slovene or Serb people in Croatia because their existence could only be expressed in the right to a separate political territory'.[42] His anti-Serbian sentiments seem to have been prompted by the Habsburg occupation of Bosnia-Hercegovina in 1878, which created a more serious possibility of a 'Greater Croatia' by adding lands which contained Catholics to the Habsburg domains.[43] In interwar Zagreb, a pro-Ustaša newspaper was printed under the title *Starčević*.[44] At the turn of the century relations between Serbs and Croats were enflamed by the publication of an article in August 1902 in the Serb nationalist newspaper *Srbobran*, which suggested that these communities could not live together and this must finally lead to the extermination 'of us or you'.[45] This particular ethnic division was incubated entirely in the minds of extremists and fanatics, with little evidence that the areas in which Serbs and Croats had lived for many centuries in close proximity, such as the Krajina, were more prone to *ethnically* inspired violence.

The extremism and methods of the Croatian fascists shocked even their German allies and provoked Serbs to retaliate: the German General Glaise von Horstenau warned in 1941 that the 'bestial behaviour of the . . . authorities is causing unrest and rebellion'.[46] Siegfried Kasche, a German minister based in Zagreb, remarked that they were 'filled with a blind destructive will against real or imagined enemies of the state, above all Serbs'.[47] Pavelić and his 'sworn Ustašas' were not purely pragmatic and interested in the maintenance of power: 'the readiness to risk their own survival proved that the[y] . . . considered genocide a fundamental duty'.[48] Many of their statements were almost millenarian in character. In Karlovac on 13 June 1941 Mile Budak exclaimed: 'The whole work of the poglavnik is a chain of events, deeds and sacrifices based on divine providence and necessity leading to success, as was the case on 10 April when the NDH was proclaimed.'[49]

Bogoljub Kočović calculated that Serb losses in the NDH amounted to one in every six Serbs killed. Commenting on these statistics Aleksa Djilas remarks, '[a]fter the Jews and the Gypsies, this is the highest percentage of losses during the Second World War in the whole of Europe'.[50] It was also the 'earliest total genocide to be attempted during the Second World War',[51] unprompted by either the Italians or the Germans. The cruelty of the regime provoked a clear backlash and ultimately Pavelić and his close associates were forced to flee Zagreb as the Partisans advanced on the city. Individuals suspected of having collaborated with the regime were brutally punished by the Communists[52] and *ustaštvo* only survived clandestinely in small pockets in Croatia and in exile in Buenos Aires, Toronto or Melbourne. Pavelić himself died in 1957 in South America, one of the legendary community of fascists that lived out their days without accounting for their crimes.[53]

In the period following the Second World War, Croatian nationalism seemed a spent force, tainted by its associations with the past atrocities. In the late 1960s until 1971 the Croatian Communist party spearheaded a nationalist revival in that republic which was chiefly focused on the language question and the status of the Church. A few isolated incidents point towards more sinister problems, especially in the Knin region where the Serbs were perceived to be privileged and too pro-

Communist.[54] The bitterness of the generation of 1971 whose mass nationalist movement (Maspok) had been suppressed by the authorities who forced individuals out of jobs and out of the arena of party privileges, resurfaced in 1990 with the election of a consciously nationalist government led by Franjo Tudjman, who had been jailed for his nationalism in the early 1970s.[55]

The return of fascism in the 1990s?

Did fascist ideology survive between 1945 and 1990? In order to justify their behaviour in the hinterland of Dubrovnik, Montenegrin fighters claimed that they found Ustaša paraphernalia in the homes that they looted such as coins and banknotes. In a sense this may have been true (although it would be hard to imagine a house where one couldn't find old family paraphernalia). Clearly memories of the Second World War survived because individuals did keep souvenirs and tell their children and grandchildren what had happened or kept in touch with relatives who were nationalists in exile. Serbian Četnici would meet in the Ravna Gora Hotel in London's Notting Hill and broadcast from radio stations in Canada (although their audiences were probably rather sparse). A pamphlet glorifying the Ustaša movement before 1941 was available 'free for the members of the Croatian Liberation Movement in the USA, Latin America, Europa [sic] and Australia'.[56] Instead of knowing too little about the past these nationalists knew rather too much and derived many of their political ideas from outdated maps and almost irrelevant political projections which ignored the fundamental human rights of those still living in the regions about which they schemed and planned. It was almost as if the achievements in terms of interethnic harmony and tolerance of the period from 1945 and 1990 had almost no impact on these crystallized hate ideologies and their practitioners.

In 1990 in the wake of the collapse of communism, a consciously fascist party, the HSP or Party of Right, which drew its name from the Starčević tradition, was launched in Zagreb. Members of the HSP wore black shirts and had U for Ustaša initialled on their caps. Their leader Dobroslav Paraga insisted that Muslims are Islamicized Croats, stressing that Croatia and Bosnia are the 'same blood, same nation'.[57] He has also openly talked about reducing Serbia's borders to Belgrade and its environs, chiming in parallel with the statements of Vojislav Šešelj who wanted to reduce Croatia to 'as much as one can see from the tower of the Cathedral in Zagreb'.[58]

In December 1990 after a plebiscite clearly indicated a popular mandate for independence, Tudjman's government made plans for a complete separation from the other Yugoslavian republics. His government was then faced with a full scale uprising by the spring of 1991 in areas of the republic populated by Serbs. For the Serbs, the events of the 1990s must have felt like the end of their prophecy. When Tudjman was elected in 1990, many of them cried 'Ustaša', claiming that Croatian nationalists in power would mean that the very existence of Serbs in Croatia was threatened. Some members of the HDZ government were not subtle about their emotional affiliations. Secretary of Defence Gojko Sušak described the ministers of the Pavelić regime as 'well-respected Croats' and at a medieval jousting festival in Sinj even gave the stiff-arm salute.[59] Tudjman was the author of various pieces of 'post-modern' history, which revised the numbers killed in Jasenovac downwards.[60] In areas that were predominantly Serb, the communities retaliated immediately with armed resistance encouraged by unscrupulous nationalists in Belgrade, organizing themselves in Serbian autonomous regions. These extremists, both in the HDZ and those supporting the rebel leaders Milan Martić and Milan Babić, precipitated one of the most vicious fraternal wars in Europe since the 1940s, in which elderly villagers were left mutilated by roadsides, vast numbers of properties burnt out, historic cities and monuments were laid waste and young people were brutally murdered by their peers or left damaged with the blue scars of shrapnel. Dubrovnik endured a siege in which its citizens suffered severe privation, including shortages of water and no electricity.[61] It is probable that Dubrovnik was spared the damage that was inflicted on the Danubian towns such as Vukovar and Vinkovci and smaller ports like Slano because it was so well known was a UNESCO world heritage site.[62]

In the years between 1990 and 1995, Croatia was a traumatized society prone to the unhealthy influence of the far right and nationalism in every sphere, even though the arrival of the United Nations Protection Force (UNPROFOR) in 1992 had made daily life less dangerous. During this period almost every aspect of daily life became ethnicized, including chocolate boxes,[63] maps, recipe books, popular and folk music and art.[64] Speakers of the Croatian language were instructed how to eliminate Serbisms from their vocabulary[65] – a practice associated also with the Pavelić regime.[66] The exoneration of Archbishop Stepinac, whose own role in the installation of the fascist regime of 1941 remains controversial and the open links between the government and parts of the Catholic Church became a central part of the new Croatian identity. The so-called 'Homeland War' between 1990 and 1995 resulted in terrible atrocities and deaths of civilians. Zagreb was attacked several times. The city of Vukovar was levelled to the ground, an unrecognizable relic of its former self. Dubrovnik was repeatedly shelled and many of the pretty Croatian coastal villages were bombed out. Many who died were killed by landmines, which became a regular feature of the war in Bosnia as well and lead to widespread loss of life and limbs. In Croatia in 1991, eighty Croat prisoners of war, arrested by a JNA reserve unit were used to clear minefields, which resulted in the deaths of seventeen people.[67] Dona Kolar Panov was informed by one Croatian soldier:

> I found the dismembered parts of my younger brother whom I saw off to a patrol only that very morning. He had complained to me again that morning that he did not have a uniform, but it was good that he did not have a uniform. That way I could recognize which parts of the bodies lying around us were his. By his shoes, his jumper, and his jeans. The only thought I had then was to collect all the parts of his body to be able to give him a decent Christian burial. I never did find all of one of his legs. You see, he stepped on a mine that those bastards . . . left behind when withdrawing from their positions.[68]

The Croatian army and irregulars retaliated with brutal acts against the Serbs and the Yugoslav People's Army (JNA) and internal dissent was quashed by murders, such as the assassination of Osijek police chief Josip Reichl-Kir who disagreed with the tactics pursued by extremists in Slavonia.[69] Twelve JNA soldiers were mutilated on Kovana bridge in Karlovac on 21 September 1991 by policemen of the Croatian Ministry of the Interior.[70] Like many other victims of ethnically inspired violence in the Balkans the bodies of these soldiers had been mutilated beyond any necessity simply to kill them. The inflicting of injuries over and above the killing of the victim may give the murderer the feeling that he has killed 'an incalculable number of times',[71] but also gave the government in Belgrade an opportunity to whip up fears of a repeat of the Ustaša atrocities. The ethnic cleansing of Serbs in Pakrac in 1991 was later discussed in the independent newspaper *Feral Tribune*. One man recalled his own involvement in the town:

> I killed 72 people with my own hands, including nine women. We didn't differentiate, we didn't ask anything, they were all Chetniks and our enemies. The most difficult thing to do is to set fire to the first house and kill the first man. Later everything becomes routine.[72]

Operation Storm or Oluja effectively ended the large scale Serb presence in Croatia. The Croatian army broke through the Serbian front lines on 4 August 1995 and in neighbouring Bosnia the tide was finally turned in the siege of Bihać. Many Serbs had left the Krajina earlier, but in the first week of August 1995 at least 100,000 Serbs vacated their homes, travelling rapidly eastwards. Ivo Goldstein comments that they assumed there 'was no room for them in the Croatian state'.[73] Only a few thousand Serbs remained, most of them too frail to travel.[74] Several hundred of those who remained were killed. Deserted by their allies in Belgrade, an exodus of thousands of people, who left the Krajina in carts and motor vehicles heading east to Serbia. President Tudjman's speech on the occasion was broadcast live by Croatian television on all channels simultaneously on 26 August. He described the exodus of the Serbs from the Krajina during Operation Storm as the solution to Croatia's 'centuries-old problem'.[75]

Mirko Grmek and his co-writers have commented that ustaštvo cannot be equated with mainstream Croatian nationalism because of the puppet nature of the Pavelić government and his dependency on the Germans and Italians.[76] In a sense this is true. The fascists had a miniscule number of supporters in pre-war Croatia and would never have gained power other than through foreign aid. But if we return briefly to Tudjman's 'centuries-old' problem of the existence of Serbian communities in Croatia, we might be able to refute these claims of qualitative difference between the nationalisms. Extremists often claim to be acting for those who do not have the courage to do the dirty deed themselves. Those who fantasized about a Croatia without Serbs, in spite of their knowledge of what happened to the Serb communities during the Ustaša period (and in the case of Tudjman an active denial of history), are an integral part of the process of ethnic cleansing, as were all those people who indulged in a discourse that suggested that the Serbs were 'aliens' in lands they had inhabited for hundreds of years. On 25 April 1941, the Pavelić regime banned the use of the Cyrillic alphabet in the NDH and designated the Orthodox Church as 'Greek-Eastern'.[77] When Stjepan Meštrović and others commented that 'Serbia insisted on maintaining the Cyrillic alphabet among its minority living in Croatia, even though Serbia is the only European nation to use this outmoded alphabet',[78] they might do well to ask themselves why indeed this alphabet became not just 'outmoded' but historic after 1995 in the Krajina.

5   The death of the hero cult

Each culture creates its own dreaming – myths which revolve and evolve around memories of social origins.[1]

Kosovo: field of Serbian dreams

The National Gallery in Belgrade has a series of stirring twilight canvases depicting various scenes from the Kosovo legends.[2] You will see paintings in a similar genre in galleries across Europe, but generally they are souvenirs of the past not living, breathing memorials. As Slobodan Milošević once remarked, 'every nation has its one love that warms its heart. For Serbia it is Kosovo.'[3] In 1912, Trotsky noticed in a shop in Belgrade, 'a huge symbolic battle picture . . . Having thrown down a frontier fence of sharp pointed palings, the Serbs, picturesque and elegant, are bursting in, mounted on powerful horses, to the realm of the Turk, crushing and smashing everything in their way.'[4]

Kosovo has had more symbolic than actual meaning in Serbian national consciousness for most of the nineteenth and twentieth centuries, with many Serbs preferring not to go there even when they had an opportunity. As a symbol it represented the recreation of the Serbian medieval kingdom, the restoration of an age of greatness and final victory against the Turks (or whoever it was that was deemed to represent Islam). When King Petar Karadjordjević visited the reconquered land of Old Serbia in 1913, at the monastery of Dečani he lit a candle that was to symbolize the avenging of the Battle of Kosovo polje.[5] This was not just an elite ritual: consciousness of the battles of the past had thoroughly permeated popular culture. In 1912, according to a Serb soldier fighting in the Balkan Wars,

> when the (Serb) soldiers entered the Plain of Kossovo [sic] they became very excited. I was even surprised at the way they reacted. Kossovo, Gracanica – these names are handed down from generations, repeated over and over in folksongs . . . the soldiers were firmly convinced that when they got to Guvno,[6] that would mean our task was over.[7]

In a sense, the accuracy of the facts concerning the Battle of Kosovo polje in 1389 are not as important as what it came to symbolize. To paraphrase Claude Levi-Strauss, Kosovo was good for thinking with (and even better for mobilizing with). If it became synonymous with Ottoman oppression and was re-crafted and woven in the nineteenth century, it was not too different from the way that the 'Norman yoke' myth was fashioned by the English in the seventeenth century, or the figure of Columbus is found in North American memorialization. The word appeared frequently in the ballads of the guslars or bards and codified culture drew on these heroic themes.

Of particular importance is the role played by the death of the medieval King Lazar at the battle of Kosovo polje, the remembrance of which became an act of faith for nationalists. Michael Sells has argued that '[D]uring the nineteenth century, Serbian nationalist writers transformed Lazar into an explicit Christ figure, surrounded by a group of disciples . . . and betrayed by a Judas . . . In this story the Ottoman Turks play the role of the Christ killers.' The facts of the battle itself are open to historical interpretation. As Noel Malcolm has remarked on the ballads that 'many of the folk epics mingle characters promiscuously from different periods'.[8] Although it is possible to unpack many of the elements of the Kosovo myth in this way (as indeed any other myth), this does not begin to explain why individual stories 'warm the heart'.

In the nationalist myth of the battle, (the betrayer) Vuk Branković, 'represents the Slavs who converted to Islam under the Ottomans and any Serb who would live with them or tolerate them'.[9] Fear and conciousness of betrayal remain central aspects of Serb and other Balkan national consciousnesses.[10] Indeed it would be difficult for any modern nation state to mobilize its citizens for war if it did not have the trump card of internal betrayal upon which to play. The Montenegrin President Momir Bulatović declined to sign the Peace Agreement brokered by Lord Carrington in 1992 because he feared being called a traitor to pan-Serbian unity.[11] A Montenegrin journalist who worked for the independent newspaper *Monitor* told me that she was driving to Dubrovnik in June 1989. She was passed on the road by a convoy who beeped at her: 'Sister, sister you're going the wrong way . . . come with us to Kosovo!'[12] In 1997, a music journalist Strahinja Maksimović was expelled from Republika Srpska after attending a rock concert in Sarajevo on the grounds that he crossed into alien territory. He was asked: 'What were you doing in Sarajevo? What were you doing among the balije? Why didn't you go to a concert in Pale instead of giving your money to Alija?'[13] A memorial in Kosovo itself proclaimed: 'Let him who fails to join the battle of Kosovo fail in all he undertakes in his fields. Let his fields go barren of the good golden wheat. Let his vineyards remain without vines or grapes.'[14] On Gazimestan in June in 1989, Milošević utilized this myth for his own political purposes when he stated that 'lack of unity and betrayal . . . will continue to follow the Serbian people like an evil fate through the whole of its history'.[15] In 2001, the former FRY Minister of Defence Dragoljub Ojdanić declared that he would rather go to the Hague Tribunal as a national hero (*kao heroj nacije*) than to be dishonoured by being tried at home in Serbia.[16] From this mind-set came the (re)interpretation of the medieval symbol of four S's (C in Cyrillic) as '*Samo sloga Srbina spašava*' (Only unity will save the Serbs).[17]

Ivan Čolović has frequently pointed out the importance of 'holy warriors' (*sveti ratnici*) in Serbian nationalism.[18] The Turkish yoke, symbolized by the battle of Kosovo was certainly one fact about the Serb and Montenegrin experience of the past, but not the only one and it was open to conscious or unconscious manipulation by nationalists. According to Jovan Cvijić,

> the Dinaric has an ardent desire to avenge Kosovo . . . and to resuscitate the Serbian Empire . . . even in circumstances where the less courageous or a man of pure reason would have despaired. Betrayed by circumstances and events, abandoned by all, he has never renounced his national and social ideal.[19]

Ivo Andrić was an admirer of the Montenegrin Vladika and poet Njegoš, who he called the 'archetype of the Kosovo fighter' . . . for the 'removal of the curse' and the fulfilment of Obilić's idea'.[20] It was not just the Serbs who indulged in the idea of 'heavenly Serbia': again the mythologizing was cheered on (in Ivan Čolović' phrase) if not actually created by foreigners. Ernest Denis, author of *La Grande Serbie*, published in 1915 regularly stated in his lectures that 'Serbia is one of the five digits on the divine hand that will make the future'.[21]

Some contemporary nationalists have presented Kosovo as a symbol for an almost Manichaean battle with the forces of contemporary Islam. On 28 June 1989, the poet Matija Bećković announced that Kosovo polje should be seen as 'a Jerusalem in which the whole of Europe has its churches'. Earlier that year he had stated: 'Six hundred years after the battle of Kosovo it is necessary for us to declare: Kosovo is Serbian and that fact depends neither on Albanian natality or Serbian mortality. There is so much blood and holy relics there that it will be Serbian even when not one Serb remains there.'[22] The irony of the Kosovo story might ultimately be the influence of Islamic spirituality on Serbian national consciousness. Tone Bringa's assertion that 'Muslim identity, seen as a spiritual possession, is more valuable than material possessions'[23] surely finds an echo Tsar Lazar's mythic repudiation of an earthly kingdom in favour of a heavenly one. While Serbs celebrated the medieval present in the run up to 1989, relations with Albanians, which might never have been as 'osmotic'[24] as relations between ethnic communities elsewhere in the Balkans, deteriorated rapidly.

Annexed by Serbia in 1912, Kosovo has had a mixed population of Slavs and Albanians since the Middle Ages and is important for both ethnic groups in different ways. Albanians were discriminated against in the 1920s and the kaçak rebels took to the hills to oppose the hegemony of Belgrade. During the Second World War, Albanians led by the nationalist Ballists committed atrocities against Serbs. Kosovo was reintegrated into Yugoslavia in 1945, although this may have been a temporary manoeuvre on the part of the Communists to dissipate Serbian nationalism. After 1948 and the schism between Yugoslavia and the Cominform countries including Albania, any changes in the borders between these states was out of the question. In the 1960s Aleksandar Ranković tried to recentralize author-ity in Kosovo, often quite brutally. After his demise and the refiguration of Kosovo's status in the 1974 Constitution, the region enjoyed a brief period of relative peace and prosperity. The University of Priština became an important centre for intel-lectually ambitious Albanian youths. After the death of Tito, the status of Kosovo as an autonomous region within Serbia looked vulnerable and police repression became a normal part of life after riots in the capital Priština in 1981. It is quite clear that the Serbs, although they were a numerical minority, could not generally accept a devolution of power away from them to the majority Albanian commu-nity. Part of the problem was a basic kind of orientalist racism felt by Serbs towards the Albanians. As Ognjen Pribičević remarked in 1999, 'the Serbs do not treat the Albanians as equal, they treat them as uncivilized, very primitive, dirty . . . as humans of a lower profile. Of course Milošević . . . opened the bottle and let these feelings out, but these feelings are much older than Milošević.'[25]

By the mid 1980s, it was asserted that the Serbs were facing 'genocide'[26] in their ancestral lands. In the rhetorical panic of this time, Serbs were continually reminded of the demographic 'encroachment' of the Albanian population (which had a higher per capita birth rate) and frightened by stories that women faced rape. The emphasis so often found in this nationalism on collective suffering under the Turks has often been seen by commentators as paranoid in psychoanalytical terms. As two Slovene writers commented in 1989: 'Everything, from the assault by the Turks on Europe and the bombardment of Belgrade to Communist takeover of the government in the heart of Serbia all amount to a single conspiracy forged by the papists, Sultan Murat, Franz Josef and the Albanians against the (Serb) nation.'[27]

From the period between 1981 and 1991, paranoia seems to have seeped into daily life and there was a kind of unofficial apartheid in Kosovo, with separate bars, cafes and other venues for Serbs and Albanians. In 1996, Shkëlzen Maliqi com-mented on the 'intense war of nerves, in which one side stops at nothing, committing the most brutal violations of human rights and civil liberties . . . while the other side bottles up it humiliations, despair, fury and hatred, but for how long before it explodes?'.[28] During this period all other aspects of life seem to have become subordinate to the 'National Question' for Serbs and Albanians alike. Julie Mertus noted that issues that concerned the quality of life for women and men (illiteracy, domestic violence, political representation, etc.) were neglected amongst Kosovo Albanians, because 'the call for solidarity . . . (was) so strong, and the cost of breaking rank so high, that most women cannot choose to emphasize their gender identity over their Albanian identity'.[29] Because of this long-term polarization, it was more difficult to reconcile the two communities after the NATO bombing of spring of 1999. One Albanian from Priština told a reporter in the summer of that year that 'it's better to burn down the Serbs' houses. With the houses still there, there's a danger they might come back.'[30] And as in the Krajina in 1995, it was the policies of the Belgrade government that effectively led to the exodus of the Serb population in the summer of 1999, which had represented about 10 per cent of the region before the late 1990s.

Serbs' attitudes were polarized by deliberate political manoeuvres on the part of Slobodan Milošević, who may have realized in advance what kind of political opportunity the six-hundredth anniversary of the battle of Kosovo polje would give him. In 1987 on a balmy April evening he had scored a propaganda coup by reassuring a group of agitated Serbs in Kosovo that they would have the full protection of the government. Effectively he adopted the political programme of the Serbian Academy of 1986, which considered the 'genocide' against Serbs to be one of the 'three agonizing questions' for their future status within a Yugoslavian state, which had discriminated against them.[31] On 28 June 1989, one million Serbs from across the world flocked to Gazimestan to mark the anniversary of Tsar Lazar's defeat. Milošević arrived in a helicopter[32] (as it were from the heavens) and sealed this as a propaganda coup for his regime.

Many individuals from both ethnic communities regretted the ethnicization of daily life and the conflation between Muslims and rapists and/or sexual deviants in a kind of Orientalist subplot.[33] Commenting on the Martinović case of 1985, in which a middle age man accused Albanian youths of torturing and sodomizing him with a broken bottle, one Albanian remarked: 'I am ashamed to think that Albanians could have done this. . . . The expert testimony conflicted so we don't know what happened for sure. Where I take offence is that Serbs automatically accused us all of being there with the perpetrators. It was as if we had all done the attack.[34] . . . The manner of the attack on Martinović tapped into a popular stereotype about the Muslim penchant for sodomy.'[35] Psychiatrist and Krajina Serb activist Jovan Rašković, whose ethno-pyschological theories had some influence at that time told *Intervju* magazine in September 1989 that 'Muslims (are) fixated in the anal phase of their psychosocial development and (are) therefore characterized by general aggressiveness and an obsession with precision and cleanliness.'[36] As Homi Bhabha has noted, the stereotype . . . 'must always be in *excess* of what can be empirically proved or logically construed . . . the essential duplicity of the Asiatic or the bestial sexual license of the African . . . needs no proof [and] can never really, in discourse, be proved'.[37]

Beneath the mild embarrassment of the unfortunate Martinović and some scepticism about whether the wounds were self-inflicted (which seems unlikely given the logistics of the wounds) lay a more sinister fear on the part of Serbs, that they were facing attack from the rear reminiscent of Ottoman juridical practices. Impalement as a metaphor for Ottoman oppression was frequently used in the 1980s to illustrate the suffering of the Serbs. As Julie Mertus comments, 'Every Serbian school child knows about the horror of impalement from national folk ballads, national novels, national plays and other national traditions.'[38] It is of course a graphic illustration of the 'otherness' of Islam, the Turks and by inference in the Martinović case, the Albanians.[39] In 1988, a group of Serbian women marched on the Skupština (Parliament) in Belgrade to lobby for the removal of Kosovo's autonomy, which had been granted under the terms of the 1974 Constitution. They proclaimed that 'We can no longer stand by while our sons are killed on their mothers' breasts; while our brothers are impaled on a sharpened stake; while our husbands are killed before the eyes of our children on the threshold of our houses.'[40] One of the ironies of the Martinović case (and indeed one of the greatest contrasts between peace time and war in general), is that it was followed by far more profound atrocities in Bosnia committed by Serb nationalists, which rarely or never made the Serbian daily newspapers.[41] In the summer of 1992, a Bosnian Muslim witnessed the execution of his neighbours Hadžić and Ismeta Ilijaz in the camp of Trnopolje. They had electric drills bored into their chests and their three children aged 1, 3 and 5 years were impaled on spikes.[42]

Kosovo remained relatively quiet but tense during the early 1990s when other parts of the former Yugoslavia were devastated by war. Due to the actions of one of the most prominent Kosovo Albanian politicians, Ibrahim Rugova, a policy of dialogue was pursued with the Belgrade regime. The status of Kosovo was left out of the Dayton Accords, signed in 1995. The already difficult situation polarized in 1998 with the killing of Adem Jashari and fifty-eight members of his family by the police. The Kosovo Liberation Army, which had been formed to oppose the Serb-dominated regime by military force the previous year and took to hiding in the border regions with Albania, retaliated by killing both Serbs and 'collaborators'.[43] By the summer of 1998, Albanians began fleeing their homes and moving into neighbouring Montenegro, Albania and Macedonia.[44] When the International Community failed to come to any lasting agreement over the status of Kosovo at Rambouillet in the first months of 1999, war then seemed inevitable. In March 1999, planes from the North Atlantic Treaty Organization began a bombing of the Federal Republic of Yugoslavia, causing extensive 'collateral damage' (the deaths of at least 500 civilians), while the paramilitaries and Yugoslavian troops moved in on Kosovo, beginning a vicious course of ethnic cleansing. Many Albanians fled for their lives into neighbouring Macedonia, Montenegro and Albania. At the height of the NATO bombing until the capitulation of Milošević in June 1999 an estimated 863,000 civilians were displaced.[45] By 2000, at least 3,000 bodies of the victims of ethnic cleansing had been exhumed and final estimates of those killed exceed 10,000.[46]

Rape and ethnic cleansing

One particular tension point that emerged in Serb–Albanian relations in Kosovo was the symbolic issue of rape. Despite the fact that the incidence of rape in the province was statistically slightly lower than the rest of Yugoslavia at the time, it became the most important single issue to enflame an already difficult situation.[47] Here again the rhetorical wars of the 1980s must be viewed with some irony when one considers that Yugoslavia as a whole had relatively low incidences of rape in peace time and the way in which rape cases escalated during the fighting, either as the result of a concerted military policy to dehumanize and scare populations or a violent by-product of war.

Rape has accompanied ethnic cleansing throughout the last two centuries in the Balkans and has been used elsewhere in the arsenal of destruction of war. Some scholars have also argued that in nationalist discourse, since women come to represent the entire nation, acts of sexual violence are also the 'symbolic rape of the body of that community'.[48] In Bulgaria in 1878, in the village of Oklanli, Turkish women were raped over several days and then burnt alive. The atrocities were carried out by their Christian neighbours in communities that had lived in the same villages for centuries.[49] In 1903, *The Times* reported widespread rapes of women during the Ilinden Uprising, adding that, '[w]hether this system of whole-sale devastation and rapine is being carried out in accordance with a settled plan or is attributable to the lawlessness of the undisciplined soldiery and Bashi-Bozouks, the result is the same'.[50]

During the Balkan Wars, Anastacia Pavlova reported that at Ghevgheli she had seen 'a number of Greek soldiers who had with them sixteen Bulgarian girls as their prisoners. All of them were crying, several of them were undressed and some were covered with blood.'[51] Her own daughter had escaped violation because she had disguised herself as a boy, something that also took place in Bosnia in the 1990s. Peter Maass reported that 'girls did their best to avoid becoming war booty by cutting their hair into a crew cut, by smearing their faces with dirt, by binding up their breasts so that they could pass as boys. It worked some of the time.'[52]

In some senses Balkan masculinity has been on trial as a result of war and crisis. Dubravka Ugrešić has written about patterns of meaning in the violence and she also points to the negative division of responsibility between men and women and states that if one was to choose an 'anthology of selections from Yugoslav literature' it would 'not infrequently (represent) textbook examples of misogyny and patriarchalism'.[53] Lydia Sclevicky wrote a pioneering series of articles about the patriarchal nature of Yugoslavian society and the postwar Communist regime.[54] Andrei Simić has argued that one legacy of the South Slav extended family, is that women exercise power within the home through 'moral superiority', 'self-abnegation' and 'devotion', thus creating a debt that can never be repaid and maintaining their power base in the household well into old age. As a result of the enforced purity of the home, 'dramatizations of masculinity' (heavy drinking, heedless hospitality, destruction of property, violence, associating with 'profane' women) 'never occur within the household', which perpetuates a distorted image of 'total male dominance' in society as a whole.[55] These interpretations may or may not be valid when we try to interpret a society in normal times, but cannot hope to explain the stark contrast between war and peacetime. Misogyny in literature, male-orientated historical accounts and bar room brawls followed by a return to the 'purity of the home' occur in societies elsewhere, without being accompanied by ethnic cleansing.

Considering 'Balkanist' constructions of masculinity Maria Todorova has stated that 'the standard Balkan male is uncivilized, primitive, crude, cruel and without exception disheveled'.[56] There may be many such accounts, but a great number of descriptions are absolutely opposite to this negative model. In the nineteenth and early twentieth centuries, descriptions of Balkan men were often rather erotic, their muscularity and the length of their legs were often remarked upon.[57] Writers frequently cast the men of the Balkans in a heroic mode, comparing them to the Classical epoch and suggesting that heroic values remained unchanged by time. The heroism of the Serbian army during its long march to the coast during the

First World War was constructed as particularly heroic by Westerners and the fighters of the Partisans were admired for their masculine prowess by the Allied Special Operations Executive. Even during the Bosnian Wars, one British MP, Sir Peter Tapsell was able to describe the Serbs as 'one of the most patriotic races on earth and always have been',[58] thus replicating a stereotype about warlike qualities that had little relevance in that cowardly conflict.

Despite a traditional reputation for heroism and bravery on the part of Balkan men, rape has become an integral part of ethnic cleansing in the Balkans (and elsewhere) because it is directed against civilian populations, intended to humiliate, traumatize and punish them for their continued existence. Rumours of rape and other atrocities also serve to drive people out. One Bosnian stated in 1992 that rapes were committed to 'scare the people off, to make them run from Brčko and make it clear . . . that there was no return for them'.[59] Rape warfare reached horrendous heights in Bosnia in the early 1990s, where many claimed that it was used as a concerted weapon by the Serbs against Muslims. In Foča, Muslim women were interned in 'rape houses' where 'Serb soldiers and paramilitaries beat and assaulted the women as part of the evening's entertainment. They would shave the women's heads, tattoo their bodies with their persecutors first names, and force them to submit to their alcohol- and drug-induced sexual-sadistic fantasies.'[60] The sexual sadism of concentration camp guards in Allach during the Second World War was captured by a Slovene artist Boris Kobè who drew his recollections of torture and perversity on playing cards:[61] such acts would appear to be part of the general repertoire of dehumanization associated with ethnically inspired violence. In Kosovo in June 1999, NATO soldiers found what appeared to be a torture cell in a police station in Priština.

> Hundreds of packaged condoms littered desktops upstairs. In the locker room – where investigators found hundreds of ethnic Albanian identity cards – pornographic magazines, some with bizarre photographs of werewolves groping women, were strewn about the floor. In one office, a nude pinup hung next to a Serbian Orthodox icon. In another office, a table was littered with empty bottles of cheap tequila and gin, shot glasses and a half-dozen long knives.[62]

Norman Naimark has remarked that the problems that this reveals may be 'psychologically complex . . . relating to a deep-seated attraction to and repulsion from women and even men of the persecuted minority'.[63]

Obrad Kesić has examined the case of rape warfare in the 1990s, asserting that 'in order to mobilize for war, political leaders need to manipulate gender imagery. Deeply patriarchal in its essence, aggressive nationalism is based on warrior mythology.'[64] Not only did these paramilitaries commit atrocities outside their republic, but once they were home in Serbia they also felt that their own ethnic community owed them a 'debt of gratitude' which could be gained by force. Kesić estimates that the number of violent crimes has quadrupled in Belgrade since 1990 and that 'most of these crimes were directed at women and could be attributed to young men either on leave or discharged from units and paramilitaries involved in the fighting in Bosnia and Croatia'.[65] The mobilization of extreme virulent nationalism violently suppresses other identities. As he continues, '[t]o the victor go the spoils, which in this case are the bodies of enemy women and their own grateful women. The linkage between the whore image manufactured at home and rape at the battlefronts is a direct one, as can be seen in the abundance of pornographic material at front-line positions.'[66] The point that Kesić made can be illustrated by turning the example to the horrific career of the Bosnian camp sadist Zoran Žigić, responsible for the cruel deaths inflicted upon hundreds of Bosnians, who was subsequently turned over to the Hague tribunal after he killed a Serb woman in Republika Srpska.[67] The cycle of violence that begun in the summer of 1992 (or possibly before) certainly did not end once he had run out of victims of ethnic cleansing to inflict suffering upon.

In his film *Montenegro*, the Yugoslavian film director Dušan Makavejev made the link between eros of military hardware and sex in a scene in the night club *Zanzibar* when an enlarged 'aggressive' phallus is attached to a small model tank in an erotic dance performance.[68] The celebrated Bosnian director Emir Kusturica has also used tanks and other military paraphernalia in his films in explicitly erotic scenes, perhaps as an oblique criticism of the militarism of post-Second World War Yugoslavia. The reality of ethnic cleansing has been more brutal with no relation whatsoever to eros, but only to humiliation, fear and violence. In the Croatian detention centre for Muslims at Kaonik in 1993, a woman was interrogated. She was then 'grabbed . . . by the hair, forced to take her clothes off, and then [he] began to stroke her naked body with a knife and threaten to insert it . . . if she did not tell the truth'.[69] In Macedonia, as the Muslim populations were expelled in 1922–3, women in the village of Guvezna 'were said to have been gathered together in the *aghora* (market) and publicly ridiculed as they were forced to dance naked at gunpoint'.[70] A Bosnian woman reported that rape attacks on her began as soon as she was taken to an abandoned high school: 'at one point I was raped with a gun . . . Others stood watching.'[71] During the recent [early 2000s] fighting in Macedonia, images of naked women have been stuck on government tanks.

Rape is also about patrimony and the destruction of one man's 'domain' by another.[72] The absence of men to protect women leaves them vulnerable to attack and victimization, especially from the viewpoint of would-be rapists. A young child from Bosnia, living in a refugee camp in Koprivnica in 1992, reported that 'in the night Croat soldiers always came and took women who were of legal age . . . or who didn't have kids . . . I don't know what the soldiers did to the women and girls, but I know it was something very bad.'[73] In Izmir in 1922 a French Officer described one of the quarters of the city where men had been killed, were in hiding or taken away. Without the protection of the men as guarantors of their safety, women were vulnerable to every kind of attack: 'the streets are heaped with mattresses, broken furniture, glass, torn paintings. . . . young women and girls . . . must submit to the whims of the patrols. One sees cadavers in front of the houses. They are swollen and some have exposed entrails. The smell is unbearable and swarms of flies cover them.'[74] Men also have often expressed the sentiment that rape offends their deeply held patriarchal moral codes. In Omarska in Bosnia in 1992, Mehmetalija Sarajlić, a man of sixty was killed after being ordered to rape a woman almost 40 years younger than him. He protested that she was young enough to be his granddaughter, a plea that led to his humiliation in front of the other prisoners and subsequently to fatal beating by the camp guards.[75] High levels of violence towards women and children have also been recorded since the Kosovo conflict in the Federal Republic of Yugoslavia.[76]

The use of rape as a method to frighten people, to destroy their cultures and to drive them out, is one of the aspects of ethnic cleansing that is the most difficult to reconcile with the past because it utterly negates traditional constructions of heroism. A Bosnian Serb soldier reported how he had shot a woman five times after raping her. 'All I can remember is that I was the twentieth, her hair was all sticky, she was disgusting and full of sperm and that I killed her afterwards.'[77] However, this behaviour contrasts with the narrative that when the Russians sacked Dubrovnik in 1806, the local women begged the Montenegrins to protect their chastity 'contre le brutalité du soldat moscovite'.[78] Traditionally, Austrians killed women in war, but Montenegrins and Turks did not.[79] Rape was often seen as a particular sign of chaos and undisciplined fighting, its practice sometimes attributed to irregulars and paramilitaries, not regular soldiers. Many denied that 'their' soldiers actually committed acts of rape. A Serb soldier claimed in 1912 in Macedonia that 'If acts of rape did actually occur . . . they were committed by the komatadji, not by the soldiers.'[80] Ceca, the widow of murdered warlord Zeljko Raznatović ('Arkan') told a journalist that her late husband was 'our greatest patriot . . . People on the front line cannot be held responsible for violence. Soldiers fighting soldiers. War crimes are acts against civilians. My husband never did any. He loved his children. He had the utmost respect for women.'[81] As Wendy Bracewell remarks, the denials of Ceca are part of what she sees as an established discourse about the behaviour of the home troops: 'What one side presented as virility, self-sacrifice and patriotism, others would soon characterize as rape, war profiteering and ethnic cleansing.'[82]

The language of heroism was appropriated by Romantic nationalists, then by communists[83] and then by reinvented nationalists in the 1990s. Heroism was finally 'ingloriously buried'[84] during the wars in the 1990s in Bosnia, Croatia and Kosovo as was the myth of male heroism during the fighting. Undoubtedly some mobilization of soldiers took place because those who signed up thought in some sense they were fighting for a higher cause. In practice, however, ethnic cleansing has not been heroic or manly: most acts of fighting associated with ethnic cleansing have been 'cowardly' even in a traditional sense. Women and children have been victims of murder, torture and rape. Haris Silajdžić estimated that by 1993, 25,000 children had been killed in the Bosnian War.[85] Journalists were also frequently targeted in Croatia and Bosnia in the 1990s. Volunteers from *Médecins sans Frontières* spent two years caring for refugees in the designated 'safe haven' of Srebrenica. In 2000, twenty people, who worked for the doctors, including drivers who had been forced off buses after the fall of the town in 1995 were still missing, presumed executed by Ratko Mladić and his troops.[86] They joined the many thousands of Muslims killed there in the summer of 1995.

A pessimistic interpretation is that war and crises bring normal 'insane' social contradictions to the fore. This may be true on one level, but another interpretation might also be true in part. Victimizers have rarely experienced rape and cowardly acts with any sense of triumph. The use of the tactic of systematic rape warfare was consistently denied by the Bosnian Serb commanders.[87] Rapists frequently excused their actions by claiming that their commanders had told them to rape. These acts violate an innate sense of human rights, held even by the perpetrators. The number of suicides among young Serb men in Bosnia since 1995 is reported to be very high.[88] As the Krajina Serbs were driven out in 1995, 'two men committed suicide by hanging themselves from trees' and another shot his wife, his children and then turned the gun on himself.[89] The cycle of violence suggested by Obrad Kesić indicates that perpetrators of violent crimes are left with a permanent self-disgust, which is reinforced by repeated patterns of violent sexual behaviour. Ethnic cleansing and the crisis of war appears to invert, not exaggerate normal behaviour, to turn normal men into murderers and rapists, leaving both victim and victimizer damaged.

6 The destruction of community

The Macedoine:[1] Neighbours and/or enemies in the Balkans

Until 2001, the Former Yugoslav Republic of Macedonia or FYROM had largely avoided the ethnic strife that had been seen elsewhere, although during the wars of the twentieth century, Macedonians have suffered a great deal from nationalist violence from within and from outside their country. Until the turn of the twentieth century, its population was a mixture of Slav Muslims, Orthodox Slavs, Catholic and Orthodox Albanians, Greeks, Jews and Turks. Furthermore, Bosnian and Serbian Muslims moved to Macedonia in the 1870s, while it still remained within the Ottoman Empire increasing its already multiethnic character. Prior to the Balkan Wars of 1912–13, Macedonia remained the last vestige of Ottoman multiethnicity until the almost complete withdrawal of the Turkish government from the Balkan peninsula (apart from a small toe hold around the Bosphorus). During these wars, Ottoman Macedonia was the focus of the territorial ambitions of the nation states of Serbia, Bulgaria and Greece with Albania as an interested party: the so-called 'four wolves',[2] who pictured it as a region where 'unredeemed (ethnic) brethren'[3] were living. After particularly vicious fighting and ethnic cleansing,[4] Macedonia was effectively dismembered at the end of the First World War with Bulgaria gaining 6,798, Yugoslavia 26,776 and Greece 34,600 square kilometres.[5]

For many writers who have described life in Macedonia, it has come to represent a multiethnic idyll. Sometimes that idyll belongs to a past time. Turkish writer Nilüfer Mizanōglu Reddy rewove her family's history in Macedonia, by tracing the path taken by her grandmother's trousseau, and in particular a splendid embroidered jacket in 'Balkan-Ottoman rococo' style with its 'unmistakable gaiety and buoyancy in the design' from Veles to Salonika and subsequently to Istambul.[6] More recently, Misha Glenny recalled a perfect evening in Skopje in 1991. 'We talk in the darkness, listen to the crickets who click their legs in time with a festival in the distance, the full-blooded celebration of a Romani marriage in Europe's gypsy capital.'[7] Although Macedonia has sometimes been used as a 'metaphor for internal multiplicity'[8] and this fact has been celebrated this is really only the case in the 'Former Yugoslavian Republic of Macedonia'. Greek Macedonia, in particular has lost its multiethnic character and by 1945 there were only a few thousand Jews left in Salonika. In the mid-1940s the 'Slavophone' population of Greek Macedonia was estimated to be about 90,000. During the Civil War, many were pro-communist and left in 1949 to live in Yugoslavia or Bulgaria. The Greek population census of 1951 stated that 41,000 Slavophones remained in Greece.[9] The Hellenization of Greek Macedonia was speeded up by the influx of over one million Greeks from the Aegean regions after the Treaty of Lausanne in 1923 and the loss of around 380,000 Muslims who left to try to rebuild their lives in Turkey, Lebanon or Syria.[10] The Slavonic speakers of Greek Macedonia were relentlessly Hellenized. In the 1930s, during the dictatorship of Metaxas, education in Slavonic languages was made illegal and individuals were made to change their family names to sound Greek.[11] As recently as 1998, the Greek Foreign Minister denied the existence of a Macedonian minority in Greece at a press conference.[12]

The practice of forced homogenization was experienced elsewhere in South Eastern Europe. In Bulgaria in the 1980s, the minority Turkish community were given lists of suitable Bulgarian names and given 24 hours to choose something suitable. If they refused they were imprisoned.[13] This policy of forcing individuals to change their family names was also carried out by Mussolini's government in Istria and Dalmatia in the interwar years. In Trieste in 1929 a book guiding people in the art of changing their names was published by Aldo Pizzagalli entitled *Per l'italianità dei cognomi*, in which Čuk was to be changed to Zucchi, Slavec to Salvi and Debeljak to Debelli.[14] Some of these changes were linguistically absurd, as were many of the concoctions dreamt up for newcomers to the United States by officials at Ellis Island, but the destruction of nomenclature is a fairly drastic step towards elimination of the memory of that community. In the interwar period Greek gendarmes effectively stopped people from speaking their Slavonic language in public and children were known to be thrashed at school if they failed to speak in Greek.[15] Greater Serb nationalists also attempted to repress the pro-Bulgarian sentiment of the Macedonians (the Macedonian Slav language is almost identical in functional terms to Bulgarian). In Prilep in 1912, the then crown prince Aleksandar (who was killed by a Macedonian VMRO revolutionary in Marseilles in 1934) apparently slapped a little girl on the face when she told him she was a 'Bulgarian'.[16] Jovan Cvijić developed the thesis that it would be possible to 'Serbianize' the Macedonians, in part because they had traces of the Kosovo epics in their folklore.[17] Many Macedonians became quite pragmatic about their taxonomy as far as the outside world was concerned. A Russian writer Vasil Vodovozov was told by an informant during the First World War: 'I was a Bulgarian, now I'm a Serb.'[18]

The remainder of the *Macedoine* in so far as it exists is threatened by the current (early 2000s) fighting in that republic. Part of the contemporary problem stems from the fact that although the Albanians are ethnically homogeneous (and clearly more so than almost any other group in this region, although there may be underlying complexities that make this statement ultimately problematic) many of their 'number' live in states outside Albania proper. The Albania created in 1912 was clearly a '*klein-Albanien*' or a small version of the nation state that had numerous 'ethnic brethren' contiguous with its border. Over the following years these regions became more Albanian in character, as for example the Turkish community of the

Ohrid region left after 1912. The high birth rate amongst the Albanian community combined with a Serbian outflux from Kosovo meant that this part of the Yugoslavian state became increasingly Albanianized. The 'Albanian National Question' became even more important in 1999 with the influx of many Albanians from Kosovo and the confident military activities of the KLA and subsequently the NLA in Macedonia. The militarization of the Albanian populated regions of Macedonia, particularly around Tetovo, has unleashed intercommunal violence which may only cease when the region is partitioned, although that seems a very drastic solution and one which is unlikely to be welcomed by the Macedonian government in Skopje.

Clearly the events of 2001 can be linked with the unleashing of painful memories and some long-term antipathies in some villages. During the Balkan Wars, the Greek army burnt down Albanian villages. The sides of the hills were covered with black patches and the corn standing in the fields was burnt in a deliberate attempt to starve people and drive them out.[19] Violent and brutal acts of ethnic cleansing have not always been committed by outsiders: as part of the reprisals for the uprisings in 1902 and 1903, Albanian irregulars burnt down some 150 villages around Bitola.[20] Jonathan Schwartz was told a story about how in the Spring of 1945 Bulgarian troops had come to a Macedonian village and 'rounded up thirty-eight Albanians – with the help of some Macedonians – took them to an all-Macedonian village and axed them to death'.[21] One of the Macedonians, who wanted to help the Albanians was also killed. Years later, 'the element of betrayal . . . is what is most remembered in my friend's narrative. It is not hatred for Bulgarians but mistrust of at least one of his Macedonian neighbours.'[22]

Many outsiders who have profound and intimate knowledge of the communities they are describing have remained optimistic about the future of Macedonia. When President Kiro Gligorov was almost killed by a bomb in Skopje in October 1995, Jonathan Schwartz remarked that

> (g)uesses as to the ethno-nationalist identity of the would-be assassins did not develop into violent conflict. Friends from many ethnic groups in Macedonia conveyed to me by phone and fax their trust that society would hold together. Their responses suggest that problems within Macedonia and across the borders can be resolved through negotiation and changes in policy.[23]

The optimism of commentators who believe strongly that a particular society will withstand crisis may come to exist because the destruction of one's 'own' society or a society which one knows and understands intimately may be the hardest thing to anticipate. There may also have been an important element of denial at work because it was suspected that those responsible were Macedonian rather than Albanian. A privileged insider always sees the nuances and complexities that practitioners of ethnic cleansing seek to eliminate.[24] Because they reproduce 'local' and 'conjectural' knowledge so successfully they sometimes fail to use the 'powerful and terrible weapon of abstraction'[25] in the right measure or perhaps fail to believe that ideologies such as nationalism, which at one level seem to be so alien to multiethnic societies, can have so much destructive impact. An idea does not have to be a particularly profound one to initiate the destruction of something that is both deep and complex.

The destruction of community

Ethnic cleansing has taken place in places where the population was profoundly integrated. Before the war of 1991–5, the Croatian town of Karlovac had a population, which included more than 30 per cent Serbs. Before 1990, many people who lived in that town did not even know whether their neighbours were precisely Serbs or Croats and religion only ever became an issue if marriage was the outcome of a relationship. This was told to the author by a former Croat resident of Karlovac, who informed me further:

> I have a reputation for being ethnically tolerant, but this in part masks my almost complete ignorance about nationalist politics. When I was a boy in the 1960s, we did not ask questions about ethnicity and we were not expected to think about it. I grew up without having to know these facts and if you were to ask me about the pupils in my class in *Gymnasium* [sic], I could hazard a guess as to who was Croat and who was Serb on the basis of surnames, but it would only be a guess.[26]

Like many of the towns of Eastern Slavonia, the Danubian town of Vukovar had a mixed population of Serbs and Croats (its German population had been expelled in 1945). Slavonian towns had a far greater level of intermarriage than the norm for the rest of Yugoslavia (at 35 per cent for Vukovar[27] as opposed to an average of about 12 per cent in the rest of Yugoslavia[28]). The almost total destruction of Vukovar in the latter half of 1991 is a tale of horror reminiscent of the annihilation of the Irish citizenry of Drogheda by the English army of Oliver Cromwell in the seventeenth century. In both cases, all adult males were classed as combatants and slaughtered en masse. On 17 November 1991 the desperate defenders of the town surrendered after several months of siege. The Yugoslav People's Army (Jugoslovenska Narodna Armija or JNA) and Četnici paraded through the utterly desolate and ruined streets. The paramilitaries apparently sung bloodthirsty songs, no doubt to distract themselves from the fact that they had gained so very little in practice.[29] Over 300 patients in the hospital, most of whom were soldiers, were executed and their bodies hastily disposed of at a sheep farm near the town; these atrocities were later to become the subject of a United Nations war crimes investigation.[30]

The war in Croatia was watched with horror in neighbouring Bosnia;[31] however many felt that this tragedy might not be repeated there because the lines between ethnic communities were so faint and difficult to 'map'. In the event, similar horrors were repeated many times over and the international community in various guises spent three years trying to remap Bosnia, while the ethnic cleansing of Muslims in particular cost the lives of perhaps up to a quarter of a million people.[32]

Because ethnic difference is 'managed' from day to day in traditional cultures (as indeed it is in modern urban cultures), this does not mean ideas of separateness between communities in the Balkans do not exist. Rather *völkisch* notions of 'ethnic totalities' continue to exist at the level of popular culture and ideas of 'race' play an important role in the popular imagination.[33] One test of this was the widespread belief that interethnic marriage was not particularly desirable, even in the Titoist period of 'brotherhood and unity'. Tone Bringa characterizes resistance to intermarriage as the ultimate boundary between groups[34] and remembers being told by one informant: 'the children from mixed marriages, who will they be? Who will be their friends? They will be neither Catholics nor Muslims.'[35] As an expert witness at the Hague Tribunal, Bringa felt that 'in a conflict, which could be anything from a quarrel about sheep that run into your property (sic), in these kinds of conflicts, relatives would often have strong loyalties to each other and would stand up for each other'.[36] In such circumstances there was a conflation between ethnic ties and kinship ties.

It would be somewhat naïve to argue that popular consciousness of difference was not a factor in ethnic cleansing and that it was only 'modern' nationalism that drove a wedge between peoples who had lived together harmoniously for centuries. The persistent indulgence in 'mutual radicalization',[37] at times bordering on narcissism in the 1980s in Yugoslavia amongst Slovenes, Croats and Serbs in particular, was an important factor in inhibiting better understanding between communities. But as Noel Malcolm has remarked, 'between low level prejudices on the one hand and military conflict and mass murder on the other, there lies a very long road'.[38] Consciousness of perceived difference is not enough to create situations of crisis and violence, although the reification and subsequent repetition of elements of difference may not ultimately be a recipe for sustained harmony. Visitors to Bosnia before the war were often struck by the ease with which the different religious groups socialized with each other. Stereotyped jokes about *Bosanci* by other former Yugoslavs usually emphasized their 'laid back' attitude and the fact that they were happy to celebrate all the religious festivals in their republic, thus gaining far more days off work.[39] Individuals from different ethnic groups socialized together, but Andrei Simić has argued there was an 'invisible psychological wall' between neighbours and 'superficial cordiality, more often than not masked a deep sense of alienation, suspicion, and fear'.[40] And it certainly is the case that individuals do not forget what happens during war and crisis and will bury hostilities until such time as it is possible to take revenge. In Kosovo in the 1990s some interpersonal relations between Serbs and Albanians survived despite the 'apartheid' around them. This in itself 'fail(ed) to dismantle stereotypes'. Thus a Serb woman living in one of two Serbian households in a village of fourteen houses 'can praise her Albanians neighbor's generosity, attesting that she would "live and die" for them, while continuing to cast the most vile slurs against Albanians' as an ethnic group[41]. After the 1999 war, extremists ensured that interethnic harmony did not return. In Priština's Talixhe district in the summer of 1999, ethnic Serbs were asked not to go to a shop run by Albanians as the shopkeepers feared getting into trouble with the KLA.[42]

The victimization of neighbours is a constant element in ethnic cleansing. Although much of the most cruel and brutal violence is reported as being committed by outsiders (soldiers, paramilitaries or mercenaries), many individuals have fallen prey to the spite, greed, lust and sadism of people they knew all too well. A Muslim woman from Bosnia reported that she had been raped by her teenage neighbour: 'so often he had sat at our place, drank coffee with us. He even worked for me.'[43] On 12 August 2001 in Ljuboten four miles north of Skopje, five unarmed Albanian villagers were shot, apparently by local police who knew them. 'Witnesses said that at least two men were called out of the cellars by name and summarily shot . . . When the police finally left Albanians claimed that they heard them singing "Long live Macedonia" and "we killed the Albanians".'[44] Bosnians were killed by their neighbours in Omarska and at Trnopolje there were times when 'Serb acquaintance would come and call for a prisoner, take him out and kill him'.[45] Peter Maass visited a Bosnian village where thirty-five Moslem men had been slaughtered: 'They were killed by Serbs who had been their friends, people who had helped harvest their fields the previous autumn, people with whom they had shared adolescent adventures and secrets, skinny-dipping in the Drina river on hot summer days . . . All of a sudden, seemingly without reason, they had turned into killers.'[46]

Other individuals experienced very different behaviour from their neighbours. The author was informed by a volunteer who worked with Bosnian Muslim refugees in London in the 1990s that many of them had escaped because they had used the identity papers of their Serb neighbours. One Muslim woman from Bijeljina reported that:

> [w]e left our rich and beautiful house to a man, a refugee, a wonderful man, a Serb who will take care of it. When we left, a Serbian woman came to see us off. She was my best friend and we had lived thirty-seven years together. She brought me oranges and tomatoes for the trip.[47]

Amongst the prisoners at Omarska were 'two Serb women arrested for protesting (sic) the behavior of Serb soldiers and reservists towards their neighbors'.[48] Relationships between Serbs and Croats were not entirely destroyed by the war in Croatia from 1991–5 and Croats who fled the war zones asked trusted Serb friends and neighbours to care for (and sometimes even to bury) their possessions during the conflict.[49] Responses to the cruelties of war and ethnic cleansing are entirely individual and, I would argue, essentially an ideological response to extreme conditions. Many individuals have refused to be ruled by hate and the destruction of tradition. As 79-year-old Branko Mulić, who had witnessed the ferocity of fighting in the Krajina region during the Second World War, exclaimed in 1990: 'Serbs and Croats will be better off if they adopt the old Indian practice and bury the hatchet forever.'[50]

The violent acts of people one has known intimately may be peculiarly traumatic for the victims. Jovan Rašković remembered such an individual in Kistanje in 1941:

One morning a strong and tall man with enormous hands appeared. He didn't talk with anybody. He sat in the sun and didn't look for shade. And in this heat he wore a warm sweater and a dark hat on his head. The story went that his neighbors who became Ustasha killed all his children and threw them in a pit.[51]

The historian Milorad Ekmečić, a Bosnian Serb and founder of the radical nationalist Srpska Democratska Stranka (SDS Serbian Democratic Party), who lost seventy-eight members of his family in 1941 in the village of Prebilovci, recalled that '[o]ver the years when I came to visit [the village] for weddings and funerals the stories they told were about the massacres during the war. They were possessed by the memories of 1941–45.'[52] Their 'possession' by memories of the war period was partly due to the horrific nature of the crimes committed, but also partly due to the fact that the Communist regime suppressed discussion of the war and ethnically inspired atrocities. A Bosnian Croat told the anthropologist Tone Bringa: 'Yes, we lived in peace and harmony (i.e. during the Tito era) because every hundred meters we had a policeman to make sure we loved one another'.[53] The Communists feared nationalism and knew that it could divide the people of Yugoslavia and plunge them into further civil wars, but failed to provide a durable ideological alternative. The ideology of brotherhood and unity (*bratstvo i jedinstvo*), which they promoted, was too heavily dependent on the memory of the partisan struggle during the war, which could not necessarily be relied upon to outlive the older generation.[54] Unlike nationalism, which more successfully mimics an essence and therefore has more durability, Partisan ideology was closely linked to a single historical experience (i.e. the Second World War) that it could not be continually reinvented.

The accounts of participants in ethnic cleansing suggest that basic 'revenge' is a common motive for committing atrocities. In September 1941, a Partisan from Sarajevo noted in his diary that, 'Some Chetniks from other areas are threatening to burn the Muslims' homes . . . for what the Ustaši are doing to the Serbs.'[55] In Izmir in 1922, the Greek archbishop Chrysostom was lynched by the Turkish soldiers on the orders of their commander Nurettin. What might appear to be a symbolic extermination of a representative of Christianity was actually a personal grudge on the part of the commander.[56] Medjugorje is a town in Hercegovina, which lost half its population in the early 1940s when it was part of the fascist Independent State of Croatia (*Nezavisna Država Hrvatska*). In 1992 a local war (*mali rat*) took place between families known to have links with Ustaša and Četnici abroad, that the Communist authorities defined in the 1970s as 'organized crime that has spread from the capitalist West'.[57] However much the 'morally decaying West' (*truli zapad*) was responsible for perpetuating extremism in exile, the fighting had a very local, personalized and vicious outcome. On 27 May 1992, three bodies were found in the yard of Djure Šivrić. Their feet had been 'tied to a pipe and their hands behind their backs [and] were suspended upside down immersed to the shoulders in a partially demolished cistern'.[58] Two weeks earlier the elderly parents of Siro Ostojić 'were found hanging from a mulberry tree in front of their house, their throats slit and their hands chopped off'.[59] Both families were linked with Ustaša and Četnici respectively and these individuals were killed in deliberately dehumanizing and humiliating circumstances in their own homes.

Sometimes this sense of revenge is artificial and short lived. A Serb soldier fighting in the Balkan Wars of 1912–13, made the following observation: 'The killing of prisoners is due partly to desire for vengeance for disappointed hopes . . . The brave and educated men among the soldiers never killed prisoners. The cowards revenged themselves on these unarmed men for the fear they had felt during battle.'[60] Writing to his brother in July 1913, a Greek soldier felt that 'we have turned out much crueler than the Bulgars – we violated every girl we met . . . I have taken what I had a right to after all they did to us at Panghaian.'[61] As Branimir Anzulović has remarked

> in a perverse way, the ideology that generates a genocide demonstrates at the same time that most people committing it believe that they are following their conscience. The self-defensive 'kill so that you may not be killed' is usually not sufficient to mobilize the masses; the victim must be seen as a demon and his killing as a universally beneficial act. Even at his worst, man likes to think that he is doing good.[62]

Revenge is carried out for acts that soldiers have been told the enemy has committed and sometimes it can be presented as a social 'good' or a settling of scores. One 16-year-old rape victim from Bosnia was told by the Serb soldier (who eventually helped her escape) that he would rape her because 'that's what your people are doing to us as well'.[63] A Greek refugee, fleeing from Turkey in 1922 reported that 'we were . . . shut up in a garden in which Turkish civilians, women and children were allowed to enter. These pointed out some among us, who, they said, maltreated Turks during the Greek occupation. These unfortunate individuals were without further process conducted to unknown destinations.'[64] The catharsis of revenge is often short lived. One Serb soldier who fought in Kosovo in 1999, reported 'We lived off revenge, sweet revenge . . . back then revenge felt very good. Especially when we killed the KLA. That was back then. Now I can't sleep, I can't eat. It hasn't lasted.'[65] Frantz Fanon, a psychiatrist and critic of French colonial government in North Africa argued that 'we are forever pursued by our actions' and describes attacks of guilt and remorse as moments of 'vertigo'. He described the fate of an Algerian revolutionary who had placed a bomb, which had killed ten people.

> He wondered with a feeling of anguish whether among the victims of the bomb there had been people like his new acquaintances. It was true that the café that it was aimed at was a meeting place for notorious racists; but there was nothing to prevent a quite ordinary passer-by going in and having a drink. From the first day that he suffered from vertigo the man tried to avoid thinking of these former occurrences. But paradoxically . . . the symptoms . . . appeared with great regularity.[66]

Heimat and landscapes of ethnic cleansing

Ethnic cleansing in not just about murder, the wanton destruction of property, theft, rape and other violations and flight. It is about the destruction of what has been there before, an attack on memory, security and *Heimat*.[67] An Albanian woman from Rahoveci in Kosovo remembered that 'when the paramilitary Serb forces drove us out . . . [t]he grief was unimaginable, the leaving of home and everything we possessed'.[68] Atatürk on hearing of the loss of Salonika during the Balkan Wars, is said to have shouted to a fellow native of the town: 'How could you leave Salonika, that beautiful town of ours? Why did you hand it to the enemy and come here?'[69] The contrast between what has been and what is now is often very poignant. Discussing the video representations of ethnic cleansing, Dona Kolar-Panov remarks that 'flashes of childhood dreams ("idyllic countryside and fields golden with ripened wheat") mix freely with other dreams with the flashes of other memories and slowly form into sequences of the present yet unreal world of hatred, madmen and war'. A British writer described the desperate flight of Muslims from Yenidje-Vardar in Macedonia in 1912 with all their property, typically evoking the Bible:

> then came a troop of barefooted Moslem [sic] peasants leading donkeys upon which were piled mattress and quilt and coffee pot, all they had saved in the rush from Yenidje, when the Greek guns set fire to the rude huts they called home . . . Two weedy oxen were dragging a creaking wooden wagon, which threatened to break asunder at every dip in the road. The worldly goods and chattels of these fugitives – beds, mats, the inevitable prayer rug, the shallow copper utensil which serves alike as cooking pan and salver even now as it did in Biblical times, a dozen unhappy ducks strung by their webbed feet to the frame – were piled high on the conveyance, and on top of this conglomeration of household effects sat wives and mothers, their sorrowful faces hidden from the sight of men, weeping and wailing as they ineffectually tried to comfort aging parents or to hold suckling babies to their breasts.[70]

Muslims driven out of the Macedonian town of Guvezna in 1922 were rounded up and taken to the *aghora* or market place,[71] which Anastasia Karakasidou has described as 'a key institution in facilitating the interaction among the local population'. The ethnic cleansing of this community was thus symbolically recognized by this ritual. Many first hand accounts describe the loss of the individuals driven out from their homes. In December 1991 at the Slovenian–Croatian border, Dona Kolar-Panov saw refugees from the Croatian war 'identified not just by the empty look in their eyes, but by the numerous packages they clung on to, mainly ordinary plastic shopping bags filled with all that remained of their world possessions'.[72] The diaries of a child from Sarajevo written in the early 1990s are filled with her own experience of living under siege, but also chronicle the destruction of her *Heimat* and memories. On Thursday 18 June 1992, she recorded that

[t]oday we heard some more sad, sad news. Our country house in Crnotina, a tower that's about 150 years old, has burnt down. Like the post office, it disappeared in flames. I loved it so much. We spent last summer there. I had a wonderful time. I always looked forward to going there. We had redone it so nicely, bought new furniture, new rugs, put in new windows, given it all our warmth and love and its beauty was our reward. It lived through so many wars, so many years and now it's gone. It has burned down to the ground. Our neighbours Žiga, Meho and Bečir were killed . . . Vildana's house also burned down. All the houses burned down.[73]

In November of the same year Zlata mourned the cutting down of all the trees in Sarajevo's beautiful parks for firewood.[74] Like so many other individuals who survived ethnic cleansing, she was then forced to recreate her identity in a new country. The collapse of the Ottoman Empire through to the Yugoslavian Wars of the 1990s created vast diaspora communities across the world, but particularly in Western Europe, Canada, the USA and Australia. These people then faced the challenge of whether to recreate the customs and culture of their old lives or to rebuild their lives entirely or to somehow create a middle way between the old and the new. Many of them continue to live with terrible trauma, poverty and despair, whereas others have made wholesale and successful adaptations to their new environment. Sometimes, but rarely, individuals attempt to return to their old villages. In the Bosnian town of Glamoč, a remote community where the majority of farmers grew potatoes, the pre-war population was over 80 per cent Serb. In 1997, a group of displaced former citizens now living in Banja Luka in the Serbian section of Bosnia grouped together, calling themselves *Zavičaj* (native country or *Heimat*). Several hundred of them voted in the municipal elections, defying instructions from the ruling party in Republika Srpska. This kind of defiance in itself may not be enough to reverse the trends of the Dayton Accords, signed in 1995, which divided Bosnia along strict ethnic lines.

Theft and destruction of property generally deters people from ever returning.[75] In parts of Bosnia, Muslims who had made money in Germany or elsewhere in Europe were particularly targeted during the ethnic cleansing campaigns in 1992–5.[76] During the war, markets in Belgrade and elsewhere were awash with stolen white goods and many Muslim houses were gutted in the attempt to find cash. Much of the destruction of property during the wars of the 1990s was gratuitous. The travel writer Paul Theroux was in Croatia in 1994 and noticed the damage to buildings in Slano, Split and Dubrovnik. In Zadar, he remembered that the town had been badly affected and some building targeted so that 'it was obvious that it had been hit from up close and vindictively: the ancient gate of the main town, a Roman relic, had been shelled – for what reason apart from malice? – and chunks blown out of it'.[77] The Roma parts of Mitrovica in Kosovo were burnt down in the summer of 1999 by Albanians in revenge for supposed collaboration with the Serbs,[78] luxury hotels in Dubrovnik were prime targets from bombing in the winter of 1991 and in Karlovac in the same year, the Yugoslav People's Army (JNA) torched orchards and burnt down houses with no military or strategic value.

Often those who dared to return to their homes found them trashed. One Albanian woman from Priština, returned to her flat in 1999 to find the rotten contents of the refrigerator on the floor, taps running, damp and insects everywhere. Her furniture had been removed by her Serb and Roma neighbours, but she subsequently recovered much of this when they themselves took flight.[79] During times of crisis, people have frequently left their homes with extreme haste. In 1999, Serbs and Albanians fled at different points during the year carrying their belongings in plastic bags and wearing their house slippers.[80] In Izmir in 1922, Greeks and Armenians desperately tried to sell their portable belongings such as carpets and jewelry to tourists for next to nothing as they made their escape from the fire and Atatürk's troops.[81]

Deaths occurred from hunger in 1999 among Kosovo Albanians who had escaped into Macedonia. Xhevahire Belia,[82] a refugee from Kacanik reported that troops had 'burned 80 per cent of the food at their home'. Elsewhere people died from starvation in the ethnic cleansing campaigns in the Balkans. In Bosnia, a British officer Garry Donaldson witnessed the people in the 'safe haven' of Srebrenica prior to the massacre in 1995. He was reminded 'of the Warsaw ghetto: the quiet hungry eyes of the children crouching around the food distribution points, the vulnerable old men and women pushed to the back of the queue by the strongest, the figures combing the rubbish dump for food'.[83] He, like many of the foreign observers, was numbed by his inability to prevent this humanitarian disaster. He could only think '(t)he sadness of the poverty and deprivation was overwhelming'.[84]

Ethnic cleansing throughout the two centuries in the Balkans and elsewhere has often been carried out with extreme haste, without obvious planning or care about later detection.[85] In the summer of 1999, Ljubica Vujović, a Serb from Priština was killed in her home. Like the Šivrić familiy in Medjugorje she had been held under water in a grotesque and very 'domestic' murder: 'Her corpse lay over the edge of the bath tub, her feet on the ground, her head in the water, where someone had held her until she drowned.'[86] In Kostajnica in Croatia in 1991, the Serbs left the village the night before paramilitaries moved in to execute the Croats. They left 'their cattle in the stables, dinners on the table, washing machines spinning'.[87] One man from the village was shocked by the betrayal, but wondered whether this was a 'conspiracy of mortal fear',[88] that they had been threatened with death if they alerted the Croats to the planned cleansing. In such cases where murder has been hasty and particularly cruel, the terrain becomes important.

The South East of Europe is covered with mountains and limestone ridges of Karst, which are often rocky and inhospitable. In Tripolitsa in Greece in October 1821, Muslim women and children were led to a ravine in the mountains and simply pushed down to their deaths. One eyewitness saw heaps of sun-bleached bones two years after the event.[89] In Bosnia in the summer of 1992, Medo Sivac was ordered to kneel on the edge of a cliff in the Koricani ridges on Mount Vlašić. He reported that 'horrible fire was heard and I felt a sharp pain in the shoulder. I was falling into the abyss.' He and six other survivors spent two days lying wounded at the bottom of the cliff.[90] It was common for those who survived such an ordeal to live because they fell on to the bodies of other victims and then were able to fain death. In Kosovo in April 1999, Arbnesha Huskaj lay in a snowy ravine while she listened to her neighbours being shot by paramilitaries.[91] Because of the haste and inefficiency of this method of killing numerous witnesses from different historical periods have survived to tell the tale, despite having lain surrounded by bodies for many hours or days in some cases.

The role of the limestone ravine both as a place of death and a symbolic burial ground for unknown numbers of victims is a central motif in the ethnic cleansing of the Balkans. For the African informants of Victor Turner one of the key symbols in their landscape was the milk trees, but in Karst regions this role was fulfilled by the rocks.[92] In Medugorje the Ostojić clan were referred to disparagingly by their neighbours as 'stone-eaters' as their land was so craggy[93] and in Montenegro there are many wistful legends about God dropping stones on the land in error.[94] An English wine-buyer who crossed Croatia and Slovenia in the early eighteenth century cursed the limestone rocks that caused his horse to lose shoes.[95] These ravines were dangerous places, even without their additional role in war and crisis. In the folk epics Kraljević Marko and other heroes frequently wander in the Karst looking for water. Animals occasionally fall down pits or caves and rock climbers usually have tales to recount of stepping on decomposing animals in unexpected places. In regions where limestone ravines exist, the lay of the land was used to dispose of bodies quickly. Ustaša pushed Serbs down the sides of mountains and pits in the Krajina in Croatia and also in Hercegovina in 1941. Individuals kept the knowledge of these events very much alive. In 1983, a play based on the short story collection *Golubnjača* by Jovan Radulović from Knin was banned and remained so until 1990. The *Golubnjača*, which means pigeon cove, is the name of a Karstic pit into which the Ustaša threw their victims, but the actual drama is set in the early 1960s. Nevertheless, it involves a number of quite violent scenes and the Karst landscape itself is quite clearly a symbol for trauma and bloodshed.[96] It was a central metaphor for the Serb population in particular who lived in these regions and had their fears of a revival of the events of 1941 whipped up by nationalist writers and politicians. In 1945, the Partisans used the caves and ravines to dispose of the bodies of Ustaša and other 'enemies of socialism'. In 1990, 80-year-old Jela Smeciklas, who was working in a nearby field, remembered that 'they came every day for two weeks and from time to time thereafter'.[97] When the excavations began at Sosice, the bodies were found in caves more than 120 feet deep.

It was not only in the Krajina region that the landscapes of violence were ethnicized. In attacks against them after the defeat of Mussolini and the collapse of the Italian front in 1943, ethnic Italians from the littoral regions of the Adriatic were pushed down Karstic holes or what they refer to as *foibe*. The fate of those thrown into pits (*infoibati*) has become controversial in the historiography of the region and was intertwined with other discourses. Cold war divisions of East and West were used by the Italians to dehumanize the Slavs and to link the fate of the *infoibati* to a lack of civilization amongst the Slavs. Old ethno-geographical distinctions between the 'Slavonic' limestone Karst as the hinterland and the warm and the sunny 'Hesperian' shores of Italy some of which dated back to the eighteenth century were also used to create an imaginary fault line between civilizations.[98] Italians who had fled from Istria and Dalmatia and were living as exiles (*esuli*), particularly in Trieste, were often reminded of the fate of their compatriots. A memorial built at Basovizza (on the outskirts of Trieste) to commemorate the fate of the victims of this ethnic cleansing 'immediately became an object of pilgrimage for nationalists and Istrian exiles who demanded national recognition'[99] Glenda Sluga has described this as 'a memorialization of the region's *italianità*'[100] and not simply of the suffering of local people during war. The fate of the Slovenes under the fascist government is forgotten here.

Symbolism and violence

Are discernable patterns of behaviour random human responses to crisis or do they point to the existence of the unitary and 'consistent' system of signs of a traditional and relatively 'unfragmented' society, as Mary Douglas argued?[101] The insurrection led by Karadjordje in 1804 was accompanied by deliberately targeted acts of atrocities against Muslims in Serbia who were to be driven out in the wake of independence. The rebels then began to (successfully) destroy all the architectural heritage of the Ottomans and now only the Barjakli Džamija mosque from this earlier period remains in Belgrade.[102] Ever since, the destruction of material culture has been a constant in ethnically inspired violence. In 1877, in Bulgaria in Yeni Zagra, '50 Turkish houses were burned as were the mosque and government buildings'.[103] Shops owned by Jews were also destroyed. In the same year in Filibe in Bulgaria, mosques were turned into latrines.[104] In Salonika the occupying Germans used one synagogue to stable their horses and blew the others up.[105] They also demolished the Jewish cemetery and used the tombstones to build roads. One eyewitness recorded that 'the vast necropolis, scattered with fragments of stone and rubbish, resembled a city that had been bombed, or destroyed by a volcanic eruption'.[106] It is well recorded that Serbian and Croatian nationalists targeted the material (i.e. symbolic) culture of the Muslims in Bosnia. The Islamic bridge at Mostar one of the finest pieces of Ottoman architecture in South East Europe,[107] was destroyed by the Croatian paramilitary Defence Force (*Hrvatsko Obrambene Snage* HOS) who had close links with the neo-fascist Party of Rights (*Stranka Prava*) in 1993, who fired at it until the pieces of stone fell into the river below. The district of Mostar around the bridge was an almost perfectly preserved Ottoman vestige which was ravaged by the war and almost all that was left of the mosque and the other buildings was a pile of rubble. In contrast, the huge church erected at nearby Medjugorje to accommodate the prayers of over one million tourists since the early 1980s remained untouched by the fighting. The destruction of this 'Islamic symbol' of the famous bridge is viewed with tragic irony by Ivo Goldstein, as he points out that it was built by Croatian stonemasons from Korčula and Dubrovnik under the direction of Muslim architects.[108]

During the Balkan wars of 1912–13, wounded soldiers were placed in the Turkish tower of Strumnitsa and set on fire before the Greeks evacuated, thus destroying not only enemy soldiers but the cultural presence as well.[109] The destruction of buildings and other material objects symbolizes the removal of the last vestiges and traces of the people who lived there. In Bulgaria in the 1980s, the tombstones of Turks were broken and the old names removed.[110] In Kosovo in June 1999, Albanians began to remove the numerous statues of Serbian kings and a few weeks earlier Serbs had blown up the house where the Albanian League of Prizren had met in 1878.[111] The destruction of property and material culture during the ethnic cleansing of the Balkans is occasionally reminiscent of the iconoclastic furies of the popular Reformation, when crowds inspired by religious radicals deliberately ruined religious buildings or even when groups of pious Protestants destroyed and even 'tortured' graven images. In Wittenberg in 1522, Gabriel Zwilling persuaded the local Augustinians to mutilate statues and 'cleanse' altars 'to avoid idolatry'.[112] Ideologically inspired hate is a powerful short-term emotion and once unleashed has a number of complex 'symptoms'. In Rwanda body parts of the victims of the genocide were organized and 'methodically . . . stacked into piles' becoming part of a series of 'macabre rituals which would (puzzle) a psychiatrist'.[113]

The nationalities of the Balkans exploited difference at the time of execution, which was often carried out with a great deal of symbolic power and atrocious cruelty. Damjan Budisavljević, a Montenegrin shoemaker and Partisan, was killed by the Četnik Sime Despotović with his own auger. It was drilled through his head.[114] Instances of the torture and abuse of people on the grounds of religious difference follow clear cultural patterns. In Rogatica during the Second World War, the 'Ustaša shoed an Orthodox priest; they nailed horseshoes to his palms and knees and then climbed on his back and rode him through the town'[115] in a grotesque attempt to dehumanize their victim and to turn him into a beast of burden. Traian Stoianovich has interpreted ethnic cleansing in very traditional terms stating that it 'brings us back to the honor–shame orientation of the Balkans' and such examples of obvious and profound humiliation of another person's cultural practices seem to fit this interpretation in part.[116] And as Pieter Spierenburg reminds us, 'honor originally depended on the body . . . appearance was crucial for one's reputation',[117] which may also help to explain why mutilations occur.

Religious personnel and manifestations of religion were frequently attacked. The fifteenth century Orthodox monastery of the Annunciation at Žitomislici in Hercegovina on the banks of the Neretva river was destroyed by Croat fighters in 1993 and its monks and nuns driven out.[118] The Ustaša were reputed to ask their potential victims to make the sign of the cross to establish whether they were Orthodox or Catholic. Violence against Muslims during the war in Bosnia in the early 1990s often emphasized very obvious differences. Peter Maass recorded in Bosnia: 'a teenage girl explained . . . how one of the Muslim men in her village had been nailed to the front door of the mosque, so that he was like Christ on the cross, and he was still alive at the time'.[119] In Bratunac in 1992, a Muslim hodža was tortured in front of his neighbours, then 'ordered to make the sign of the cross, had beer forced down his throat, and then was executed'. Bulgarians were accused of crucifying Greeks in the village of Doxato in 1913.[120] Crucifixion occurred during the Balkan Wars in Macedonia, apparently committed by the Turks. Officer Penev reported that a soldier of the tenth Rhodope infantry had been crucified on a poplar tree by means of telegraph wires.[121] In Bosnia Muslims in the 1990s were made to urinate in the mosque and had crosses carved into their flesh.[122] In 1922, during the ethnic cleansing of Turkey spearheaded by Atatürk, one Greek priest was blinded, then crucified and had horseshoes nailed to his hands and feet by Turkish soldiers.[123]

Clear patterns of anti-Muslim behaviour were played out during ethnic cleansing in the Balkans, including a mental dehumanization of Muslims and vice versa (quite apart from the actual physical destruction). Robert Hayden discusses the case of a Serb soldier forcing a fez onto the head of a 'distraught' Muslim prisoner in Banja Luka in 1994. He explains the episode thus: 'the visible mark of Islamic culture ensured that "Muslim" was more than simply a label of difference, but rather indicated a culture not only apart, but in the Orientalist rhetorical structure . . . also inferior to that of Europe'.[124] The town of Zvornik, with a rich Muslim heritage going back to the sixteenth century, had all its mosques dynamited in 1992, prompting the new Serb major of this ethnically cleansed town to announce that 'there were never any mosques in Zvornik'.[125] As Michael Sells remarks, destroying the mosques not only destroyed the evidence of Islamic heritage but a sign of 500 years of 'shared living' between Christians and Muslims.[126] International human rights lawyer Payam Akhavan remembered the destruction of the village of Ahmići by Croat paramilitaries in 1993:

> One could sense that there were still many bodies which had not been recovered from underneath the rubble, there was virtually not a living creature in the village. Even cats and dogs and cattle had been killed and were lying all over the roads. So I think on the whole, what struck me was the total and all-embracing form of the destruction of this village and its inhabitants.[127]

In Bosnia in the 1990s, women were particularly targeted by Serb and Croat fighters, who raped them en masse and subjected them to other forms of gender specific humiliation. Anthropologist Tone Bringa noted during her fieldwork that Muslim women were generally more devout than men and more likely to fast and make traditional ablutions.[128] Their reputation for piety may be, of course, additional reason why they were targeted. Muslim kitchens were subjected to stricter dietary regulations than their Christian counterparts. Cooking with lard, in particular, was seen as 'unclean'[129] and the forcing of Muslims to eat pork[130] as part of the dehumanization ritual of ethnic cleansing might again be seen as an attack on their 'high standards'.[131] In Bosnia in 1992, in Novo Selo, Serb troops

> rounded up 150 women, children and old people and forced them at gun point into the local mosque. In front of the captives they challenged the local community leader to desecrate the mosque . . . they told him to make the sign of the cross, eat pork and finally have sexual intercourse with a teenage girl . . . [he] refused all these demands and was beaten and cut with knives.[132]

In this single episode all the elements of Muslim alterity were emphasized: chastity, aversion to pork[133] and the sacredness of the mosque. Not content with humiliating their victims, the tortured man was beaten and then disappeared. He has never been seen since.

Muslims also punished Christians in a symbolic fashion, by selecting key motifs of cruelty. In 1821, the Greek Patriarch of Constantinople Gregorius was hanged in his sacred vestments after celebrating the Easter Day mass to the horror of the Christian public of Europe,[134] even though he had expressly called for loyalty to the Ottoman state from the Orthodox millet of the Empire. Such persecution reappeared in the twentieth century in the population transfers of 1922–3. One Greek survivor of the ethnic cleansing of Turkey in 1922 remembered that 'the peasants conceived the diabolical idea that . . . victory against the Christians should be celebrated by a *Courban* (sacrifice or holocaust) of one or two Christians in each village . . . Many prisoners were put to death in an atrocious manner.'[135] This persecution seems to be a particularly grisly imitation of the passion of Christ. Occasionally, the Turks were blamed by Christians for atrocities they did not commit. A Serb soldier told Leon Trotsky in 1912, 'as a rule the Turks don't touch churches . . . priests or women . . . They undoubtedly possess some elements of chivalry.'[136] The same soldier had earlier reported that the village of 'Sorovic . . . was completely wiped out [by the Greeks]. True, the Greeks say that the Turks burnt it. However at Sorovic, mosques were also destroyed – buildings sacred to the Turks – and that's a sure sign.'[137] When Muslims did commit atrocities they also emphasized the very obvious differences between the two groups in terms of the liturgy or cultural difference. During reprisals for the Ilinden massacre in Macedonia in 1903, peasants were squeezed to death in their own wine-presses.[138] Thus markers of difference (in this case for the production of alcohol) became instruments of execution. Victims of ethnically inspired murder have also constructed their persecutors as behaving in a symbolic fashion, perhaps as a result of images that appear in the mind in extreme circumstances. One woman, questioned by the anthropologist Pam Ballinger, retold a story of how the partisans had menaced and then driven out the Italian shopkeepers in Koper who were described as dancing a 'kolo'[139] around them. (In this reconstruction of events, the traditional south Slavonic dance is mutated into a macabre modern version of the medieval dance of death, intended presumably to denote their ethnic difference from their victims.)

Between Christians of different denominations, there were also concerted efforts to destroy religious heritage. In 1991, the Serb Orthodox church in Tovarnik in Croatia was blown up.[140] In the same year a mortar shell badly damaged the roof of the cathedral in Šibenik, a jewel of Renaissance architecture in part designed by Jurij Dalmatinac and a potent symbol of the Catholic culture of the Croatian littoral.[141] Serbs in Krajina fired rounds of ammunition into the graveyards of the ancestors of the Croats they drove out in 1991 in an effort to erase not just their physical existence but arguably the memory of their existence as well.[142] It is true that these gravestones often contained pictorial representations of the dead on the tombstones, but the significance of these acts is probably more closely linked to the survival of udalism in these regions (the belief that land is owned by those who have farmed it and are buried there).[143] In the Serbian language, there is even an expression '*Gdje je sahranjen Srbin, tude je Srbija*' (wherever there is a Serb interred, this place is Serbia). During the rise of virulent nationalism among Serbs in the late 1980s and early 1990s, '*ovo je Srbija*' (this is Serbia!) was frequently sprayed on walls in areas which were patently ethnically mixed and not part of Serbia.[144] If it is the case that udalism survived among rural dwellers in the Balkans, then obliterating the memory of the dead seems more explicable. In 1941, Milovan Zanić claimed he wanted to settle the Krajina with Croats from America: 'they will occupy the home hearth we will have cleansed'.[145] There were many examples in which an apparently bizarre fury was vented on inanimate objects during the 1990s, suggesting that the perpetrators of the acts were deeply unstable rather than sadistic (although the two phenomena are not mutually exclusive). In Sarajevo, a Serb army officer went to the home of an artist, who was also a Serb. One of the works of art had a representation of a page from the Koran. 'Infuriated, he had all the artwork taken out into the street, lined up and shot to pieces with automatic weapons fire.'[146]

Despite its apparent religious nature, patterns of behaviour have little to do with traditional religious teaching, although undoubtedly the appropriation of religious symbolism is important. During the 1920s and their rise to power in the 1930s the Nazis metaphorically alluded to atonement and expiation. 'Hitler was presented as a great purifier, the one who could bring "salvation".' He was also called 'the great sacrificer'.[147] Even their euphemism for genocide, the 'final solution' has messianic overtones. Analysing the language of the Ustaša, John Allcock has noted the conjunction of the words for slaughter of animals (*klanje*) and sacrifice (*žrtvovanje*). He argues that 'killing of this kind is more than mere killing: it is the offering of the slain as if they are sacrificial animals. It is atrocity raised to the level of sacrament.'[148]

Tragedy hardens division. Before 1922, the Greek island of Lésbos had a population of about 10 per cent Turks, who left during the population expulsions of this period. In the early 1990s an anthropologist doing fieldwork on Lésbos, only a few miles from the Turkish Aegean coastline, noted that elderly people remembered 'having eaten bread and tomatoes together', although she noticed very hostile attitudes towards Turks from the younger inhabitants, suggesting that borders and bad experience can reify difference.[149] The Vrbanja bridge in Sarajevo has now been renamed the Suada Dilberović bridge, after a Muslim girl who was killed there. Although it was not the intention of those who chose to remember this girl's final suffering, it is possible that in the future it could become a 'Muslim' symbol rather than simply a symbol of the suffering of the entire town.[150] In this case the war has clearly had an important effect in creating a stronger and more cohesive Bosnian Muslim identity, a project that the government of Aljia Izetbegović explicitly distanced itself from early in 1992.

There are many first hand and graphic accounts of violence that accompanied ethnic cleansing in the Balkans and undoubtedly many of these accounts have similarities in terms of their symbolic content. Radovan Haluzik has cast a sceptical eye over reports of atrocities and massacres in the Balkans and Transcaucasia, especially given that many war rumours follow patterns and are spread to make people fearful of the enemy or of returning to their homes.[151] The head of the French General Delgorges was reported to have been turned into a football after the siege of Herceg-Novi.[152] Over several generations, this story expanded. A Montenegrin Četnik, Kristo Punoshevitch told George Sava in 1939 that he could remember his grandfather telling him that the Russian Tsar had enlisted the aid of many Montenegrins to fight with him against Napoleon on account of their ferocity and bravery. He recalled being told that 'one of the things the French troops could not stand was the sight of our men dangling three or four French heads from their belts and rushing to the attack'.[153] Rumours are established as historical fact and then occasionally magnified or transformed over time into different, but related events. Ferocity towards the enemy thus becomes a general explanatory category for other occurrences. Similar stories about a boat floating on the Sava river, piled high with corpses, with the lable 'meat for Belgrade market' fastened to it, were circulated both in the early 1990s and during the Second World War,[154] suggesting that the story was a myth created and then recreated to demonize Serb fighters in Bosnia. A journalist from the independent Montenegrin journal *Monitor* told me she had spoken to 'weekend warriors' from Podgorica who went thieving in Bosnia and who recounted stories of bodies floating in the Sava.[155] Each time the 'text' of the tale was very similar. During the Balkan Wars, Montenegrins were reputed to take the noses of Ottomans if they captured them, having been forbidden to take heads by their ruler, the Vladika and their reputation for carrying out such deeds was firmly established in the literature of that time. However, other explanations may exist to explain facial mutilation in this region. The Irish writer and military volunteer Joyce Cary saw the deformed faces of Turkish soldiers during the Balkan Wars, but as he pointed out, many of the mutilations he saw on corpses could have been caused by the environment ravages or by scavengers.[156]

However, war stories are exploited or expropriated by the participants in any given struggle, it is clear that we are dealing here with many thousands of genuine individual tales of tragedy. If such killings were purely 'primordial' in nature, then they would happen regularly and not be confined to moments of extreme and provoked crisis such as war. The way in which these acts were committed does suggest a less sophisticated explanation for murder, even when it has a symbolic element. Themes may reoccur and be exploited in a mythological sense, but the weight of evidence and the sheer number of similar incidents imply that many people in the Balkans met their deaths from the hands of their previously friendly neighbours and these murders were often carried out with extreme haste and in deliberately humiliating and cruel circumstances. The population in Macedonia remains thoroughly mixed together within villages and regions and any partition or cantonization would be impossible without changing its basic character. It remains 'one of the most complex'[157] regions in the Balkans. If the *Macedoine* is to survive then it will certainly be exceptional in the Balkan region.

Plate 2 Mostar (Hercegovina) with temporary bridge over the Neretva river, 2001, reproduced with the permission of Florian Bieber.

Plate 3 Damage to buildings in Mostar (Hercegovina), 2001, reproduced with the
permission of Florian Bieber.

Plate 4 Burnt out buildings in former United Nations 'safe haven' of Goradže (Bosnia), 1998, reproduced with the permission of Florian Bieber.

Plate 5 Bridge at Mostar (Hercegovina) over the Neretva river, by Csontvary Kosztka Tivadar, 1903, reproduced with kind permission of the Csontvary Museum, Pecs, Hungary.

7 Ethno-psychology

What does the earth look like in places where people commit atrocities? Is there a bad smell . . . something about the landscape that might incriminate?[1]

The Cvijić thesis

During the twentieth century, writers from outside and inside the Balkans came to view the inhabitants of the Dinarics, a mountain range, which stretches from the Istria down to the highlands of Albania as rougher and more inclined to violent behaviour than lowlanders. This thesis was initially developed by the geographer Jovan Cvijić, who was motivated by a desire to create a symbolic spine for any future South Slav[2] state by constructing the Dinaric Karst as a region.[3] By using a mixture of geographical conjecture, anthropology and elements of folk culture, he deduced that the Dinaric types were forceful and brave, had a strong historical consciousness, linking their own daily struggles to the 'memory' of the battle of Kosovo polje, that they had an almost inbred desire to kill Turks and a sense of revenge, freedom and bloody-minded independence.[4]

Cvijić was not drawing entirely from his imagination. He spent years undertaking a form of anthropological fieldwork in the region and had a detailed and intricate knowledge of his subject. His magnum opus *La péninsule balkanique* is of its era and steeped in greater Serbian nationalism, but remains arguably one of the most profound books on the subject of the Balkans. Cvijić was also influenced by what had been written before about this region and extant stereotypes in Italian, German, French and British travel writing and topography: in particular the idea of the primitivism of the 'Morlacchi'[5] who inhabited the Dinaric Hinterland and were constructed within Venetian discourses as barbaric and uncivilized.[6] The image of wild mountaineers versus sophisticated urbanites was certainly used in previous discourses. In Thomas More's *Utopia*, the mercenaries who do all the fighting for the citizens of that state are 'hideous, savage and fierce, dwelling in the wild woods and mountains'.[7] In the 1516 edition of the book, More added a marginal note that they were 'a nation not so unlike the Swiss', a comment that was later removed.[8] Fernand Braudel's construction of the Mediterranean region relied heavily on a juxtaposition between the culture of the mountains and that of the littoral, a theme that he developed after reading Cvijić.[9] In 1876, in Britain, a pro-Ottoman writer publicist H.A. Munro-Butler-Johnstone wrote a pamphlet entitled *The Turks: Their Character, Manners and Institutions*, describing the uprising in Hercegovina as being 'in a highland district inhabited by wild mountaineers'.[10]

A paradigm was established by Cvijić,[11] which exercised great power on subsequent writers and was utilized by Serb, Croat and Bosnian writers as well as a liberal number of foreign writers who used the thesis as a substitute for engaging their minds. Vasa Čubrilović, a committed Serb nationalist who made it part of his lifework to promote the removal of Muslim populations from Yugoslavia thought that Dinaric Montenegrins could be used to drive Albanians out of Kosovo since they exhibited many of the necessary violent 'traits' to do the job.[12] Bojan Baskar has characterized these motives of Čubrilović as 'cynical' stating that the Karadjordjević regime had 'in their conception of ethnic cleansing, anticipated such a cultural determinism and made it part of their plans'.[13] Here as Stephanie Schwander-Sievers has remarked, '[i]n some settings, "tradition" is effectively used to justify, excuse and direct violence'.[14] Like Stojan Protić, Čubrilović may well have had purely cynical motives for advocating the use of force and forceful individuals, but at some level the myth of the violent Dinaric type became quite deeply embedded in the minds of many writers.[15]

After the Second World War, the Cvijić thesis gained a second wind in the writing of the Croatian American émigré writer Dinko Tomašić, who had been active in the Croatian Peasant Party in the 1930s.[16] He also emphasized the link between human geography and the land in his own ethnographic writings on what he called the 'power seeking' Dinaric personality. Irrational and violent behaviour was imagined to be an integral part of the construction of this personality type whose 'traditions and practices, supported by the fierceness of the Dinaric temper made professional banditry flourish until present times . . . a certain restlessness among the Orthodox in Hercegovina made men most eager to fight whenever the occasion arose.[17] He continued,

> treachery and violence are aspects of the same mental process of the Dinaric warrior. His traditions and his own experience teach him to identify self-aggrandizement with power and power with violence. But if violence does not seem expedient to him at the moment, the socially recognized way to fight superior strength is to outwit his opponents by resorting to craftiness and deceit.[18]

Tomašić also states that a disproportionate number of Ustaša fascists came from this region as well as OZNA agents.[19] By virtue of this thesis, many of Yugoslavia's problems could be blamed on its geography, which is paradoxical given that Cvijić' aim had been to unite the region. It is fair to say that, according to Dennison Rusinow,[20] by the time he was at Bloomington in the 1960s, Tomašić had come to regret the extremism of his earlier views, but he was certainly not alone in his use of self-orientalizing categories. After the Second World War, Montenegrin writer Milovan Djilas also contributed to the further elaboration of the Dinaric 'ethnopsychological type' with his autobiographical renditions of a violent and brutal

Montenegrin childhood.[21] When the Croatian writer Ante Ciliga recalled his brutal experience in Jasenovac, he drew on ethno-psychology to explain this.[22] Foreign writers about the Balkans have often been consciously or subconsciously attracted to the exotic and have interpreted informants rather too literally. Edith Durham, whose work on the Dinaric region is particularly well known and often quoted, had her own theories linking *pobratimstvo* (ritual brotherhood) to cannibalism[23] and this wild and totally unsubstantiated assertion is repeated almost en passant by Tomašić.[24] Writers from other cultures have also very frequently replicated and reinforced stereotypes about violence, masculinity and heroism.[25]

When Yugoslavia's communist system broke down in the mid 1980s, older exclusivist ideologies were readily available in the portfolios of extremists who had previously been in exile or on the alcoholic fringes of society. The potential of the thesis to become a discourse of alterity can be seen by its revival by contemporary writers. The Slovene psychologist Alenka Puhar has made a link between abuse in childhood and patterns of violence in the Dinaric region.[26] Croats and Bosnian Muslims have also used this motif of barbaric backwoodsmen versus the urbane sophistication of the town dwellers, and this 'mountain men' thesis was picked up from them and used by Western journalists during the recent wars.[27] The commander of a Bosnian military unit, Djordje Krčun commented that the siege of Sarajevo was 'about civilization. It's not an ethnic war, it's a war of ordinary people against primitive men who want to carry us back to tribalism.'[28] The poetry of Radovan Karadžić has sometimes been interpreted as the protest of a village boy against the urban environment of Sarajevo, although this view is not without irony as Stevan Weine has pointed out.[29] John Kifner writing in the *New York Times* in 1994 asserts that 'the rocky spine of the Dinaric Alps . . . nurtured the most extreme and combative elements from each community . . . these were wild, warlike, frequently lawless societies whose feuds and folklore have been passed on to the present day like the potent home-brewed brandy that the mountain men begin knocking back in the morning.'[30] Here I must agree with David Norris' assessment that the Bosnian War 'nearly became an archetypal battle between civilization and non-civilization between mountain and city, in which one headline reads "Sarajevo repels the mountain menace" relying on a sign system in relation to the Balkans and the Serbs which has been periodically reinvented'.[31] On the occasion of the bombardment of Dubrovnik in 1991, Norman Stone had declared that '[n]ow the Balkans, in a traditional semi-savage sense, are getting their own back, wrecking the city and setting back the level of their own civilization by 50 or 60 years'.[32] As Misha Glenny remarked in characteristically witty style, '(t)he villages that are scattered down the Dinaric mountain range enjoy a similar reputation to that of the Gallic village where Astérix and Obélix lived. Feuds are endemic in the area – within families, between families, between villages and of course, between national groups . . .'[33] The reputation for feuding and revenge has frequently been seen as a kind of Balkan 'habit of the heart' alongside violence, although as John Allcock points out 'The tradition of vengeance has been largely associated with those parts of the Balkans which were formerly under Turkish rule and in which the state for long periods was both ineffective and illegitimate.'[34]

Another example of this discourse about mountain types being used perhaps rather too creatively is found in the work of Stjepan Meštrović, Slaven Letica and Miroslav Goreta who have tried to prove there was some kind of link between the war in the former Yugoslavia and the Dinaric personality in the book *Habits of the Balkan Heart*, which includes a lengthy discussion of the sociology of Tomašić.[35] For instance it is stated that 'the Yugoslav civil war exhibited barbaric acts of cruelty – massacres and the mutilation of the living as well as corpses that they beg for an explanation. Our explanation is that when one examines the history of the Balkans, such savagery appears to be fairly typical.'[36] As Florian Bieber has argued the Meštrović approach has 'no explanatory value': it serves only a rhetorical purpose.[37] The chief instigators of the recent wars in Yugoslavia for the most part were not particularly 'Dinaric' at all, but urbane, sophisticated ideologues who cynically drew upon the past and tradition as a way of legitimizing their own brand of nationalism. Vojislav Šešelj, one of the chief theorists of the Cetnik movement in the 1990s was the youngest person ever to be awarded a doctorate in Communist Yugoslavia.[38] Franjo Tudjman was from Zagorje and not Hercegovina. Voices prophesying and provoking war were far more likely to have come from universities than mountainous regions.

Bojan Baskar has persuasively argued that 'depicting war as an accomplishment of anti-urban savages from the Dinaric region is . . . a standard interpretation by the Belgrade opposition, which is desperately interested in situating the evil in the rural area in order to be capable of believing in its own innocence'.[39] As Mirjana Prošić-Dvornić has argued, the opposition *Druga Srbija* (Alternative Serbia) had its 'own arsenal of internal "Orientalizing" labels' which drew on the Cvijić notion of the peace-loving farmers of Šumadija and Vojvodina, and the 'restless, violent and militant' Dinaric types.[40] It was not only in Belgrade that mountaineers were blamed for the savagery of the fighting in the 1990s. 'In times of crisis, wildness . . . becomes a space, a territory.'[41] The issue of the Dinaric personality is an ambivalent one in the Croatian national consciousness,[42] especially as the region was traditionally ethnically mixed and the Croats could be said to share many of these personality traits. Ivo Žanić marks this ambivalence thus: 'On the one hand, "the best Croats" are thought to live here. On the other hand Hercegovinians are thought to be "the worst Croats", inclining towards extremism and with little appreciation for the complexity of democratic pluralism.'[43] Croat historian Ivo Rendić-Miocević has attempted to blame the historical and cultural cleavages in Croatian society for the war and violence. The raison d'être for this work is to effectively distance the Croatian nation (as the author constructs them) from patriarchal Dinaric society, which is depicted as being exiled from historical time, an example of barbarism within.[44]

During the Second World War, the Ustaša used the term 'Vlach'[45] to refer to Serbs as if they were aliens in the NDH. Undoubtedly may of the Orthodox and Catholic inhabitants of the region had been Vlach speaking until the early modern era and this ancient language which is related to Latin and Romanian is found across the Balkans, especially in Macedonia and Greece and only died out in Istria in recent years. Nevertheless, the term 'Vlachs'[46] to describe the Orthodox peoples of the Dinarics, particularly Krajina was used in the 1940s and then revived by nationalists in Croatia in 1990s, to delegitimize their presence in the region and to separate them from the rest of the Orthodox peoples who might define themselves as Serbs. Rendić-Miocević even refers to the inhabitants of the Dinaric region as the 'tribe with no name', thus delegitimizing their actual and historical presence still further.[47] Archbishop Stepinac also expressed fairly standard anti-Serb sentiments in his diary of 17 January 1940: 'it would be best if the Serbs would return to the faith of their fathers . . . then we could finally breathe easily in this part of Europe, in whose history Byzantium and the Turks have played a terrible role'.[48] The concept of 'Byzantism' was also used frequently in Croatia in the 1990s to denote undemocratic political practices and the use of violence within political life, which further undermined and delegitimized the presence of Orthodox peoples.[49] To imagine the peoples inhabiting the Dinaric region as a kind of ethnic fifth column undermining the fabric of the Croatian state rather closely parallels the intellectual remarginalization of Yugoslavia's Muslims by Serb nationalists in the late 1980s. That a reworking of the thesis should have found its way into recent sociological writing is a testament to the fact that we have not all yet been able to dispense with radicalizing categories, despite decades of scholarship on the nature of modern European nationalism.

Collective 'madness': the 'curse' of the Balkans (*balkanski klet*)?

Other attempts to relocate responsibility for the violence and fighting have come from nationalists themselves who have frequently used the idea of general chaos and madness to obfuscate the discernable patterns of social behaviour, which have emerged over time. Željko Raznatović, usually known by his nom de guerre Arkan ran as a candidate for the party of Serbian Unity in 1992. 'I don't promise you new telephone lines. I don't promise you new highways. But I pledge to defend you with the same fanaticism that I've used so far in defending the Serbian people.'[50] Martin Bell was told in Bosnia by a Serb commander who had previously been a social worker that 'this is a war, and in wars bad things happen. We have emptied our prisons and asylums; what did you expect?'[51]

Serbs themselves were told by Jovan Rašković in 1990, that they were a mad people (*'lud narod'*)[52] and he himself expressed a wish to create a link between psychoanalysis and the language and metaphors of politics.[53] The films of the Bosnian director Emir Kusturica usually have manic soundtracks to suggest a sort of collective madness and this was certainly a theme in his highly successful film *Underground* (1995). The idea of collective madness during periods of war and crisis has been viewed very cynically by some critics. During the NATO bombing of the Federal Republic of Yugoslavia in 1999, Serbs attended rock music concerts and displayed humourous slogans taunting Bill Clinton about his sexual behaviour. In Kragujevac, a town in Southern Serbia that was targeted because of a suspicion of an overlap between car and military production at the Zastava plant, a banner telling NATO to 'surrender' was displayed at an anti-war demonstration. Slavoj

Žižek compares these defiant actions to that of a mad person who instead of appearing mad themselves inflicts suffering and despair on all the people around them: 'this obscene (Bakhtinian) carnivalisation', he continues, 'is effectively the other, public, face of ethnic cleansing. While in Belgrade people defiantly dance on the streets, three hundred kilometers to the south, a genocide of monstrous proportions is taking place. . . . When people wear paper "target" signs, the obscene falsity of this gesture cannot but strike the eye: can one imagine the REAL targets years ago in Sarajevo or now in Kosov@ wearing such signs?.'[54] It may be true that Sarajevans did not wear paper target signs, but they developed a rich genre of jokes about the siege, many of which had quite ribald themes, which could be interpreted as a kind of defiance to the terrible fate that befell them during those years. Twelve-year-old Zlata Filipović nicknamed the sniper that fired on their district 'Jovo'. On Wednesday 28 April 1993, over one year into the siege that had killed many of her childhood friends and relatives, she recorded 'Our own tiresome sniper . . . was in a playful mood today. He's really out of his mind. There he goes! Just fired another bullet to shake us up.'[55] The criticisms of Žižek are also odd given the role of satire in recent Slovene political culture. In June 1989, the staff at the satirical magazine *Mladina*, Erwin Hladnik-Milharčič and also Ivo Štandeker (who was subsequently killed in Sarajevo), dressed up as Serbian knights, mocking the celebrations of anniversary of the battle of Kosovo polje that was taking place on Gazimestan that week. The playful text accompanying the picture was as follows: 'Slovenes and Serbs are brothers. We don't like Albanians either. Tito messed up everything (*je zajebal vse*).'[56] Slovenes can hardly be said to have invented the use of political irony, so should have Žižek have been so surprised by its reappearance in 1999?

The analysis of Dubravka Ugrešić of these kinds of 'Bakhtinian' rites that have been seen in demonstrations in Serbia in particular, seems more convincing, in that she interprets them as reactions to 'enforced oblivion' and nationalist madness. These patterns of behaviour predate 1999 and the NATO bombing. Djordje Balašević, the popular singer, is said to have attended the Milošević rally in the late 1980s carrying a placard 'Save Isaura the Slavegirl!' as his own 'gesture of protest at encroaching stupidity'.[57] One should also remember that given the nature of the Milošević regime, his use of '*squadristi*'[58] at rallies in the late 1980s, threats against individuals, his manipulation of extremists in politics,[59] the growth of political gangsterism (in the form of anonymous assassinations) and state robbery of national assets, that Serbs themselves were victims of the regime as well as their neighbours. Surely those Serbs who took to the streets in 1999 were protesting about their own incarceration under a 'mad' regime?

Rašković and other Serb writers did manage to skilfully manipulate the idea of collective madness in the late 1980s and early 1990s. They also exploited a genuinely traumatized collectivity, particularly in Krajina.[60] It is no coincidence that the end of Yugoslavia coincided with the opening up of graveyards and the digging up of the victims of the Second World War particularly those individuals whose bodies had been thrown into limestone caverns or pits. As Svetlana Slapšak has remarked, 'the symbolic vocabulary of nationalist discourse, mainly invented by intellectuals in the late 1980s, includes many identical terms, expressions and stylistic figures . . . and parallelisms between Croatian and Serbian nationalist discourses are often stunning'.[61] She mentions the digging up of bones as crucial to both Serb and Croat discourses and the revival of painful memories may have triggered some of the behaviour that has been interpreted as irrational, obscene or cynical on both sides.

The revision of history that the digging up of bones triggered may have left individuals very confused. Speaking of the revelations about the caves of Sosice in Croatia, which were reported to contain the bones of over 4,000 wounded soldiers brought from hospitals in Zagreb, Nikola Hranilović exclaimed: 'When I heard that the Partisans carried out the killings, it made my head spin because it went against everything I learnt at school.'[62]

The use of the idea of collective madness has taken on the character not so much of sociological analysis, but of self-fulfilling prophesy. As Slaven Letica stated in 1991: 'there is a tradition of oral aggression in the Balkans. Someone will say, "I'm going to kill him. I'm going to kill him." But then they will add, "please stop me before I kill him" . . . If the killing starts nobody will be able to stop it.'[63] Serbian writers have utilized quite violent and dramatic metaphors in their prose, although it is unlikely that any of them has directly taken part in bloodshed. The poet Kosta Bulatović cries during his performances about historical events he has not personally experienced. Montenegrin poet Matija Bećković once stated that 'it is as if the Serbian people have waged only one battle – by widening the Kosovo charnel-house, by adding wailing upon wailing, but adding new martyrs to the (Kosovo) martyrs. (It) is the Serbianized story of the Flood.'[64] These notions are essentially literary conceits. In 2001, the Serbian people showed themselves to be fed up with nationalists in power and quite pragmatic over the issue of handing Milošević over to the Hague Tribunal and not at all slaves to their 'historical' or 'traditional' national consciousness.[65]

It is difficult to extract anything meaningful from the study of the Dinaric personality type, other than a consciousness of the danger of using ideas that construct different levels of humanity, either for the victims or the victimizers. According to Vera Stein Erlich, Dinaric men were

> robust only in physique, while mentally they are extremely sensitive and susceptible to nervous troubles. An inflexibility of a different kind and an extraordinary sensibility endangers their emotional equilibrium. When people emigrated from the Dinaric Alps, they also took with them their specific sensitivity and spread it to other regions.[66]

If people from the Dinaric region did indeed have different psychological attributes (and none of the advocates of this thesis have furnished very convincing evidence for this and often seem to have quite explicit nationalist agendas themselves), it may well originate in the atmosphere created by living on the margins of the Habsburg, Ottoman and Venetian domains – which must have been a kind of liminal and insecure existence. In the context of the legacy of French colonialism in Northern

Africa, the psychiatrist Frantz Fanon considered the issue of the 'sensitivity' of his patients and concluded that 'the Algerian's criminality, his impulsivity and the violence of his murders are not . . . the consequence of the organization of his nervous system nor of a peculiar trait in his character, but the direct product of the colonial situation'.[67] Furthermore as Maria Todorova has remarked that 'for all the stereotypes about virulent Balkan nationalism, most . . . are essentially defensive, and their identity is the direct result of problems of unconsolidated nation-states and identities in crisis'.[68]

Balkan violence

The Balkans as a whole has frequently been constructed as somehow more prone to violence than elsewhere in Europe or indeed the rest of the world. The facts used to establish this idea are for the most part methodologically dubious and non-anthropological, in that they establish different grades of humanity according to which century and which region an individual lived. Traian Stoianovich has grounded the implicit racism of such constructions by linking these ascribed tendencies to discernable historical development, stating that 'like the peoples of other European pre-modern societies, Balkan man was impulsive and inclined to violence'.[69] In the forty-five years of its existence, Communist Yugoslavia was not notably a violent society. United Nations figures on homicides indicate that pre-war Yugoslavia actually had a less violent culture than the industrial developed world with proportionally less than half the number of murders in 1987–8 than Britain and less than a quarter of the USA.[70] During the recent wars there was a tendency by both insiders and outsiders towards essentialist demonization of all ethnic groups by their corresponding 'others' or more partisan commentators in the West.

In the late 1980s when it became clear to both the people of Yugoslavia and citizens of other states that the country created by Communists on the ashes of the Royalist Yugoslavia was about to collapse, it became necessary to search for explanations for the failure of this state. Historical and cultural arguments were often deployed, often without care or attention or with what Thanasis D. Sfikas has called 'blatantly racist, ahistorical and anachronistic deployment of an "orientalist" logic and discourse on the Balkans by outside observers'.[71] Indeed, many writers have preferred to deal in the older explanatory categories (that Sfikas describes) and have privileged these over and above the actual and future relations between states and communities in the Balkans. 'Balkan' people were constructed by Western politicians as violent by nature who interpreted conflict as primarily the result of 'centuries old ethnic conflicts'.[72] If Balkan society is constructed as tiresomely violent, it is as if structures, local peculiarities and events have no meaning. George Bush stated that the war in Bosnia was 'a complex convoluted conflict that grows out of age-old animosities'.[73] Secretary of State Warren Christopher in February 1993 described the situation thus: '. . . the end of communist domination of the former Yugoslavia raised the lid on the cauldron of ancient ethnic hatreds. This is the land where at least three religions and half a dozen ethnic groups have vied across the centuries. . . . It has long been the cradle of European conflict and remains so today.'[74]

Ethnic complexity is also often singled out as an explanatory cause of Yugoslavia's collapse as if it were unnatural to live in multiethnic societies. John D. Treadway states that

> four years of warfare, accompanied by ethnic cleansing and flights of population, have 'simplified' the arrangement and composition of its population. The ethnic and religious crazy quilt that was the 'old' Yugoslavia is not quite as intricate or as confusing as in years past. But the current regional admixtures of peoples and confessions constitute a witch's brew – the stuff of which powder kegs were (and are) made.[75]

The inappropriate use of stale historical categories interferes with our ability to treat all the subjects of enquiry with equal respect and (to use that heavily loaded word) 'dignity'.[76] And by reminding ourselves that the 'traditional' Balkans has been destroyed, sometimes obliterated, we can see the situation not as a timeless cycle of violence, spite and revenge, but a set of specific historical circumstances with causes, a course and a conclusion, namely 'cleansed' nations across the region.

State formation was usually accompanied by blood in the nineteenth and twentieth centuries; there is barely another European state that did not experience violence and extreme dislocation prior to formation in the same historical period. Despite this, endemic violence as an explanatory category has been commonplace in the last decade. The then Secretary of State James Baker told a hearing of the Senate Foreign Affairs Committee on 23 June 1992: 'It is hard to believe, *in this day and age* that armed forces will fire artillery indiscriminately into the heart of the city, flushing defenseless men, women and children out into the streets and shooting them. It is an absolute outrage. It is barbaric and it is inhuman.'[77] He was describing Bosnia, but could equally well have been describing US troop actions in Vietnam less than a generation earlier.[78] However, this problematic has not prevented the publications of 'numerous commentators, who indulged the sort of naturalizing tropes that underwrote the (implicitly racist) rationalizations with which Western politicians and diplomats tried to justify their governments' complacency'.[79]

The rise of Balkan nationalism can be characterized in terms of a fusion of ideologies both from other parts of Europe with 'autonomous' trends. Once scholars from the Balkans became nationalists in the modern sense, it would be hard to separate their ideas from the European mainstream. In the longer term, other supranational ideologies such as Orthodox Christianity, Catholicism, various forms of Islam, Protestantism (in parts of Dalmatia, Istria, Transylvania and Slovenia) were crucial in the formation of mentalities in South East Europe. Other than the fact that the Balkans represented a frontier between not only different states, but different religions, it is difficult to see in which sense the Balkans were different from the rest of Europe except for the fact that this region became the area of rather intense international rivalry in the nineteenth and twentieth centuries. It is probable that this status as a border region is responsible for the instability, not some predisposed penchant of the population towards violence.

Mark Mazower has argued that there is a tendency in assessing levels of Balkan violence to conflate violence with cruelty,[80] although given the range of methods still used by some Western states to execute their citizens, it is hard to imagine circumstances in which murder is not cruel (but undoubtedly injection of fatal chemicals is less visually violent and therefore 'cruel' than decapitation). Writers about the Balkans have often been consciously or subconsciously attracted to the exotic and have interpreted informants rather too literally. This tendency predates the 1990s and perhaps has more to do with the need to provide good copy than good knowledge. Edith Durham repeated that a Miss F. Wilson had told her that in 1915 Serb soldiers had boasted about drinking the blood of Bulgars, not perhaps realizing that this was a metaphor for victory over the enemy.[81] If we analysed the contemporary English language vocabulary for sport (thrashing, beating, slaughtering, etc.) we might also in certain naïve circumstances come to the conclusion that people were actually being hurt out there on the pitch (outside the usual run of accidents). As we also know, sometimes people tell tall tales to outsiders.[82]

In the context of the warfare in Yugoslavia since 1990, there have been heinous and dreadful crimes committed, probably with the aim of frightening populations to leave or with what James Gow has called 'the demonstrative capacity of violence',[83] as much as for the sake of the violence itself (although no doubt the prospect of 'real' killing attracted many sadists not just from Yugoslav ranks but from foreign mercenaries). Similarly, Richard Hall defines the atrocities during the Balkan Wars as 'deliberate terror created by arson, looting, murder and rape was intended as a spur to move populations out of a particular piece of territory'.[84] Gow has also pointed out that violence has clear military objectives if civilian populations are seen as being support networks for guerrilla operations as was the case in Bosnia during 1992–5.[85] In practice the fighting in the Balkans in the 1990s was strategic and certainly not primordial upsurges of 'ethnic fury', as one British newspaper declared when it stated: 'The practices of territorial displacement, massacre, deliberate desecration of cultural symbols and systematic mistreatment of women, all evident in recent non-state warfare in the Balkans and Transcaucasia, undeniably resemble those of the surviving Stone Age peoples of the world's remote regions – at their most savage.'[86]

Another problematic is the selective use of individual atrocities to establish facts about national personality. For Tim Judah, '(T)he burning of villages and the exodus of the defeated population is a normal and traditional incident of all Balkan wars and insurrections. It is the habit of all these peoples. What they have suffered themselves, they inflict in turn upon others.'[87] For a start, I think this is factually inaccurate but it also relies on looking at a cross section of violence in extreme circumstances. It is pointless to make generalizations about violence in the Balkans or even individual national or ethnic groups if the devil is indeed in the detail. Thus, the approach adopted by Glen Bowman missed a very important political point:

The amount of violence now raging between communities of the former Yugoslavia was not manifest before nationalist mobilization . . . If we explain the extreme levels of brutality evident in the former Yugoslavia today as something endemic to the Balkans we not only deny and ignore the recent history of modernization in Yugoslavia but also effectively cast Yugoslavs out beyond the pale of what we must term 'human society' . . . [but] we are still left with the question of 'where has this penchant for extreme violence come from?'.[88]

If one characterized all the groups in the former Yugoslavia as 'raging' during the 1990s then one might seriously come to ask this question. However, in reality, there was certainly not a cult of violence amongst Bosnian Moslems, nor among Macedonians, nor in Slovenia, nor amongst the hundreds of thousands of *vojski begunci* (war exiles) who took flight from Montenegro, Serbia and Croatia.[89] Some draft dodgers in Serbia even hid in the cellars of their houses, a theme which was latter depicted in a popular play by Vladimir Arsenijević published in 1995.[90] In the Serbian city of Valjevo, only two men turned up to register as volunteers to fight in Croatia in 1991 although at least 2,000 were expected.[91] In numerical terms, perhaps only a few thousand individuals were actually involved in the fighting in the wars of dissolution, although the victims number hundreds of thousands. On 6 April 1992, 20,000 unarmed people marched in Sarajevo as a protest against nationalist politics, demanding that Bosnia remain 'as one'. They were fired upon by perhaps only a couple of dozen snipers in the Holiday Inn.[92] It would therefore be as plausible to represent Balkans peoples as unarmed victims as much as perpetrators of violence. In the terrible logic of ethnic cleansing, a few armed individuals can kill many times their number very quickly. In the town of Zegra in Kosovo in 1999, 260 police and paramilitaries killed between 6,000 and 7,000 people. One eyewitness described how '(T)hey took about a minute a house . . . It's the worse kind of war.'[93]

To combat the tendency to burden a large region with almost insurmountable legacies and an overarching reputation for pathological violence, it may be necessary to examine specific cases very carefully and to ask questions such as how it was that certain micro-regions largely avoided problems of violence and others have suffered immensely. Clearly some areas have been more badly affected than others. Fighting in the 1990s in parts of Kosovo, Bosnia and Krajina by Serb paramilitaries clearly fed upon memories of atrocities committed by Albanians, Muslim Handžars and Croatian Ustaša during the Second World War: their populations were certainly more vulnerable to nationalist manipulation than, say for example, Serbs in Vojvodina, which remained relatively peaceful throughout the 1990s. In Medjugorje, an Ustaša cell was said to be active until the 1970s and much of the recent violence in this locality can be seen as a direct result of the violence of the 1940s.[94] Recent fieldwork in Hercegovina by Mart Bax[95] has emphasized variation even at the parish or village level, while still locating the region within the Dinaric, Mediterranean and Balkan context. To avoid essentialization and over-generalization may require, as Mark Thompson suggests, 'a tiresome level of vigilance within our saturated discourse'.[96] Comparative fieldwork, for example, between peaceful Bela krajina and war-ravaged Vojna krajina or even a comparison between the Szeklers of Transylvania with the Orthodox community of Krajina might be instructive here (although the ethnic cleansing of the Knin area has made this subject somewhat difficult in practice). We need a science of human behaviour *in extremis*, which is sensitive to locality, history and politics. We also need to make a clear distinction about what has happened *in* the Balkans and what is *of* the Balkans. When the Germans dynamited the synagogue in Salonika, their actions were part of the same intellectual and cultural process that led to the destruction of Bosnia's material culture in the 1990s. It is far easier for a writer, when faced with a complex problem to look for an 'essence' such as Balkan violent behaviour and dig up stale historical categories than to actually learn about specificities, but if we persist in using generalized categories about the Dinaric personality and/or Balkan violence we will be responsible not for breaking down barriers between people, but for building new ones.

8 Conclusion

> Nothing that has taken place should be lost to history . . . only to redeemed human-
> ity does the past belong in its entirety.
>
> (Walter Benjamin)[1]

Following on from Walter Benjamin, this study has argued that the facts about the
series of events in the South East of Europe that we have defined as 'ethnic cleansing' are to some extent knowable, recordable and that it is possible to analyse
them as a single historical problematic. Furthermore, if we do not record these
details, we may find that revisionist writers will begin to claim that many of the
things that are discussed here are beyond real knowledge. As Jean-François Lyotard
once notoriously remarked of Auschwitz, 'its name marks the confines wherein historical knowledge sees its competence impugned'.[2] It may well be that the name of
'Bosnia' becomes a symbol of discursive inaccuracy for the next generation, with
some individuals attempting to deny what happened in that country or to clothe
any discussion about it in ironic or quasi-poststructuralist rhetoric. Already some of
the events of the 1990s have been disputed. The photograph of a half-starved
Fikret Alić in Trnopolje in the summer of 1992, which some British newspapers
compared to Belsen, has become the subject of a vast and bizarre 'holocaust
denial' on the Internet, with scores of dedicated websites stating that the picture is
a fake.[3] The Serbian President Vojislav Koštunica, who has been feted in the
NATO countries (no doubt on account of a general guilt about civilian deaths
during the bombing of Serbia in 1999), has been ambivalent in some of his public
statements about the events of the Bosnian war. As Norman Cigar has noted,

> asked about an earlier statement that Srebrenica (where over 3,000 Muslim
> men were massacred by the Bosnian Serb army) had been 'a defensive action
> by the Serb Army', he retorted that 'I probably added some "perhaps". Even
> today there is some "perhaps" about Srebrenica', with so much 'media manip-
> ulation that anyone who thinks for himself must be forced to reflect a little'.[4]

By being evasive about the events of the 1990s in Bosnia, Kosovo or elsewhere,
Koštunica is not promoting any kind of serious patriotic political course, which

could be constructed as beneficial to Serbs or anyone else living in the region. Indeed some of his statements have added serious grist to the mills of a number of relentless anti-Serbian 'workshops' publishing in the West under the guise of academic debate. Young people in the region, many of whom were not even adults at the start of the last decade will not be able to rebuild their societies and their own sense of self-esteem, if they are made to carry any kind of collective guilt by association for the sins of their fathers and mothers. Nor will they benefit from listening to politicians who lie about or manipulate the facts of history.

The main thesis that has been pursued in the book is the one that the Balkans suffered ethnic quakes, largely because the impact of European ideas (initially nationalism, then fascism and communism) was so profound and clashed so indelibly with older 'autochthonous' ideas found in religious practice and traditional culture. Although the forms that violence took during ethnic cleansing were often 'traditional' in the sense that they had a large symbolic content and involved the honour of the individuals involved, the ideas that inspired this violence were modern and European in their origins.

It is not my wish to present the inhabitants of the region in a wholly mimetic sense or argue that their ideologies were entirely epigonal. Nor would I want to suggest that most individuals after 1800 (but particularly the literate) became de facto 'intellectual national-workers'.[5] It is clear that the state projects that culminated in ethnic cleansing were linked to important historical circumstances, such as Ottoman oppression and a genuine feeling of community between co-religionists and people who spoke the same language. And yet it is hard to imagine that ethnic cleansing would have taken place in the Balkans without the intellectual influence of modern European nationalism and the idea that any individual has a single genetically predisposed national identity and not multiple and complex loyalties to region or religion, language, monarch, state, etc. Most recent scholarship on nationalism has emphasized its recent vintage and socially constructed nature. Ideologies of identity can lead to social intolerance, because they are not recognized by their devotees as being ephemeral and constructed: they mimic an essence or a truth.[6] Nationalists become extreme in shared territorial circumstances when they fail to recognize the rights of other groups, see their own rights as given and eventually come to construct the 'other' as somehow less than human with lesser human rights. In every sense therefore, nationalism as a group identity, which implicitly or explicitly excludes other groups who may inhabit the same space has been an 'alp' or 'nightmare on the brain'[7] of the last seven or eight generations of people in the Balkans (as it has been elsewhere in Europe). As Mark Mazower has argued 'the triumph of nationalism brought bloodshed, war and civil war in its train'.[8] In this respect as in many others this triumph has come with the 'Europeanization' of the Balkans.

The actions, thoughts and words of the nationalists have been studied here, not to elevate them to the level of something worthy, but to reveal something about the theory and practice of ethnic cleansing. If we refuse to examine their language and practices on the grounds that they are tasteless, offensive or even intellectually ridiculous, we can fail to grasp what ideologies that provoke wars are about. Wars are about ugly borders forced on populations by extremists, degenerates and psychotics encouraged and egged on by ideologues who use crisis to push many sane and well-balanced people into taking actions that they would not even dream of in normal circumstances. These people may be unrepresentative in a strictly numerical sense. For every sworn nationalist on each side there may be one hundred others who refuse such ascription. These individuals may feel great pride in their cultures and feel a strong sense of *Heimatliebe*, without necessarily feeling the need to humiliate, dehumanize or kill their neighbours. Thousands of young men from the former Yugoslavia left in the 1990s to avoid conscription and many thousands still live in semi-permanent exile. Frequently former Yugoslavs of all national groups mix together in other countries without reproach, hatred or bitterness – many regard nationalist politics as insane or as a kind of Biblical plague that came upon them undeserved, which they had little control over. But however many people have refused to be ruled by essentialist ideas, these ideas have still ruled them. Nationalism has had more power over individuals' lives in the Balkans than any other political force in the last two hundred years. Nationalism will continue to determine the fate of the individual, whether he or she believes in its 'truth'. To mock or deconstruct nationalism simply is not enough. It is discourse without power.[9] To combat destructive ideas, one has to provide a positive alternative.

One of the most difficult things to explain when looking at the actions of the nationalists is their own cynical manipulation of the truth and the enormity of the crimes committed in the name of the nation. Hannah Arendt's celebrated description of the evil of Nazism as 'banal' is an apt description of much of nationalist discourse in the Balkans. When President Franjo Tudjman was asked to comment on the exodus of the Serbs from Krajina during Operation Storm in August 1995, he replied: 'We didn't ask the Serbs to leave. And it's their problem if 90 per cent of them packed their bags.'[10] Given that the Croats of the Knin region sprayed the sign 'HK' (*Hrvatska kuća* – Croat home) on their houses in the path of the advancing Croatian army, it is fairly clear that *they* knew what fate would await any Serb who stayed in the region.[11] The Croatian Ambassador to France described the actions of the Serbs as 'auto-nettoyage ethnique' (self-cleansing) in 1999, glossing over the fate of the unfortunate individuals who stayed behind.[12] United Nations Special Rapporteur Tadeusz Mazowiecki remarked at the Hague Tribunal that 'ethnic cleansing seems to be not a by-product of war . . . but rather its aim',[13] which makes statements of these kind seem at best insincere, but at worst obfuscation to detract from the real purpose of the operation they were planning. Cynical obfuscation became rather commonplace during the war in Bosnia in the 1990s. A desire to level off all the dramatis personae in the recent wars and to deny responsibility for what was really happening was rarely as morally banal as the bureaucrat Miloš Bojinović, Director of the Banja Luka 'Bureau for the Removal and Exchange of Material Goods' who told journalist Peter Maass that Muslims were leaving Bosnia during the height of the war of their free will.

'But why do these people want to leave?' I asked.

'It's a fashion,' he said.

'A fashion?'

'Yes. You must understand that this agency helps people for humanitarian reasons. You cannot use words like ethnic cleansing to describe the voluntary movement of people.'[14]

Some philosophers, including Richard Rorty have concluded that an education which promotes empathy for the 'other', sentiment and relativism is the best hope for a tolerant society as well as the preservation of individual human rights.[15] Jonathan Glover[16] has also emphasized the importance of moral education. In a newspaper article he remarked that 'if you look at the people who sheltered Jews under the Nazis, you find a number of things about them. They tended to be brought up in a non-authoritarian way, brought up to have sympathy with other people and to discuss things rather than just to do what they were told.'[17] Such an education might break the destructive cycle of revenge and the apparent need to settle the scores between national and ethnic groups. There appear also to be strong psychological reasons for this kind of approach as well. In the context of Bosnia in the 1990s, Stevan Weine discusses the negative role of 'polarizing war mentalities', and argues that survivors must 'find non-dichotomizing ways of making sense of the history that they have lived through'.[18]

A respect for the rights of the other individuals and groups involves taking an ideological position, which might then find its ultimate test during times of crisis. If multiethnic societies are to survive, then the principle of mutual assistance in times of crisis should be learnt, prior to learning the national anthem or the canon of national literature. This is a universal lesson and not one that pertains only to the South East of Europe. If we identify ourselves in monolithic ethnic terms first and foremost how can we ever hope to defend the rights of the other? Dubravka Ugrešić, writing somewhat rhetorically about the wars in Yugoslavia (and in an unfairly personalized way, since she herself was a consistent voice against divisive nationalism), is quite clear that the defence of human rights has to be collective and non-national:

> I did nothing to stop the war. Just as I did nothing when some ten years or so ago, I watched television shots of police beating up Kosovo Albanians. . . . I did not react to the permanent production of lies; I let them wash over me like dirty water. . . . I did not pour petrol over myself in protest at the war and set myself alight in the city square. The list of omissions is long. My actions are negligible; on the whole they had a written character. And I did not even manage to die of shame. The fact that others did not either is no excuse . . .[19]

The actions of politicians are crucial in a moral and ethical sense. It may well be the case that the 'Ghandhian' approach of the Kosovo Albanian leader Ibrahim Rugova was instrumental in maintaining an uneasy peace in Kosovo before 1998 and the violent actions of the KLA and subsequently NATO as well as the response of the Milošević regime to the KLA and NATO campaigns effectively militarized and radicalized a situation that might have been solved slowly and peacefully if there had been any concerted will on the part of the international community before 1998. Although the existence of authoritarian and non-democratic states makes the notion of collective responsibility difficult to sustain, individual narratives of resistance to hate and discourses of alterity are crucial and may be the only real way that future ethnic wars can be resisted (especially if states continue to use war to legitimize themselves). In Greece during the Second World War, on the Island of Lefkada, 'the local population tried to feed [the Jews] . . . by pushing bread and vegetables through the barbed wire' where they had been caged by the Nazis.[20] In this case, the local people refused to construct the imprisoned Jews as less than human, with less than human rights. They looked at the people in the cage not as something different, but as if they were looking in a mirror. In Sarajevo during the siege of 1992–5, some 50,000 Serbs continued to live with their neighbours in appalling conditions as the Bosnian Serb army pounded the city with mortars. It was only after the war and the effective partition of Bosnia that these individuals actually left. One Muslim victim of the war recalled: 'When an anti-tank shell hit . . . my apartment, [a] Serb neighbour was the first one to come and help, to clean it up. He, and another neighbour . . . Two fine people. Not because they helped me, I thought the same also earlier.'[21] Importantly, some clearly recognize that what they do in the present will have an impact on how they live in the future. In Banja Luka, an American journalist recalled a conversation with a Serb, Spasoje Knežević, who spoke as if he were addressing a 'jury':[22]

> In history, progress is only possible with the mixing of nationalities . . . I'm not only mad and embarrassed about this stupid war, but disappointed. What is being done here is not in the favor of Serbs. We are losers too. Look at the number of Serbs who have died or been forced out of their homes. Look at the destruction. We used to go to Italy for vacation. Now we can't afford gasoline to drive our cars across town . . .'[23]

Perpetrators of violence are rarely consistent in the execution of their task as total genocides without recourse to scientific and impersonal means risk being sabotaged by an individual soldier who simply misses the point of widespread killing. Dražen Erdemović, who was tried for war crimes at the Hague tribunal in 1996 claimed that 'he did not want that crime . . . but he had no choice'. He argued that he had taken part in the massacre of Bosnian Muslim men at the Pilica farm near Srebrenica in July 1995 because he felt a 'concrete danger to his own life and the life of his family'. Furthermore, he claimed to have attempted to save at least one of the captives led out for execution. Psychiatrists working on the case reported that he exhibited clear signs of post-traumatic shock.[24] A number of individuals survived the Ustaša massacres because they were so hastily attacked and a handful of men survived the Srebrenica tragedy because they feigned death. At other times, soldiers have hesitated and helped individuals to escape death if not actual ethnic cleansing. In Kosovo in 1999, one woman was told by policemen who robbed her that she would be 'safer in Albania' and warned to stick to the white lines in the middle of the road, perhaps to avoid landmines.[25]

Constructions of ethnic hatred and exclusion are not 'natural' and furthermore, they often contradict experience and tradition. In Republika Srpska after the Dayton Peace Treaty in 1995 that split Bosnia and Hercegovina into two uneasy statelets, Serbs have struggled to speak the *ekavski* dialect of Serbian, which they deem to be more authentically 'Serb' than their native *ijekavski* dialect. The historical dialect of most Bosnians, whether Serbs, Croats or Muslims is *ijekavski*, rendering this behaviour a bizarre and somewhat impractical form of 'invented tradition'. It is believed by many Serbs and Croats that *ekavski* dialect is authentically Serbian, whereas the *ijekavski* dialect is authentically Croatian. If one examines the actual distribution of these dialect forms, another pattern emerges. In parts of Southern Baranja it is the Croats who speak *ekavski* and the Serbs who speak *ijekavski*.[26] Occasionally people in Republika Srpska will forget that they should be speaking *ekavski* and slip back into the patterns of speech learnt in childhood. This example seems to illustrate the very artificial and shallow nature of denying the past and creating a travesty of invented tradition in the present. Until 1945, Salonika was

> a typical polyglot Ottoman port whose bootblacks could make themselves understood in half a dozen languages, but it had one unique feature: of the ethnic kaleidoscope which made up its population, the largest single group were not Greek, Turks, Albanians or Slav but Sephardic Jews.[27]

In July 1992, the ethnological museum in Salonika had no exhibit to commemorate the Sephardic Jewish element in the city's population, which was annihilated during the Nazi occupation. When the anthropologist Jonathan Schwartz 'asked a member of staff about this absence . . . they could not understand what the question was about. It was taken for granted that the Museum is Greek. Ethnology is apparently a scientific euphemism for Nationalism.'[28]

Ethnic cleansing in its most extreme form – genocide – can be adjudged ultimately successful if it expunges evidence of the richness and variety of past history. Such a 'cleansed' society is, however, an incomplete one[29] because memory cannot be suppressed indefinitely, nor can people hate the 'other' for eternity, without the implementation of an artificial crisis or fear. The mobility of populations in modern times and the preservation of 'community memory' amongst the survivors of ethnic cleansing mean that – eventually – a society may be roused from what is described in John Sturges' 1955 film *Bad Day at Black Rock* as a 'settled melancholy' by subsequent events.[30]

As far as the international community is concerned the lessons from the ethnic cleansing of the Balkans may be clear: that is to make an 'early engagement with societies in the midst of human rights crises'[31] in order to prevent war and recognize these crises for what they are, without resorting to essentialism about the character of the people living in these countries and their innate propensity for violence. In addition, the impetus is also clearly now upon Western governments, particularly those in the NATO alliance, to end their support for represssive regimes that might or might not be their allies. The active participation of Non-Governmental Organizations without active political policies to pursue may also prove to be important in preventing future humanitarian disasters.

Sentimental education might be nationalism's ultimate destroyer, especially as the information technology revolution encourages communication across national boundaries. But will the forging of new and supranational identities allow peaceful coexistence? Can individuals be patriotic and express genuine *Heimatliebe* without threatening the rights of groups of others?[32] Only one thing is certain. Most of the Balkan States might be closer to being 'ethnically clean' at the beginning of the twenty-first century, but the human capacity for cultural change and development will probably not alter. The citizens of Albania, Macedonia, Kosovo, Bulgaria, Serbia, Montenegro, Croatia, Greece, Turkey and Bosnia could certainly find ways of communicating and living together without interference from extremist intellectuals and politicians. They will manage and negotiate their differences if they have peace, prosperity, a positive image of cohabitation of shared lands, but even more fundamentally a 'complementary and ennobling'[33] antithesis to ethnic cleansing.

Notes

1 Nationalism, violence and the destruction of tradition

1 Throughout the text, I use Ernest Gellner's definition of nationalism as 'primarily the principle which holds that the political and national unit should be congruent' in his *Nations and Nationalism*, Oxford: Blackwell, 1983, p. 1.

2 Here discussions of the Crimea, Armenia and other regions which have a clear Ottoman legacy but are geographically outside Europe have been omitted, although in historical terms the experiences of these regions is undoubtedly important and in many respects similar.

3 The term 'Balkans' is not used here in either a negative or positive sense, but as a historical term.

4 The terms Balkans and 'Balkanism' have been discussed at some length, often with reference to Edward Said's *Orientalism. Western Conceptions of the Orient*, Harmondsworth: Penguin, 2nd edn, 1995, which first appeared in 1978. See in particular, John Allcock, 'Constructing "The Balkans"', in J.B. Allcock and A. Young (eds), *Black Lambs and Grey Falcons: Women Travellers in the Balkans*, Bradford: Bradford University Press, 1991, pp. 170–91, Robert Hayden and Milica Bakić Hayden, 'Orientalist Variations of the Theme "Balkans": Symbolic Geography in Recent Yugoslav Cultural Politics', *Slavic Review*, vol. 1, no. 1, 1992, 1–15, Rastko Močnik, 'Eden nov orientalizam: Crnata mitologija na Balkanot', *Naše pismo*, vol. 11, no. 2, 1996 and Maria Todorova, *Imagining the Balkans*, New York/Oxford: Oxford University Press, 1997.

5 Todorova, op. cit., p. 13.

6 I have included the Krajina because it existed as a military frontier created by the Habsburgs against the threat of Ottoman incursion. Had it not been for the Ottoman Balkans, the Krajina would simply not have existed and its unique social composition and legacy not a part of the history of ethnic cleansing in this region.

7 Scholars have disagreed about appropriate terminology and some have preferred other terms (Ethnocide, genocide, ethnic cleansing, population transfer) to described similar phenomena. The death or victimization of any individual is a human tragedy and it is an individual tragedy even when the person in question is murdered in the name of the collectivity. Some of the most outstanding work on the analysis and reporting of ethnic cleansing has been written by Jews or individuals with a strong Jewish heritage. This may be a coincidence, but I suspect that it is a quiet testimony to the lessons of history learnt by a religious/ethnic community that has had to face the terrible consequences of the worst ethnically inspired crime in history, the Shoah.

8 Carrie Booth Walling, 'The History and Politics of Ethnic Cleansing', in Ken Booth (ed.), *The Kosovo Tragedy. The Human Rights Dimension*, London: Frank Cass, 2001, p. 48.

9 Norman M. Naimark, *Fires of Hatred. Ethnic Cleansing in Twentieth Century Europe*, Cambridge, Massachusetts: Harvard University Press, 2001, p. 3.

10   Ahmed Akbar, 'Ethnic Cleansing: a Metaphor for Our Time?', *Ethnic and Racial Studies*, vol. 18, no. 1, 1995, 2–25.

11   Mirko Klarin, 'The Case Against Karadžić', *Tribunal*, August/September, 1997, 3.

12   This term is used in the East European context by Mark Mazower in his, *Dark Continent: Europe's Twentieth Century*, Harmondsworth: Penguin, 1998, p. 224.

13   Andrew Bell-Fialkoff has argued that it is an ancient phenomenon found in the ancient world in his study *Ethnic Cleansing*, New York and Oxford: St. Martin's Press, 1996.

14   Roy Gutman, *A Witness to Genocide: The First Inside Account of the Horrors of Ethnic Cleansing in Bosnia*, Shaftesbury: Element, 1993, p. xix.

15   As Immanuel Wallerstein states, 'in the tradition of *Annales*, all historical writing should be organized as *histoire-problème*', in 'Fernand Braudel, Historian, "homme de la conjoncture"', *Radical History Review*, vol. 26, 1982, 105.

16   Lucien Febvre, quoted in Wallerstein, op. cit., p. 117.

17   Although it is quite clear that the many opponents of this state regarded its character as Serbian hegemonistic in character.

18   This is, of course, meant in the hermeneutic sense.

19   Clifford Geertz, *Interpretation of Cultures*, New York: Basic Books, 1973.

20   'Military Court in Niš raises, issues of "cleaning up" in Kosovo, 6 November, 2000 found at <http://groups.yahoo.com/group/balkanhr/message/1276> on 2 May 2001.

21   The following paragraph owes a great deal to the methodology used by Robert Darnton in his, *The Kiss of Lamourette: Reflections in French History*, New York: Norton, 1990, especially chapter 1.

22   Robert Walsh, quoted in Misha Glenny, *The Balkans 1804–1999. Nationalism, War and the Great Powers*, London: Granta, 1999, p. 28. In Montenegro, killing an enemy by decapitation was the sign of a hero, celebrated in folk poetry, although it is likely that this practice originated from the Turks. See Božidar Jezernik, *Dežela, kjer je vse narobe. Prispevki k etnologiji Balkana*. Ljubljana: Znanstveno in publicistično središče, 1998, p. 147 ff.

23   Vladimir Dedijer, *The Yugoslav Auschwitz and the Vatican*, Buffalo, New York: Prometheus Books, 1992, p. 248.

24   Tim Judah, *The Serbs. History, Myth and Destruction of Yugoslavia*, New Haven: Yale University Press, 1997, illustration 44 between pp. 238–9.

25   Mary Douglas, *Purity and Danger: An Analysis of the Concepts of Pollution and Taboo*, London: Routledge and Kegan Paul, 1966, p. 69.

26   Rezak Hukanović, *The Tenth Circle of Hell. A Memoir of Life in the Death Camps of Bosnia*, London: Abacus, 1998, pp. 64–5.

27   In traditional English law, the traitor was mutilated before execution and in the 1820s, the Cato Street Conspirators were decapitated, although their bodies were not displayed in public. On the cultural politics of execution see Jezernik, op. cit., p. 163.

28   Vladimir Dedijer, *The War Diaries of Vladimir Dedijer*, Ann Arbor: University of Michigan Press, vol. 1, 1990, p. 43.

29   Vladimir Dedijer, *Dnevnik*, Belgrade: Jugoslovenska knjiga, 1951, 2 vols.

30   Any teacher who has taught courses on nationalism, fascism or ethnic cleansing might legitimately fear that for every thousand students who are genuinely appalled by the events in Nazi Germany, Fascist Croatia or elsewhere, there may be the odd individual who admires fascism and the goals of these regimes. Vojislav Šešelj wrote theoretical work on fascism before he turned into a practitioner.

31   Laura Silber and Allan Little, *The Death of Yugoslavia*, Harmondsworth: Penguin, 1995, p. 155.

32   Silber and Little, op. cit., p. 155.

33   Judah, op. cit., p. 187.

34   Slavenka Drakulić, *Balkan Express. Fragments from the Other Side of War*, London: Hutchinson, 1993, p. 79.

35 British soldiers are rumoured to have cut off the ears of Argentinians in the Falklands war as trophies and certainly gory war stories are an established part of pub folklore in the United Kingdom, but this never makes the mainstream press. On 14 November 2001, the author was informed by a former British soldier, named here as GT, who served in the Falklands that the British would send in the Gurkhas to Kabul in Afghanistan to sort out any remaining Taliban fighting. He informed me further that it was the *reputation* of the Gurkhas for cruelty that was most effective and the fact that once they had drawn their knives, they were obliged to make a cut.

36 John B. Allcock, *Explaining Yugoslavia*, London: Hurst, 2000, p. 402.

37 Christian Giordano, 'The Balkans: European Periphery, Epicentre of Ethnicity and Landscape of Feuds', *Anthropological Journal on European Cultures*, vol. 4, no. 2, 1995, 104–5.

38 Leon Trotsky, *My Life*, Penguin, Harmondsworth, 1980, pp. 181–2.

39 Mikhail Bakhtin argued about the 'carnivalesque' and popular festive forms as well as 'transgression' from social norms in *Rabelais and His World*, Bloomington, Indiana: Indiana University Press, 1984, and in Michael Holquist (ed.), The *Dialogic Imagination Four Essays by M.M. Bakhtin*, Austin: University of Texas Press, 1981. His theories have frequently been used to interpret patterns of behaviour that seem to invert social norms (such as the wearing of vestments and habits in Catholic countries during the carnival to mock the authority of the priesthood or the ways in which gays at the Sydney *mardi gras* dress up as policemen). These are seen as socially controlled transgression or inversions.

40 Philip Gourevitch, *We Wish to Inform You that Tomorrow We Will Be Killed with Our Families. Stories from Rwanda*, London: Picador, 1998, describes the promotion of 'genocide as a carnival romp' in Rwanda. In the build-up to the 1994 genocide, the 'Hutu Power' movement organized rallies at which '. . . military drills were conducted like the latest hot dance moves' and retreats 'to practice burning houses, tossing grenades and hacking up dummies with machetes' (p. 94).

41 Gutman, op. cit., p. 74.

42 Ed Vulliamy, *Seasons in Hell. Understanding Bosnia's War*, London: Simon and Schuster, 1994, photograph opposite p. 132. As the author notes, 'In a cruel war between neighbours, men donned military gear to carve out a patchwork of territories with a maze of roadblocks and checkpoints, often personalised or decked out to intimidate.'

43 Joanna Bourke, *An Intimate History of Killing. Face to Face Killing in Twentieth Century Europe*, London: Granta, 1999, especially pp. 42, 116–32.

44 The Hamlet metaphor is used by Ed Vulliamy, op. cit., p. 85. Mark Thompson, writing in *The Independent* on 25 March 2000, 10, compared Milošević to Macbeth and Richard III, 'so far in blood that sin plucks sin'. He maintains that 'Shakespeare remains the best guide to Balkan politics in the 1990s'.

45 Philip Gourevitch, op. cit., p. 115.

46 Gérard Prunier *The Rwanda Crisis: History of a Genocide 1959–1994*, London: Hurst, 1995, p. 247.

47 Dubravka Ugrešić, *The Culture of Lies*, Pennsylvania: Penn State Press, 1998, p. 118.

48 Richard Norton-Taylor, 'Croats Jailed for Ethnic Slaughter', *Guardian Weekly*, 20–26 January 2000, 4.

49 During his time in jail in the Hague, Tadić was given painting materials and produced pictures with explicitly nationalist themes. Stephen Bates, 'Blood stained hands dabble in paint', *The Guardian*, 15 July 1997, 11.

50 Stephen Bates, 'Serb fury at jail for killer', *The Guardian*, 15 July 1997, 11.

51 Slavenka Drakulić, op. cit., p. 67.

52 Norman Cigar, 'The Serbo-Croatian War', in Stjepan Meštrović (ed.), *Genocide after Emotion. The Postemotional Balkan War*, London, Routledge, 1996, p. 75.

53 Dimitrije Bogdanović, *Knjiga o Kosovu*, Beograd, Srpska akademija nauka i umetnosti, 1985, p. 269. The use of the term 'genocide' in a 'physical', 'legal', 'political' and

'cultural' sense received more widespread attention after the circulation of the notorious 'memorandum' of the Serbian academy. See '"Memorandum" (grupa akademika Srpske akademije nauka i umetnosti o aktuelnim društvenim pitanjima u našoj zemlji)', in Bože Čović (ed.), *Izvori velikosrpske agresije*, Zagreb: August Cesarec & Skolska knjiga, 1993, pp. 296–300.

54 Smiljan Simac, 'Croatie, Serbie: les fausses symétries', *Le Monde*, 25 May 1999, 13–14.

55 Dubravka Ugrešić, *The Culture of Lies*, Pennsylvania: Penn State Press, 1998, p. 100.

56 Vitomir Miles Raguz, 'International-brand Justice earns bad marks in Zagreb', *The Wall Street Journal Europe*, 13–14 July 2001, 7.

57 Here I am partly drawing on the term employed by Max Weber to mean a pre-modern society, which has not undergone bureaucratic, legal, political, economic and social 'rationalization' and that is still spiritually integrated. On this see, H.H. Gerth and C. Wright Mills, *From Max Weber. Essays in Sociology*, London: Routledge and Kegan Paul, 1985.

58 Todorova, op. cit., pp. 177–8. There may also be a parallel here to the self-definition and construction by Gentiles of the category of Jew in nineteenth- and twentieth-century Eastern Europe.

59 Ibid., p. 13.

60 Robert Redfield, *Peasant Culture and Society*, Chicago: University of Chicago Press, 1965, pp. 41–3.

61 Christopher Boehm, *Montenegrin Social Organization and Values: Political Ethnography of a Refuge Area Tribal Adaptation*, New York: AMS Press, 1983, p. 7.

62 Mirjana Gross, 'The Union of Dalmatia with Northern Croatia: A Crucial Question of the Croatian National Integration in the Nineteenth Century', in Mikulas Teich and Roy Porter (eds), *The National Question in Europe in Historic Context*, Cambridge: Cambridge University Press, 1993, pp. 270–92, which discusses the role of primary education in the hinterland of Split, which had up to 95 per cent illiteracy rates at that time. Rates in rural Serbia, Montenegro and Albania and elsewhere in the Balkans were probably as high.

63 Custom (*običaj* or *adet* in its Muslim sense) was frequently invoked in village discourse in Bosnia in the 1980s. Tone Bringa, *Being Muslim the Bosnian Way*, Princeton, Princeton University Press, 1995, p. 81.

64 Although there is some evidence for a strong continuity of the idea of Kosovo amongst the singers of ballads, the moulding of these scattered tales into a national literary canon in the nineteenth century by Vuk Karadžić amongst others had a clear 'nationalist' purpose. On the subject of the making of the Kosovo myth, see Noel Malcolm, *Kosovo: A Short History*, London: Macmillan, 1998, especially chapter 4.

65 J.G.C. Michin in *The Growth of Freedom in the Balkan Peninsula*, London: John Murray, 1886, p. 13 quoted in Jezernik, op. cit., p. 158 noted the vogue for nose-taking in Montenegro had precedents in the *Odyssey*. The practice of taking noses in Montenegro during battle was, however more recent, introduced after the Vladika (ecclesiastical ruler of Montenegro) banned his people from taking heads during battle, a practice they may well have learnt from the Turks.

66 Todorova, op. cit., p. 63.

67 See for instance, Mary Edith Durham, *Some Tribal Origins, Laws and Customs of the Balkans*, London: George Allen and Unwin, 1928, and numerous other books and journals devoted to Balkan ethnology.

68 Colonel L.C. Vialla de Sommières, *Voyage historique et politique au Montenegro*, Paris: Alexis Eymery, 1820, 2 vols.

69 Jovan Erdeljanović, *Stara Crna Gora* Belgrade: Rodoljub, 1926, p. 26.

70 Joyce Cary, *Memoir of the Bobotes*, London: Michael Joseph, 1964.

71 See, for example, Monica Krippner, 'British Medical Women in Serbia during and after the First World War', J.B. Allcock and A. Young (eds), *Black Lambs and Grey Falcons: Women Travellers in the Balkans*, Bradford: Bradford University Press, 1991, pp. 65–81.

72 Robert W. Seton-Watson, *The Problem of Small Nations and the European Anarchy*, Nottingham: Nottingham University Montague Burton International Relations Series, 1939, p. 7.

73 Here terms used by Roland Barthes to describe the codification of knowledge in the eighteenth century have been borrowed. See 'The Plates of the Encyclopaedia', in R. Barthes, *New Critical Essays*, translated by Richard Howard, New York: Hill and Wang, 1980, pp. 222–3.

74 Robert Hamilton Lang, *Roumelian Coup D'état, Servo-Bulgarian War, and the Latest Phase of the Eastern Question*, London: Harrison, 1886, p. 4.

75 Fanny Copeland, 'Who are the Yugo-Slavs?', *Balkan Review*, vol. 1, 1919, 41.

76 Stevan K. Pavlowitch, *A History of the Balkans 1804–1945*, London: Longmans, 1999, p. 28, fn 3.

76 Jovan Cvijić, *La péninsule balkanique. Geographie humaine*, Paris: A. Colin, 1918, p. 297.

77 Arnold J. Toynbee, 'The Western Question in Greece and Turkey', quoted in Mazower, op. cit., p. 129.

79 Sergio Bonazza, 'Austro-Slavism as the Motive of Kopitar's Work', *Slovene Studies*, vol. 5, 1993, 155–64.

80 This view of the past was portrayed in the popular work of history by Jovan Rajić, which appeared under the title, *Istoriya raznih slovenskih naradov*, and was published in Vienna in 1794.

81 These nationalists looked back to various 'golden ages' in the past. On this phenomenon, see Anthony D. Smith, 'Chosen Peoples', in John Hutchinson and Anthony D. Smith (eds), *Ethnicity*, Oxford: Oxford University Press, 1996, pp. 189–97.

82 Jezernik, op. cit., (1998), p. 115.

83 Sometimes Western travellers were disappointed by the real Greeks, who were more usually fishermen, bakers and merchants than latter day heroes and were found to be suffering from 'frustrated philhellenism', as was obviously the case with Chateaubriand who when asked by a Turk about the reasons for his journey said that he had 'come to see people and especially the Greeks who were dead'. Todorova, op. cit., p. 92.

84 Andrew Mango, *Atatürk*, London: John Murray, 1999, p. 10.

85 Peter Trudgill, 'Greece and European Turkey: From Religious to Linguistic Identity', in Stephen Barbour and Cathie Carmichael (eds), *Language and Nationalism in Europe*, Oxford: Oxford University Press, 2000, pp. 240–63.

86 'The Constitution of the Republic of Croatia, December 22nd 1990', in Gale Stokes (ed.) *From Stalinism to Pluralism: A Documentary History of Eastern Europe since 1945*, Oxford: Oxford University Press, 2nd edn, 1996, pp. 285–6.

87 Jezernik, op. cit. (1998), pp. 176–7.

88 Cathie Carmichael, 'Conclusions: Language and National Identity in Europe', in Stephen Barbour and Cathie Carmichael, op. cit., p. 286.

89 Georg Elwert: 'Nationalismus und Ethnizität: Über die Bildung von Wir-Gruppen', *Kölner Zeitschrift für Soziologie und Sozialpsychologie*, no. 3, 1989, 440–64.

90 Slobodan Reljić, 'Demagogue in Waiting', *Transitions*, March 1998, 72–3.

91 Photograph reproduced in Lenard J. Cohen, *Serpent in the Bosom. The Rise and Fall of Slobodan Milošević*, Boulder, Colorado: Westview, 2001, p. 226.

92 Sabrina P. Ramet (ed.), *Balkan Babel: The Disintegration of Yugoslavia from the Death of Tito to Ethnic War*, Boulder, Colorado: Westview, 1996, p. 210.

93 Anthony D. Smith, *Nationalism and Modernism: a Critical Survey of Recent Theories of Nations and Nationalism*, London: Routledge, 1998, p. 130.

94 At the 'rallies of truth' organized in the late 1980s, in which would-be supporters were taken on free buses and supplied with food (which the witty derided as the 'yoghurt revolution'), Milošević would occasionally appear not to hear what was said, egging sections of the crowd on '*Ne čujem dobro*', ('I can't hear (you) well'). On Milošević's use of rhetoric more generally and his mutation from Communist bureaucrat to

nationalist, see Ivo Žanić, *Prevarena povijest. Guslarska estrada, kult Hajduka i rat u Hrvatskoj i Bosni i Hercegovini 1990–1995. Godine*, Zagreb: Durieux, 1998, pp. 25–32.

95 '"Memorandum" (grupa akademika Srpske akademije nauka i umetnosti o aktuelnim društvenim pitanjima u našoj zemlji)', in Boze Čović (ed.), op. cit., pp. 296–300.

96 As Gale Stokes has observed the transformation of the superstructure preceded that of the base in the Balkans. See *Nationalism in the Balkans. An Annotated Bibliography*, New York: Garland, 1984, p. ix.

97 Ivo Žanić, op. cit., p. 29.

98 Stefan Troebst, 'IMRO + 100 = FYROM? The Politics of Macedonian historiography', in James Pettifer (ed.), *The New Macedonian Question*, Basingstoke: Palgrave, 2000, 2nd edn, p. 60.

99 Omer Ibrahimagić, *Srpsko osporavanje Bosne i Bošnjaka*, Sarajevo: Magistrat, 2001, pp. 203–4. Ivo Andrić contributed to keeping a negative view of Muslims alive through his fictional work, especially *Na Drini Ćuprija*, (Bridge on the Drina) read by generations of young Yugoslavs and translated into almost all the other languages of the Balkans.

100 Nebojša Čagorović, 'Montenegrin Identity: Past, Present and Future', *Journal of Area Studies*, vol. 3, 1993, 134.

101 On the use of the medieval past in Croatia in the early 1990s, see Ivo Žanić, 'The curse of King Zvonimir and Political Discourse in Embattled Croatia', *East European Politics and Societies*, vol. 9, no. 1, 1995, 90–122.

102 James Gow, *Triumph of the Lack of Will: International Diplomacy and the Yugoslav War*, London: Hurst, 1997, p. 43.

103 This phrase is adapted from Michael Burleigh and Wolfgang Wippermann, *The Racial State: Germany 1933–1945*, Cambridge: Cambridge University Press, 1991, p. 26, who use the term 'squatter' to discuss the discourse concerning the German mission to resettle territories inhabited by Slavs which were once populated by ancient Germanic tribes.

104 Some diplomats were more pragmatic in their attitude towards the Ottomans. 'Lord Stanley, echoing Canning's sentiments of forty years earlier, wrote in some exasperation, of Greeks and Turks in 1867 that "in point of civilization there is little to choose".' G.D. Clayton, *Britain and the Eastern Question: Missolonghi to Gallipoli*, London: Lion Library, 1974, p. 125.

105 'Extract of a Letter from Orschowa, in Servia, dated January last', *The Times*, 25 August 1815, 3.

106 Clayton, op. cit., p. 142.

107 This is discussed in Branko Horvat, *Kosovsko Pitanje*, Zagreb: Globus, 1989, pp. 42–52.

108 Benedict Anderson, *Imagined Communities*, London: Verso, 1991.

109 Tony Barber, 'A Call to Save Sarajevo', *The Independent*, 26 July 1993, 1.

110 Cohen, op. cit., p. 263.

111 Alex Renton, 'Chamber of Horrors Jails a Real Villain of Bosnia at Last', *Evening Standard*, 3 March 2000, 17.

112 Chris Bird, 'Chief of "Balkan Auschwitz" gets 20 years in Jail', *The Guardian*, 5 October 1999, 16.

113 Fernand Braudel, *The Mediterranean and the Mediterranean World in the Age of Philip II*, vol. 1, London: Fontana, 1982, pp. 2–3.

2 Mountain wreaths: anti-Islam in Balkan Slavonic discourses

1 Justin McCarthy, *Death and Exile, The Ethnic Cleansing of Ottoman Muslims 1821–1922*, Darwin Press, Princeton, NJ, 1996, p. 338.

2 Michael Sells, *The Bridge Betrayed: Religion and Genocide in Bosnia, 2nd edn*, Berkeley: University of California Press, 1998, p. 119.

3 Milica Bakić Hayden refers to this negative view of Muslims as a 'betrayal syndrome' in her article 'Nesting Orientalisms: The case of the Former Yugoslavia', *Slavic Review*,

vol. 54, no. 4, 1995, 927. Clearly the category of Muslim in the Balkans is not in itself unproblematic or monolithic. The village Muslims who went to Sarajevo after 1995 are clearly different in cultural terms from the more urban and secular inhabitants of the city. Ivana Maček, 'Predicament of war. Sarajevo experience and the ethics of war', in Bettina E. Schmidt and Ingo W. Schröder (eds), *Anthopology of Violence and Conflict*, London: Routledge, 2001, p. 218.

4   On 'the unmixing of peoples', a phrase originally used by Lord Curzon in the 1920s, see Rogers Brubaker, *Nationalism Reframed. Nationhood and the National Question in Europe*, Cambridge: Cambridge University Press, 1996, pp. 148–78.

5   In the Sandžak in Serbia, in the autumn and winter of 1992–3, pressure was put upon Muslim villagers to leave. By March 1993, only three Muslim households remained in Sjeverin. Mark Thompson, *Forging War. The Media in Serbia, Croatia, Bosnia and Hercegovina*, Luton: University of Luton Press/Article 19. International Centre Against Censorship, 1999, p. 94.

6   Turkish minister Sukru Kaya Bey in 1934, in Brubaker, op. cit., p. 156.

7   Andrew Mango, *Atatürk*, London: John Murray, 1999, p. 11.

8   Jovan Cvijić, *La péninsule balkanique. Geographie humaine*, Paris: A. Colin, 1918, p. 353, quoting a saying about what he refers to as 'islamicized Serbs' attributed to Orthodox Serbs.

9   Catherine Wendy Bracewell, *The Uscoks of Senj. Piracy, Banditry and Holy War in the Sixteenth Century Adriatic*, Ithaca: Cornell University Press, 1992, p. 160.

10   Jonathan Matthew Schwartz, *Pieces of Mosaic. An Essay on the Making of Makedonija*, Intervention Press, Højbjerg, Denmark, 1996, pp. 31–2.

11   J.A.R Marriott, *The Eastern Question: an Historical Study in European Diplomacy*, Oxford, Clarendon Press, 1940, 4th edn, p. 205. On the other hand, some Balkans peoples had a sense in which they might miss the Turks, their old adversaries. The Serbs have a popular saying : *'Drumovi će pozeljeti Turaka, al' Turaka nidje biti neće'* – The roads will long for the Turks, but there won't be any of them on them.

12   Ivan Čolović *Bordel ratnika. Folklor, politika i rat*, Belgrade: Biblioteka XX vek, 1993, especially pp. 99–117.

13   Vesna Goldsworthy, *Inventing Ruritania: the Imperialism of the Imagination*, New Haven, Yale University Press, 1998, p. 37.

14   Goldsworthy, op. cit., p. 37 .

15   Samuel P. Huntington, *The Clash of Civilizations and the Remaking of the New World Order*, New York: Simon and Schuster, 1996. The relevance of this thesis to the Balkans is discussed in Florian Bieber, 'The Conflict in Former Yugoslavia as a "Fault Line War"? Testing the Validity of Samuel Huntington's "Clash of Civilization",' *Balkanologie*, vol. 3, no. 1, 1999, 33–48.

16   On the development of Serbo-Croat see, Cathie Carmichael, '"A People exists and that People has its language". Language and Nationalism in the Balkans', in Stephen Barbour and Cathie Carmichael (eds) *Language and Nationalism in Europe*, Oxford: Oxford University Press, 2000, pp. 221–39.

17   South Slav Muslims themselves were slow to adopt European nationalism, although there were some Islamic fascists in Bosnia during the Second World War. (On this see, Francine Friedman, *The Bosnian Muslims. Denial of a Nation*, Boulder, Colorado: Westview 1996, pp. 122–5.) Many Slav Muslims migrated to Turkey after periods of significant political change such as the 1870s or 1910s. There was also never a significant Moslem South Slav diaspora agitating for a separate 'Bošnjak' state and even in 1992 the many Muslims in Bosnia saw their primary alliance with other Bosnians (Serbs and Croat) who accepted the legitimacy of the Izetbegović government. On Muslim identity, see Florian Bieber, 'Muslim National Identity in the Balkans before the Establishment of Nation States', *Nationalities Papers*, vol. 28, no. 1, 2000, 13–28.

18   Aleksandar Pavković, 'The Serb National Idea: a Revival 1986–92', *Slavonic and East*

European Review, vol. 72, no. 3, 1994, 444.

19 Vuk Karadžić, 'Serbi sve i svuda', in Mirko Grmek, Marc Gjidara and Neven Šimac (eds), *Etničko Čišćenje. Povijesni dokumenti o jednoj srpskoj ideologiji*, Zagreb: Nakladni zavod Globus, 1993, p. 29. Tone Bringa has argued that in the case of the Bosnian Muslims, 'the weaker emphasis on descent' and 'common blood' as defining their 'ethnic identity' partly excluded them from an ethnonationalist discourse, which resolves around such principles. See ibid., *Being Muslim the Bosnian Way*, Princeton: Princeton University Press 1995, p. 31.

20 Asim Peco, *Turcizmi u Vukovim Rječnicima*, Belgrade: Vuk Karadžić, 1987.

21 Tim Judah, *The Serbs. History, Myth and Destruction of Yugoslavia*, New Haven and London: Yale University Press, 1997, p. 75.

22 Malcolm, op. cit., pp. 79–80.

23 Ivo Žanić in his study, *Prevarena povijest. Guslarska estrada, kult Hajduka i rat u Hrvatskoj i Bosni i Hercegovini 1990–1995. Godine*, Zagreb, Durieux, 1998, has argued that the symbol of the gusle has remained vital in nationalist imagery and was revived in the 1990s. He reproduces a photograph (p. 390) of Radovan Karadžić proudly holding a gusle at the birthplace of his forebear Vuk in 1992. See also Čolović, op. cit., pp. 83–92.

24 Celia Hawkesworth, 'The Study of South Slav Oral Poetry: a Select Annotated Bibliography of Works in English (1800–1980)', in Michael Branch and Celia Hawkesworth (eds), *The Uses of Tradition: A Comparative Enquiry into the Nature, Uses and Functions of Oral Poetry in the Balkans, the Baltic and Africa*, London: School of Slavonic and East European Studies Occasional Paper, no. 6, 1994,, pp. 37–8.

25 Petar Petrović Njegoš, *Gorski Vijenac*, Sarajevo: Svjetlost, 1990, p. 155, ll. 2604–6.

26 Vladeta Popović, 'Introduction', in *The Mountain Wreath of P. P. Nyegosh, Prince Bishop of Montenegro, 1830–1851*, translated by James William Wyles, London: G. Allen and Unwin Ltd, 1930, p. 11.

27 Popović op. cit., p. 17.

28 Grmek *et al.* (eds), op. cit., p. 25.

29 Bakić Hayden, op. cit., pp. 927–8.

30 Omer Ibrahimagić, *Srpsko osporavanje Bosne i Bošnjaka*, Sarajevo: Magistrat, 2001, pp. 209–10.

31 Branimir Anzulović, *Heavenly Serbia: From Myth to Genocide*, London: Hurst 1999, p. 92.

32 Nationalist writers created self-image of a perpetual state of mental struggle against the Turks (who were then partially replaced by the Austrians in the latter part of the nineteenth century. See T.G. Jackson, *Dalmatia, the Quarnero and Istria with Cettigne in Montenegro and the Island of Grado*, Oxford: Clarendon Press, 1887, p. 67.

33 Cvijić, op. cit., p. 296, quoted in Bojan Baskar, 'Made in Trieste. Geopolitical Fears of an Istrianist Discourse on the Mediterranean', *Narodna Umjetnost*, vol. 36, no. 1, 1999, 123.

34 Zorka Milich, *A Stranger's Supper: an Oral History of Centegenarian Women in Montenegro*, New York/London: Twayne Publishers/Prentice Hall International, 1995, p. 29.

35 Milich, op. cit., pp. 100–2.

36 Ibid., p. 102.

37 Ibid., p. 40.

38 Ivo Banac, *The National Question in Yugoslavia: Origins, History, Politics*, Ithaca: Cornell University Press, 1984, p. 377.

39 Judah, op. cit., p. 78.

40 This concept is discussed with reference to Bosnia in Stevan M. Weine, 'Redefining Merhamet After a Historical Nightmare', Joel M. Halpern and David A. Kideckel (eds), *Neighbors at War. Anthropological Perspectives on Yugoslav Ethnicity, Culture and History*, Pennsylvania: Penn State Press, 2000, p. 412.

41 Cathie Carmichael, 'Conclusions: Language and National Identity in Europe', in Barbour and Carmichael (eds), op. cit., p. 285.

42 Anthony D. Smith, 'Chosen Peoples', in John Hutchinson and Anthony D. Smith (eds), *Ethnicity*, Oxford: Oxford University Press 1996, p. 195.

43 Vladimir Dedijer, *The War Diaries of Vladimir Dedijer*, Ann Arbor: University of Michigan Press, vol. 1, 1990, p. 272. Elsewhere in the same volume (p. 62), he refers to Montenegrin traditions, . . . heir struggle for freedom, . . . the Mountain Wreath'. If it was not never actually a strictly historical account in the positivist sense, *Gorski Vijenac* certainly came to resemble one in terms of its social functions.

44 Bringa, op. cit., p. 77.

45 Ibid., p. 61. There was even a trend for throwing away traditional kelims and other craft products as they were also deemed to be old-fashioned.

46 Božidar Jezernik, '"Evropeizacija" Balkanskih mest kot vzrok za njihovo "Balkanizacijo"'; *Glasnik slovenskega etnološkega društva*, no. 35, 1995, 2–13.

47 Radoslav Radenkov, 'The Turkish Minority in Bulgaria', *East European Reporter*, vol. 3, no. 4, 1989, 28.

48 Radenkov, op. cit., p. 28.

49 Brubaker, op. cit., p. 155. From 1934–9, some 100,000 Turks or Muslims left, followed by a further exodus in 1950–1.

50 Norman Cigar, 'The Serbo-Croatian War', in Stjepan Meštrović (ed.), *Genocide after Emotion. The Postemotional Balkan War*, London: Routledge, 1996, p. 67, characterizes Serb nationalism in 1990–1 as being led by a 'small nucleus (of) hard-core (activists)'. Similarly he notes, (p. 59), that the neo-fascist Party of Rights (*Hrvatska Stranka Prava* HSP) in Croatia gained only 5 per cent of public support in the 1990 elections.

51 Black crows are a symbol of bad luck in South Slavonic culture, somewhat similar to magpies in Western Europe.

52 Norman Cigar, op. cit. (1996), p. 57.

53 In a final sense it will be difficult for historians to judge the overall impact that Milošević made as an individual in the 1980s and 1990s. Many scholars believe that the wars in the former Yugoslavia simply would not have occurred without his manipulation of the national question, especially with regard to Kosovo. Others have sought to find the causes of the war in the *longue durée* and from within cultural phenomena. For a discussion of 'instrumentalist' versus the 'primordialist' viewpoints on the conflict see Lenard J. Cohen, *Serpent in the Bosom. The Rise and Fall of Slobodan Milošević*, Boulder, Colorado: Westview, 2001, especially chapter 6.

54 Ivo Rendić-Miočević, *Zlo velike jetre: povijest i nepovijest Crnogoraca, Hrvata, Muslimana i Srba*, Split: Književni krug 1996, pp. 126–7.

55 Anzulović, op. cit., p. 49.

56 Dunja Rihtman-Auguštin, 'Ugledna etnologinja i antropologinja govori o instrumentalizaciji folklora i teroru mitologijom', *Feral Tribune*, 23 studenoga, 1998, 22–3.

57 Nevertheless as Ken Parker reminds us, accounts of the Ottomans were often 'disorientated' and the 'them-and-us binary, with the Turks as the embodiment of everything that is the antithesis to Christianity, was never as clear-cut as some present day accounts of that "West" versus "East" story would have it', in ibid. (ed.), *Early Modern Tales of Orient*, London: Routledge, 1999, p. 3.

58 Xavier Marmier, *Lettres sur L'Adriatique et le Montenegro*, tome deuxième, Paris: Imprimerie Ch. Lahure, Société de Geographie, 1853, p. 120. The Western European obsession with headhunting in the Balkans is discussed by Božidar Jezernik, *Dežela, kjer je vse narobe. Prispevki k etnologiji Balkana*. Ljubljana: Znanstveno in publicistično središče, 1998. He points out (p. 163) that British and other nineteenth-century writers often constructed these activities as archaic and primitive, despite the fact that the public display of criminals' heads has died out only in the recent past in their own countries.

59 Alfred Lord Tennyson, *Poetical Works*, London: Macmillan, 1926, pp. 533–4.

60 Edward Said, *Orientalism. Western Conceptions of the Orient*, Harmondsworth: Penguin, 2nd edn, 1995.

61 This concept of Balkanism is explored at some length by Maria Todorova, *Imagining the Balkans*, New York/Oxford: Oxford University Press, 1997.

62 Ryan Gingeras, 'Macedonia in Crisis: British Press Coverage of the Ilinden Uprising of 1903 and the Conceptualization of the Balkans', Paper delivered at the 6th World Congress of the Association for the Study of Nationalities (ASN), Columbia University 5–7 April 2001.

63 Todorova, op. cit., pp. 163–4.

64 Zvane Crnja, *Cultural History of Croatia*, translated by Vladimir Ivir, Zagreb: Office of Information, 1962, p. 278.

65 Vera Mutafchieva, 'The Notion of the "Other" in Bulgaria: The Turks. A Historical Study', in *Anthropological Journal on European Cultures*, vol. 4, no. 2, 1995, 53–74.

66 Vuk Drašković tried to revive the cult of Sveti Sava amongst Serbs in the late 1980s.

67 Traian Stoianovich, *Balkan Worlds: The First and Last Europe*, New York and London: Sharpe, 1994, pp. 168–9.

68 In his memoirs about a pogrom against Jews in his native Ukraine, Nikita Khrushchev remembered that for three days it was announced that there would not be any enforcement of law against the violent troublemakers, suggesting this period of time would lead to the settling of scores and individual atrocities, without entirely destroying the rule of law and leading to widespread revolt and chaos. See, *Krushchev Remembers*, London: Andre Deutsch, 1971, pp. 234–5.

69 'Frontiers of Servia', *The Times*, 27 February 1815, 2.

70 The role of the border and banditry in South Slavonic history is discussed by Xavier Bougarel, 'La "revanche des campagnes", entre réalité sociologique et mythe nationaliste', *Balkanologie*, vol. 2, no. 1, 1998, 17–36.

71 Jezernik, op. cit., pp. 79–114 has argued that it was the Slav Christians themselves who scratched out the eyes of saints in Orthodox Churches to make medicinal poultices, although the occurrences were usually blamed upon the Turks.

72 Jovan Cvijić, op. cit., p. 351. Muslims in Bosnia will say 'if God wills (i.e. gives)' (ako Bog da), often adding the Arabic 'inshallah' (if Allah/God wills it) as it were for extra protection. See Bringa, op. cit., p. 68.

73 For a discussion of the relationship between 'truth' and 'history' see in particular Hayden White, *Tropics of Discourse. Essays in Cultural Criticism*, Baltimore: Johns Hopkins University Press, 1985, especially chapters one and five in his discussion of the work of the historical vision of Jakob Burckhardt.

74 On the manipulation of myths about the past see Ivan Čolović, 'Vreme i prostor u savremenoj političkoj mitologiji', in Mirjana Prošić-Dvornić (ed.), *Kulture u tranziciji*, Belgrade: Plato, 1994, pp. 122–3.

75 Roy Gutman, *A Witness to Genocide: The First Inside Account of the Horrors of Ethnic Cleansing in Bosnia*, Shaftesbury: Element, 1993, p. x.

76 Dobritsa Tchossitch, *L'Effondrement de la Yougoslavie. Positions d'un Résistant*, Lausanne: L'Age d'Homme, 1994, p. 41, cited in Florian Bieber, *Serbischer Nationalismus vom Tod Titos zum Sturz Miloševićs*, Unpublished Doctoral Dissertation, Vienna University, March 2001, p. 206.

77 As Gale Stokes remarks in *Three Eras of Political Change in Eastern Europe*, Oxford: Oxford University Press, 1997 p. 74.

78 Leon Trotsky, *The Balkan Wars 1912–13*, New York: Monad Press, 1980, p. 209.

79 Mark Mazower, *The Balkans*, London: Weidenfeld and Nicolson, 2000, p. 80.

80 Jonathan Schwartz, '"Contested Identity" or "Ethnic War"? The Endurance Test in the Republic of Macedonia'. Workshop on 'Macedonian Knots', Mediterranean Ethnology Conference, Piran, 20 September 2001.

81 Julie Mertus, Jasmina Tesanović, Habiba Metikos and Rada Borić, (eds), *The Suitcase. Refugee Voices from Bosnia and Croatia*, Berkeley: University of California Press, 1997, p. 125.

82 Sava, op. cit., p. 36.

83 Misha Glenny, *The Fall of Yugoslavia. The Third Balkan War*, Harmondsworth: Penguin 1992, p. 169.
84 John B. Allcock, *Explaining Yugoslavia*, London: Hurst, 2000, p. 390.
85 Maggie O'Kane, 'One Family's Story of the Terror Inside Kosovo. And of the Friendly Bus Driver Who Turned into a Mass Murderer', *Guardian Weekly*, 27 June 1999, 1.
86 Ibid., 12.
87 The relationship between 'local rivalries' and the 'terrorizing tactics of outside extremists' is discussed by Susan Woodward in her, *Balkan Tragedy. Chaos and Dissolution After the Cold War*, Washington: Brookings Institute, 1995, pp. 242–3 .
88 John Reed, *War in Eastern Europe. Travels Through the Balkans in 1915*, London: Orion 1999, p. 26.
89 Turbofolk is a kitsch genre of popular music in Serbia, which utilizes traditional 'oriental' tunes and traditional gender imagery.
90 Marko Živković, 'Too Much Character, too Little *Kultur.* Serbian Jeremiads 1994–95, *Balkanologie* vol. 2, no. 2, 1998, 77.
91 Ibid., 79.
92 Judah, op. cit., p. 49.
93 Grmek *et al.* (eds), op. cit., p. 82. Given the behaviour of the Croatian military in Bosnia in 1993 in particular, the comment by Marcus Tanner in his *Croatia. A Nation Forged in War, New Haven*: Yale University Press, 1997, p. 116 that this dialogue is 'an ominous reminder of the difference between Croat and Serb political culture' is erroneous.
94 Rastko Močnik, 'Balkan Orientalisms', in Bojan Baskar and Borut Brumen (eds) *Mediterranean Ethnological Summer School*, vol. II, Ljubljana: Inštitut za multikulturne raziskave, 1998, pp. 157–8.
95 Močnik, op. cit., pp. 157–8.
96 Quoted in Norman Cigar, *Genocide in Bosnia. The Policy of 'Ethnic Cleansing'*, College Station: Texas A&M University Press, 1995, p. 18.
97 Vasa Čubrilović, Iseljavanje Arnauta', in Bože Čović (ed.) *Izvori velikosrpske agresije*, Zagreb: August Cesarec and Školska knjiga, 1991, pp. 106–24.
98 On the ethnic cleansing of Muslims during the Second World War, see Vladimir Dedijer, *Genocid na muslimana 1941–45, Zbornik documenta i svjedočenja*, Sarajevo: Svjetlost, 1990.
99 *Srbadija*, vol. 29, no. 2, November 1924, quoted in Nusret Šehić, *Četništvo u Bosni i Hercegovini (1918–1941). Politička uloga i oblici djelatnosti četničkih udruženja*, Sarajevo: Akademija nauka i umjetnosti Bosne i Hercegovine, 1971, p. 109.
100 Šehić, op. cit., p. 120.
101 Branko Horvat, *Kosovsko Pitanje*, Zagreb: Globus, 1989, p. 35.
102 Philip J. Cohen, *Serbia's Secret War. Propaganda and the Deceit of History*, College Station: Texas A&M Press, 1996, p. 440.
103 Šešelj, cited in Grmek *et al.* (eds), op. cit., p. 203.
104 Miroljub Jevtić, *Savremeni džihad kao rat*, Belgrade: Nova knjiga, 1989, p. 42ff.
105 Sabrina P. Ramet, 'Islam', in ibid., *Balkan Babel: The Disintegration of Yugoslavia from the Death of Tito to Ethnic War*, Boulder, Colorado: Westview, 1996, p. 185.
106 Cigar, op. cit., p. 27.
107 Ibid., pp. 30–2.
108 This was published in Belgrade by Serb nationalists and appeared in English translation as Alija Izetbegović, 'The Islamic Declaration: A Programme for the Islamicisation of Muslims and the Muslim Peoples', *South Slav Journal*, vol. 6, Spring 1983, 56–89.
109 Sells, op. cit., p. 118.
110 Vojislav Šešelj, *Pravo na istinu*, Belgrade: Multiprint, 1988, p. 8.
111 Bieber, op. cit., 2000, p. 21.
112 On interethnic relations and the question of rape see, Wendy Bracewell, 'Rape in

Kosovo: Masculinity and Serbian Nationalism', in *Nations and Nationalism*, vol. 6, no. 4, 2000, 563–90.

113 When Slovene public demonstrated in favour of the Albanian miners of Trepca in Spring 1989, this was seen as a 'racial' betrayal by many Serbs.

114 Judah, op. cit., p. 79.

115 John Allcock, op. cit., p. 398 comments that 'Yugoslavs have spontaneously talked about people being "put to the knife" as a synonym for ethnic extermination'.

116 Mark Thompson, *A Paper House. The Ending of Yugoslavia*, London: Hutchinson Radius, p. 130.

117 Judah, op. cit., p. 199.

118 Ed Vulliamy, *Seasons in Hell. Understanding Bosnia's War*, London: Simon and Schuster, 1994, p. 49.

119 Jan Willem Honig and Norbert Both, *Srebrenica. Record of a War Crime*, Harmondsworth: Penguin, 1996, pp. xviii–xix. Vojislav Šešelj also took on a messianic tone when discussing the position of the Serbs. He has warned that 'their struggle for national liberation may take . . . years, but ultimately Serbs will emerge victorious, with their nation intact and their state reconstructed', Jill Irvine, 'Nationalism and the Extreme Right in the Former Yugoslavia', in Luciano Cheles *et al.* (eds), *The Far Right in Eastern and Western Europe*, London: Longman, 1995, p. 149.

120 Florence Hartmann, *Milošević. La Diagonale du Fou*, Paris: Denoël, 1999, p. 247.

121 Homi K. Bhabha, 'By Bread Alone: Signs of Violence in the mid-Nineteenth Century', in ibid., *The Location of Culture*, London: Routledge, 1994, p. 200.

122 Dragan Popadić and Mikloš Biro, 'Autoostereotipi i Heterostereotipi Srba u Srbiji', *Nova Srpska Politička Misao*, Nr. 1–2 (1999), pp. 98–9, cited in Bieber, op. cit., (2001), p. 493.

123 Mitar Debelonogić, *Balije*, Jahorinski potok, 1997.

124 Margaret Vandiver, 'Reclaiming Kozarac. Accompanying returning refugees', in Dzemal Sokolović and Florian Bieber (eds), *Reconstructing Multiethnic Societies. The Case of Bosnia-Herzegovina*, Aldershot: Ashgate, 2001, p. 178.

125 Michael Sells, *The Bridge Betrayed: Religion and Genocide in Bosnia*, 2nd edn, Berkeley: University of California Press, 1998, p. 4.

126 Stanley Cohen, *States of Denial. Knowing about Atrocities and Suffering*, Cambridge: Polity Press, 2001, p. 5.

127 'Military Court in Niš raises issues of "cleaning up" in Kosovo', 6 November 2000 found at <http://groups.yahoo.com/group/balkanhr/message/1276> on 2 May 2001.

128 Marcus Tanner, *Croatia. A Nation Forged in War*, New Haven: Yale University Press, 1997, pp. 127–8.

129 Joško Caleta, 'Gusle moje, "nova" davorijo: Trends and Processes in the Music Making of Croatian Guslari at the Beginning of the 21ˢᵗ Century'. Paper delivered at the Mediterranean Ethnology Conference, Piran, 20 September 2001. The publication of a Turkish grammar by Ekrem Čaušević in Zagreb in 1996 evoked a similar reaction from the Croatian guslar Željko Šimić. See Žanić, op. cit., p. 40.

130 Sells, op. cit., pp. 118–19.

131 Obituary of Franjo Tudjman by Ian Traynor, *The Guardian*, 13 December 1999, 18.

132 Ivan Mazuranić, *Smrt Smail-age Čengijića*, Zagreb: Matica Hrvatska, 1952.

133 Marc Biondich, *Stjepan Radić, the Croat Peasant Party and the Politics of Mass Mobilization, 1904–1928*, Toronto: University of Toronto Press, 2000, pp. 102–3.

134 Hrvoje Matković, *Povijest Nezavisne Države Hrvatske*, Zagreb: Nakalda Pavičić, 1994, p. 119.

135 Tanner, op. cit., pp. 148–9.

136 Matković, op. cit., p. 119.

137 Misha Glenny, *The Rebirth of History. Eastern Europe in the Age of Democracy*, Harmondsworth: Penguin, 1990, p. 129.

138 Franjo Tudjman cited in Cornelia Sorabji, 'Islam and Bosnia's Muslim Nation', in F.W. Carter and H.T. Norris (eds), *The Changing Shape of the Balkans*, London: University College Press, 1996, p. 51.
139 Norman M. Naimark, *Fires of Hatred. Ethnic Cleansing in Twentieth Century Europe*, Cambridge, Massachusetts: Harvard University Press, 2001, p. 172.
140 Naimark, op. cit., pp. 172–3.
141 *Dom i Svijet*, Broj 291, 10, travanj, 2000 at <http://www.hic.hr/dom/291/dom22.htm> on 10 October 2001.
142 'Kordić and Cerkez trial: HVO tactics in central Bosnia' at <http://www.bosnet.org> on 10 October 2001.
143 Merima Nosić, quoted in Julie Mertus, Jasmina Tesanović, Habiba Metikos and Rada Borić, (eds), *The Suitcase. Refugee Voices from Bosnia and Croatia*, Berkeley: University of California Press, 1997, pp. 62–3.
144 Sorabji, in Carter and Norris (eds) op. cit., p. 59.
145 Stevan M. Weine, 'Redefining Merhamet after a Historical Nightmare', in Halpern and Kideckel (eds), op. cit., p. 404.
146 George Sava, *The Chetniks*, London: Regular Publication, 1955, p. 31.
147 Marjorie Housepian, *Smyrna 1922: the Destruction of a City*, London: Faber, 1972, p. 35.
148 Elisabeth Barker, 'The Origin of the Macedonian Dispute', in James Pettifer (ed.), *The New Macedonian Question*, Basingstoke: Palgrave, 2001, 2nd edn, p. 10.
149 Misha Glenny, *The Balkans 1804–1999. Nationalism, War and the Great Powers*, London: Granta, 1999, pp. 230–1.
150 Including the behaviour of Mujahedin who tortured and killed five Croats in Miletici. See, Kupreskić Judgement, VII–VIII, International Tribunal for the Prosecution of persons Responsible for serious Violations of International Humanitarian Law committed in the Territory of the Former Yugoslavia since 1991, 14 January 2000, at <http://www.pict-pcti.org/. . . CTY.01.14.kupreskic.html> on 10 October 2001.

3 Bandits and paramilitaries

1 Andrew Purvis, Dejan Anastasijević, James Graff and Massimo Calabresi, 'A Valley Full of Dangers', *Time*, 19 March 2001, 28.
2 Xavier Bougarel, in 'La "revanche des campagnes", entre réalité sociologique et mythe nationaliste', *Balkanologie*, vol. 2, no. 1, 1998, 17–36.
3 Traian Stoianovich, *Balkan Worlds: The First and Last Europe*, New York and London: Sharpe, 1994, pp. 167–8.
4 Catherine Wendy Bracewell, *The Uscoks of Senj. Piracy, Banditry and Holy War in the Sixteenth Century Adriatic*, Ithaca: Cornell University Press, 1992, p. 10.
5 Andrew Mango, *Atatürk*, London: John Murray, 1999, p. 11.
6 Stevan K. Pavlowitch, *A History of the Balkans 1804–1945*, London: Longman, 1999, p. 12.
7 George Sava, *The Chetniks*, London: Regular Publication, 1955, p. 105.
8 William Lithgow, *Discourse of a Peregrination in Europe, Asia and Affricke*, Amersterdam: Theatrum Orbis Terrarum: Da Capo Press, 1971, pp. 44–5.
9 David Urquhart, *The Spirit of the East, Illustrated in a Journal of Travels Through Roumeli During an Eventful Period*, Philadelphia: 1839, vol. II, pp. 118–19.
10 Stoianovich, op. cit., pp. 167–8.
11 Ibid., p. 169.
12 Misha Glenny, *The Balkans 1804–1999. Nationalism, War and the Great Powers*, London: Granta, 1999, p. 203.
13 Omer Ibrahimagić, *Srpsko osporavanje Bosne i Bošnjaka*, Sarajevo: Magistrat, 2001, pp. 255–6.
14 Mart Bax, 'Barbarization in a Bosnian Pilgrimage Center', in Joel M. Halpern and David A. Kideckel (eds), *Neighbors at War. Anthropological Perspectives on Yugoslav Ethnicity,*

Culture and History, Pennsylvania: Penn State Press, 2000, p. 199.

15 Mirjana Prošić-Dvornić, "'Druga Srbija": mirovni i ženski pokret', in ibid. (ed.), *Kulture u tranziciji*, Belgrade: Plato, 1994, p. 196, fn 17.

16 It has become common to assess the violent nature of states on whether their violence is central or peripheral. The violence of the British state is traditionally marginal to Westminster itself, but nonetheless its existence is crucial for the maintenance of the status quo, for example in Ulster.

17 In 1903, the gruesome assassination of Aleksandar Obrenović and his retinue 'sent a thrill of horror through the courts and countries of Europe', J.A.R Marriott, *The Eastern Question: an Historical Study in European Diplomacy*, Oxford: Clarendon Press, 1940, 4th edn, p. 425.

18 Pavlowitch, op. cit., p. 28.

19 Ivo Banac, *The National Question in Yugoslavia: Origins, History, Politics*, Ithaca: Cornell University Press, 1984, p. 304.

20 C.M. Woodhouse, *The Greek War of Independence: its Historical Setting*, London: Hutchinson, 1952, p. 74.

21 Leon Trotsky, *The Balkan Wars 1912–13*, New York: Monad Press, 1980, p. 234.

22 Sava, op. cit., p. 142.

23 Tim Judah, *Kosovo. War and Revenge*, New Haven: Yale University Press, 2000, p. 21.

24 Banac, op. cit., p. 303.

25 Ibid., p. 303.

26 Nusret Šehić, *Četništvo u Bosni i Hercegovini (1918–1941). Politička uloga i oblici djelatnosti Četničkih udruženja* Sarajevo: Akademija nauka i umjetnosti Bosne i Hercegovine, 1971, p. 10.

27 Matteo Milazzo, *The Chetnik Movement and Yugoslav Resistance*, Baltimore and London: Johns Hopkins University Press, 1975, p. 49.

28 Dedijer, op. cit., (1990), p. 392.

29 Mark Mazower, *Inside Hitler's Greece*, New Haven: Yale University Press, new edn, 2001, p. 129.

30 Ivo Goldstein, *Croatia: A History*, London: Hurst, 1999, p. 240.

31 Gordana Igrić, 'In Search of the Indicted', *Tribunal*, August/September, 1997, 4.

32 This thesis has been given extensive treatment in a brilliant monograph by Ivo Žanić, *Prevarena povijest. Guslarska estrada, kult Hajduka i rat u Hrvatskoj i Bosni i Hercegovini 1990–1995. Godine*, Zagreb: Durieux, 1998.

33 Mark Thompson, *Forging War. The Media in Serbia, Croatia, Bosnia and Hercegovina*, Luton: University of Luton Press/Article 19. Index Against Censorship, 1999, p. 352.

34 See Šehić, op. cit., p. 11.

35 Trotsky, op. cit., p. 61.

36 Dedijer, op. cit., (1990), p. 186.

37 Milazzo, op. cit., p. 21.

38 On the alternative culture in Slovenia in the 1980s, see James Gow and Cathie Carmichael, *Slovenia and the Slovenes. A Small State in the New Europe*, London: Hurst, 2000, pp. 94–101.

39 Pedro Ramet, 'The Rock Scene in Yugoslavia', *East European Politics and Societies*, vol. 2, no. 2, Spring 1988, 396–410.

40 Misha Glenny, *The Fall of Yugoslavia. The Third Balkan War*, Harmondsworth, Penguin: 1992, p. 43.

41 Mirjana Prošić-Dvornić, 'Serbia: the Inside Story', in Halpern and Kideckel (eds), op. cit., p. 330.

42 From my own memories of Zagreb in September 1994, there were also many visible signs of grief and trauma. I saw innumerable individuals with blue shrapnel wounds and in many public places there were small shrines and candles lit to the memory of those who had been killed. For a sensitive analysis on the impact of war on Croatian society see, Dunja Rihtman-Auguštin, "'We were proud to live with you and are now

immensely sad to have lost you". A chronicle of the war through newspaper death notices', *Narodna Umjetnost*, vol. 30, 1993, 279–302.

43 Marcus Tanner, *Croatia. A Nation Forged in War*, New Haven: Yale University Press, 1997, p. 265.

44 Kupreskić Judgement, VII-VIII, International Tribunal for the Prosecution of persons Responsible for serious Violations of International Humanitarian Law committed in the Territory of the Former Yugoslavia since 1991, 14 January 2000, at <http://www.pict-pcti.org/. . .CTY.01.14.kupreskic.html> on 10 October 2001.

45 Susan Woodward, *Balkan Tragedy. Chaos and Dissolution After the Cold War*, Washington: Brookings Institute, 1995, p. 355.

46 Norman M. Naimark, *Fires of Hatred. Ethnic Cleansing in Twentieth Century Europe*, Cambridge, Massachusetts: Harvard University Press, 2001, p. 161.

47 Laura Silber and Allan Little, *The Death of Yugoslavia*, Harmondsworth: Penguin, 1995, p. 247.

48 Andrew Purvis, Dejan Anastasijević and Massimo Calabresi, 'The Bloody Red Berets', *Time*, 19 March 2001, 28.

49 This concept was discussed with reference to the way in which historical practices have been revived and utilized for specifically nationalist purposes by Eric Hobsbawm and Terence Ranger (eds), in *The Invention of Tradition*, Cambridge: Cambridge University Press, 1992.

50 Stevan M. Weine, *When History is a Nightmare: Lives and Memories of Ethnic Cleansing in Bosnia-Herzegovina*, New Brunswick, New Jersey: Rutgers University Press, 1999, p. 46.

51 Julie Mertus, Jasmina Tesanović, Habiba Metikos and Rada Borić (eds), *The Suitcase. Refugee Voices from Bosnia and Croatia*, Berkeley: University of California Press, 1997, p. 32.

52 Zlata Filipović, *Zlata's Diary. A Child's Life in Sarajevo*, Harmondsworth: Penguin, 1994. p. 92.

53 Robert Thomas, *Serbian Politics in the 1990s: Between Authoritarianism and Pluralism*, London: Hurst, 1999, p. 58.

54 Slobodan Reljić, 'Demagogue in Waiting', *Transitions*, March, 1998, 72.

55 Anthony Grafton, 'Introduction', in Nicolo Machiavelli, *The Prince*, Harmondsworth: Penguin, 1999, p. xix.

56 Photograph reproduced in Lenard J. Cohen, *Serpent in the Bosom. The Rise and Fall of Slobodan Milošević*, Boulder, Colorado: Westview, 2001, between pp. 316–17. In the autumn of 2000, many newspapers carried a picture of newly elected Yugoslavian Prime Minister Vojislav Koštunica carrying a gun, exclaiming that although he was a 'nationalist' that he was also a 'democrat'.

57 Jill Irvine, 'Nationalism and the Extreme Right in the Former Yugoslavia', in Luciano Cheles *et al.* (eds). *The Far Right in Eastern and Western Europe*, London: Longman, 1995, p. 149.

58 Nina Dobrković, 'Yugoslavia and Macedonia in the Years 1991–6: From Brotherhood to Neighbourhood', in James Pettifer (ed.), *The New Macedonian Question*, Basingstoke, Palgrave, 2001, 2nd edn, p. 89.

59 Reljić, op. cit., pp. 72–3.

60 Correspondence supporting the nationalist viewpoint was collected in Vojislav Šešelj, *Pravo na istinu*, Beograd: Multiprint, 1988.

61 Šehić, op. cit., p. 11.

62 The term 'inat' which has come into Serbian and Croatian from Turkish is often used to describe the kind of bloody-mindedness of Balkan men in particular, although this trait is psychologically widespread and the word actually came to Serbian through Turkish from Sanskrit. Lack of fear or even a contempt for death was a traditional sign of bravery in the Classical epoch. For a discussion of the term see, Marko Živković, 'Inverted Perspective and Serbian Peasants: the Byzantine Revival in Serbia', at <http://www.ac.wwu.edu/~kritika/Anthro.html> on 1 June 2001.

63 Slavenka Drakulić, *Balkan Express. Fragments from the Other Side of War*, London: Hutchinson, 1993, pp. 99–100.
64 Branko Horvat, *Kosovsko Pitanje*, Zagreb: Globus, 1989, p. 35.
65 Georg Rosen, *Die Balkan-Haiduken*, Leipzig: F.A. Brockhaus, 1878, p. 117.
66 Ustaša carried elaborate knives forged in their factory in Serin with ornaments, braid work and the letter U. See Vladimir Dedijer, *The Yugoslav Auschwitz and the Vatican*, Buffalo, New York: Prometheus Books, 1992, p. 232.
67 Jozo Tomasević, *Četnici u drugom svjetskom ratu 1941–1945*, translated Nikica Petrak, Zagreb: Sveučilisna Nakalda Liber, 1979, p. 234.
68 Igrić, op. cit., p. 4.
69 Trotsky, op. cit., (1980), p. 187–91.
70 Ibid., p. 194.
71 The fact that the Turks did not always use bayonets was also observed by Walter Crawfurd Price in his study, *The Balkan Cockpit, the Political and Military Story of the Balkan Wars in Macedonia*, London: T. Werner Laurie, 1914, pp. 102–3.
72 Joanna Bourke, *An Intimate History of Killing. Face to Face Killing in Twentieth Century Europe*, London: Granta, 1999, pp. 89–93.
73 Slavoj Žižek has argued this in *NATO kao lijeva ruka Boga?/NATO as the Left hand of God?*, Ljubljana- Zagreb: Bastard Biblioteque, 1999, p. 27.
74 Fikreta Jelić-Butić, *Četnici u Hrvatskoj 1941–1945*, Zagreb: Globus, 1986, p. 162.
75 Jelić-Bulić, op. cit., p. 157.
76 Milazzo, op. cit., p. 103.
77 Šehić, op. cit., p. 11. Intoxication from the 'russet wine *(rujno vino)* so often poured for the heroes in epic ballads' was an important element in one incident of excessive violence in 1605, for which the Uskoks blamed themselves. Bracewell, op. cit., p. 167.
78 A Macedonian JNA officer told Misha Glenny, op. cit. (1992), p. 125, that Croats took drugs and drunk during the war in Croatia in 1991.
79 Martin Bell, *In Harm's Way. Reflections of a War-Zone Thug*, Harmondsworth: Penguin, 1996, p. 20.
80 Ed Vulliamy, *Seasons in Hell. Understanding Bosnia's War*, London: Simon and Schuster, 1994, p. 46.
81 Laura Silber and Allan Little, *The Death of Yugoslavia*, Harmondsworth: Penguin, 1995, p. 109.
82 Roy Gutman, *A Witness to Genocide: The First Inside Account of the Horrors of Ethnic Cleansing in Bosnia*, Shaftesbury: Element, 1993, p. 71.
83 Mary Douglas, *Purity and Danger: An Analysis of the Concepts of Pollution and Taboo*, London: Routledge and Kegan Paul, 1966, pp. 35–7.
84 Hobsbawm, E., *Bandits*, Harmondsworth: Penguin, 1985, p. 78.
85 Tim Judah, *The Serbs. History, Myth and Destruction of Yugoslavia*, New Haven: Yale University Press, 1997, p. 50.
86 Vladimir Dedijer (ed.), *The War Diaries of Vladimir Dedijer*, Ann Arbor: University of Michigan Press, vol. 1, 1990, p. 43.
87 As Dunja Rihtman-Auguštin has noted ironically in her, *Ulice moga grada. Antropologija domaćeg terena*, Belgrade: Biblioteka XX vek, 2000, p. 19.
88 Vulliamy, op. cit., p. 54.
89 Dona Kolar-Panov, *Video, War and the Diasporic Imagination*, London: Routledge, 1997, p. 161.
90 Kolar-Panov, op. cit., p. 161.
91 Vitomir Belaj, 'Jokes about the Serbs, Autumn 1991', *Etnološka stičišča*, vols 5 and 7, 1997, pp. 49.
92 Dubravka Ugrešić, *The Culture of Lies*, Pennsylvania: Penn State Press, 1998, p. 61.
93 Many Yugoslavs in the early 1990s prefaced remarks about the atrocities committed by Serb paramilitaries with comments like 'they [i.e. the Serbs] were the best'. The author was informed by a Slovene doctor, DČ, in October 1989, that she had lived in Serbia

as a refugee from the Third Reich from 1941 until 1945 (parts of Slovene ethnic territory were redefined as part of the *Altreich* at this time and the Slovenes deemed suitable for Germanization). What had most impressed her about the family who had taken her in was that they had looked after her entirely free of charge (*'brezplačeno'*) and had never expected any kind of financial compensation. The vogue for choosing Serb Christian names in Slovenia after the war must in part be linked to a genuine popular Serbophile sentiment.

94 Cohen, op. cit., p. 135.
95 Glenny, op. cit. (1992), p. 39.
96 Peter Finn and R. Jeffrey Smith, 'Kosovo's Hit-and-Run Ground War', *Guardian Weekly*, 2 May 1999, 15.
97 Naimark, op. cit., p. 172.
98 Mirko Grmek, Marc Gjidara and Neven Šimac (eds), *Etničko Čišćenje. Povijesni dokumenti o jednoj srpskoj ideologiji*, Zagreb: Nakladni zavod Globus, 1993, p. 82.
99 Kupreskić Judgement, VII–VIII, International Tribunal for the Prosecution of persons Responsible for serious Violations of International Humanitarian Law committed in the Territory of the Former Yugoslavia since 1991, 14 January 2000, at <http://www.pict-pcti.org/...CTY.01.14.kupreskic.html> on 10 October 2001.
100 Stanoje Jovanović and Dragan Jerković, *Zločin Hrvatske države '91*, Belgrade: Vojni muzej, 1991, p. 10.
101 Jelena Lovrić, 'Dario Kordić: the Croatian Karadžić', *Tribunal*, November/December, 1996, 5.
102 Misha Glenny, op. cit. (1999), pp. 108–9.
103 Mango, op. cit., p. 329.
104 Judah, op. cit., p. 248.
105 Jill Irvine, 'Nationalism and the Extreme Right in the Former Yugoslavia', in Luciano Cheles *et al.* (eds), *The Far Right in Eastern and Western Europe*, London: Longman, 1995, pp. 159–60.
106 Gabriel Partos, 'Macedonia rebels fear reprisals', BBC News 4 September 2001, at <http://www.bbc.co.uk>
107 Noel Malcolm, *Bosnia: a Short History*, London: Macmillan, 1994, p. 252.
108 John B. Allcock, *Explaining Yugoslavia*, London: Hurst, 2000, p. 407.
109 '. . . the Second World War in Yugoslavia was several civil wars . . . extreme nationalists on all sides were able to indulge their wildest fantasies', Chris Bennett, *Yugoslavia's Bloody Collapse Causes, Course and Consequences*, London: Hurst, 1995, pp. 47–8.
110 Given the regular thuggish behaviour by the England team 'supporters' across Europe and the activities of the far right amongst this group, some instructive parallels might be made here.
111 Naimark, op. cit., p. 161.
112 Tim Judah, *The Serbs. History, Myth and Destruction of Yugoslavia*, New Haven: Yale University Press, 1997, p. 186.
113 Judah, op. cit., p. 186.
114 Florian Bieber, *Serbischer Nationalismus vom Tod Titos zum Sturz Miloševićs*, Unpublished Doctoral Dissertation, Vienna University, March 2001, p. 208. On the rise of bandit culture see also the important work of Ivan Čolović, especially *Bordel ratnika. Folklor, politika i rat*, Belgrade: Biblioteka XX vek, 1993, especially pp. 61–70.
115 Martin Bell, *In Harm's Way. Reflections of a War-Zone Thug*, Harmondsworth: Penguin, 1996, p. 20.
116 Purvis, Anastasijević and Calabresi, op. cit., pp. 28–9.
117 Some of the observations in this paragraph are based on discussion between the author and the Montenegrin journalist Rada Stojanović, who interviewed a number of 'amateur fighters' during the war in Bosnia for the journal *Monitor*.
118 Stevan M. Weine, *When History is a Nightmare: Lives and Memories of Ethnic Cleansing in Bosnia-Herzegovina*, New Brunswick, New Jersey: Rutgers University Press, 1999, p. 53.

119 Gérard Prunier, *The Rwanda Crisis. History of a Genocide 1959–1994*, London: Hurst, 1995, p. 243.

120 Jonathan Steele, 'They Tracked Us Day and Night. Then They Gunned Us Down', *Guardian Weekly*, 15–21 July 1999, 3.

121 Žanić, op. cit., pp. 169–70.

122 In Bosnia, Muslims had a spell to return the 'evil eye' to Romanija, which was associated with extreme Serb nationalism. Tone Bringa, *Being Muslim the Bosnian Way*, Princeton: Princeton University Press, 1995, p. 180.

123 Pawel Pawlikowski, dir. *Serbian Epics*, BBC films, 1992.

124 Jan Willem Honig and Norbert Both, *Srebrenica. Record of a War Crime*, Harmondsworth: Penguin, 1996, p. 36–7.

125 Ugrešić, op. cit., p. 125.

126 Judah, op. cit., p. 19.

4 Fascism and Communism

1 Ante Pavelić assembled and published his views in Berlin in 1941 as *Die Kroatische Frage* to align them with mainstream Nazism.

2 The most spectacular example of this was the assassination of Aleksandar Karadjordjević in 1934, by a Macedonian VMRO agent who was supported by the Ustaša in exile in Italy and ultimately by the Italian government.

3 For the case of Yugoslavia see, Laslo Sekelj, 'Anti-Semitism in Yugoslavia, 1918–1945', *East European Quarterly*, vol. 22, no. 2, 1988, 159–172.

4 On the history of the Balkan Jews, see Esther Benbassa, *Juifs des Balkans: espaces judéo-ibériques, XIVe-Xxe siècles*, Paris: La Découverte, 1993.

5 Some of the variety of Jewish life among the Ladino speakers of Bulgaria is conveyed by Elias Canetti in his autobiographical reminiscences, *Die gerettete Zunge: Geschichte einer Jugend*, Frankfurt am Main: Fischer, 1979.

6 Ivo Goldstein, *Croatia: A History*, London: Hurst, 1999, p. 158.

7 Daniel Elazar, 'The Sunset of Balkan Jewry', in Daniel Elazar et al. (eds), *The Balkan Jewish Communities: Yugoslavia, Bulgaria, Greece and Turkey*, Lanham, Maryland: University Press of America, 1984, p. 6.

8 Misha Glenny, *The Balkans 1804–1999. Nationalism, War and the Great Powers*, London: Granta, 1999, p. 502.

9 Walter Manoscek, cited in Glenny, op. cit., p. 502.

10 Mark Thompson, *A Paper House: The Ending of Yugoslavia*, London: Hutchinson Radius, 1992, p. 224.

11 Artan Peto, 'La communauté juive en Albanie avant et durant la seconde guerre mondiale', in Ioannes K. Chasiotes et al. (eds), *The Jewish Communities of Southeastern Europe: From the Fifteenth Century to the End of World War II*, Salonika: Institute for Balkan Studies, 1997, pp. 427–31.

12 Mark Mazower, *Inside Hitler's Greece*, New Haven: Yale University Press, new edn, 2001, p. 241.

13 Mazower, op. cit., p. 240.

14 Ibid., pp. 237–8.

15 Michael Sells, *The Bridge Betrayed: Religion and Genocide in Bosnia*, 2nd edn, Berkeley: University of California Press, 1998, p. 2.

16 Sells, op. cit., p. 2.

17 Jacques Klein, Press statement on the UNMIBH-UNESCO Sarajevo Haggadah Project, at <http://www.unmibh.org/news/srsgspe/2001/06apr01.htm> on 15 December 2001.

18 Goldstein, op.cit., p. 136.

19 Adolf Dressler, *Kroatien*, Essen: Essenerverlangsanstalt, 1942, pp. 157–9.

20 The conditions at Jasenovac are discussed extensively and illustrated by a series of

graphic photographic records in Vladimir Dedijer, *The Yugoslav Auschwitz and the Vatican*, Buffalo, New York: Prometheus Books, 1992, p. 130. From the late 1980s onwards the issue of whether the Communists had manipulated the 'symbol' of the deathcamp was discussed quite heatedly. On this see the exchange between Ljubo Boban, 'Jasenovac and the Manipulation of History', *East European Politics and Societies*, vol. 4, no. 3, 1990, 580–92 and Robert Hayden, 'Balancing Discussion of Jasenovac and the Manipulation of History', *East European Politics and Societies*, vol. 6, no. 2, 1992, 207–17.

21 Goldstein, op. cit., p. 158.
22 Glenda Sluga, *The Problem of Trieste and the Italo-Yugoslav Border. Difference, Identity and Sovereignty in Twentieth Century Europe*, New York: SUNY, 2000, pp. 90–1.
23 Josip Mirnić, *Nemci u Bačkoj u drugom svetskom ratu*, Novi Sad: Institut za izučavanje istorije Vojvodine, 1974, pp. 341.
24 Borislav Pekić, *Godine koje su pojeli skakavci*, vol. II, Belgrade: BIGZ Jedinstvo, 1991, pp. 140–5.
25 Two scholars at the conference 'Ethnic Cleansing in Twentieth Century Europe' at Duquesne University, Pittsburgh, 16–18 November 2000, suggested that treatment of Germans in 1944–6 was extremely brutal. Raymond Lohne, 'The Experience of Ethnic Cleansing. The Case of the Danube Swabians of Yugoslavia' and John Schindler, 'Yugoslavia's First Ethnic Cleansing. The Expulsion of Danubian Germans, 1944–46'. These papers will appear in a forthcoming volume edited by Hunt Tooley and Steven Vardy under the title *Ethnic Cleansing in Twentieth Century Europe*.
26 Marcus Tanner, *Croatia. A Nation Forged in War*, New Haven: Yale University Press, 1997, p. 228.
27 Fikreta Jelić-Butić, *Četnici u Hrvatskoj 1941–1945*, Zagreb, Globus, 1986, p. 28.
28 Goldstein, op. cit., p. 137.
29 Aleksandar Pavković, *The Fragmentation of Yugoslavia. Nationalism and War in the Balkans*, London, Macmillan, 2000, p. 32.
30 This footage was used to dramatic effect by Emir Kusturica in his film *Underground*, which won a Prix d'Or in Cannes in 1995. He used the background music *Lili Marlene*, with all its Nazi associations throughout the film to remind the audience of the fascist legacy and the achievements of the Partisans.
31 Tanner, op. cit., p. 151.
32 Dedijer, op. cit., (1992), pp. 157–8.
33 Srdja Pavlović, 'Understanding Balkan Nationalism: the Wrong People, in the Wrong Place, at the Wrong Time' *Southeast European Politics*, vol. 1, no. 2, 2000, 120.
34 Dedijer, op. cit., (1992), p. 289.
35 Aleksa Djilas, *The Contested Country: Yugoslav Unity and Communist Revolution 1919–1953*, Cambridge, Massachusetts: Harvard University Press, 1991, p. 121.
36 Francine Friedman, *The Bosnian Muslims. Denial of a Nation*, Boulder: Colorado: Westview, 1996, p. 124.
37 Djilas, op. cit., p. 120.
38 Dinko Tomašić, 'Croatia in European Politics', *Journal of Central European Affairs*, vol. 2, 1942, 76.
39 Misha Glenny, *The Balkans 1804–1999. Nationalism, War and the Great Powers*, London: Granta, 1999, p. 434.
40 Glenny, op. cit., p 434.
41 Ivo Banac, *The National Question in Yugoslavia: Origins, History, Politics*, Ithaca: Cornell University Press, 1984, p. 87.
42 Banac, op. cit., p. 88.
43 John B. Allcock, *Explaining Yugoslavia*, London: Hurst, 2000, 332.
44 Miron Krešimir Begić, *Ustaški Pokret 1929–1941: pregled njegove poviesti*, Buenos Aires: Naklada Smotre Ustaša, 1986, p. 94.
45 Nikola Stojanović, quoted in Marc Biondich, *Stjepan Radić, the Croat Peasant Party and the*

Politics of Mass Mobilization, 1904–1928, Toronto: University of Toronto Press, 2000, p. 20.

46 Goldstein, op. cit., p. 147.

47 Srdja Trifković, 'Rivalry between Germany and Italy in Croatia', *Historical Journal*, vol. 36, 1993, 539.

48 Djilas, op. cit., p. 123.

49 Dedijer, op. cit., (1992), p. 130.

50 Djilas, op. cit., 127.

51 Ibid., p. 127.

52 Some controversial details about the murder of non-Communists and the British role in helping the Communists by 'returning' non-Communists to Yugoslavia are discussed in Nikolai Tolstoy, 'The Klagenfurt Conspiracy: War Crimes and Diplomatic Secrets, *Encounter*, vol. 60, no. 5, 1983, 24–37.

53 On Pavelić' final years see, Bogdan Križman, *Pavelić u bjekstvu*, Zagreb: Globus, 1986.

54 Sabrina P. Ramet, *Nationalism and Federalism in Yugoslavia 1962–1991*, Bloomington: Indiana University Press, 2nd edn, 1994, pp. 98–135.

55 It has been suggested to me by an acquaintance of Tudjman's that the experience of imprisonment adversely affected his mental health. Similarly there are claims that the 'insanity' of Vojislav Šešelj was activated after he was abused in prison in the mid-1980s. Certainly the ability of the Communist regime to break down its opponents should not be underestimated, but nor should the 'method in madness' that these opponents subsequently displayed.

56 Begić, op. cit., text on inside cover.

57 Jill Irvine, 'Nationalism and the Extreme Right in the Former Yugoslavia', in Luciano Cheles *et al.* (eds), *The Far Right in Eastern and Western Europe*, London: Longman, 1995, p. 151.

58 Irvine, op. cit., p. 149.

59 Ian Traynor, 'In the Cause of Croatia. Obituary of Gojko Sušak', *The Guardian*, 5 May 1998, 16.

60 See, for example, Franjo Tudjman, *Bespuća povijesne zbiljnosti: Rasprava o povijesti i filozofiji zlosilja*, Zagreb: Hrvatska Sveučilisna Naklada, 5th edn, 1994.

61 The ethnologist Maja Povrzanović was a resident of Dubrovnik during the siege. See her, 'Crossing the Borders: Croatian War Ethnographies', *Narodna umjetnost*, vol. 32, no. 1, 1995, 91–106.

62 A memorial beside the town wall in Dubrovnik reminds visitors of the destruction wreaked by 'Serbs and Montenegrins' to the city in 1991. It is in part through memorialization that relations with the neighbouring states are historically fixed by the actions of a few individuals during war and all Montenegrins (or Serbs) thus become indelibly linked with the terrible winter of 1991.

63 In 1994, I received a gift of a box of chocolates manufactured by Kraš in Zagreb, in which the chocolates had been arranged in the shape of the Croatian chequerboard (*šahovnica*), with a lurid mixture of white and red wrapped pralines to represent the colours of the flag.

64 A parallel process of ethnicization took place in Serbia, particularly after 1991. On this see, Lenard J. Cohen, *Serpent in the Bosom. The Rise and Fall of Slobodan Milošević*, Boulder, Colorado: Westview, 2001, especially pp. 101–3.

65 Vladimir Brodnjak, *Razlikovni rječnik srpskog i hrvatskog jezika*, Zagreb, 1993.

66 On the subject of the 'cleansing' of the Croatian language in the early 1940s see, Marko Samardžija, *Jezični purizam u NDH*, Zagreb: Hrvatska Sveučilisna Naklada, 1993.

67 Norman Cigar, 'The Serbo-Croatian War', in Stjepan Meštrović (ed.), *Genocide after Emotion. The Postemotional Balkan War*, London, Routledge, 1996, p. 75.

68 Dona Kolar-Panov, *Video, War and the Diasporic Imagination*, London: Routledge, 1997, p. 172.

69　Laura Silber and Allan Little, *The Death of Yugoslavia*, Harmondsworth: Penguin, 1995, p. 157.

70　Stanoje Jovanović and Dragan Jerković, *Zločin Hrvatske države '91*, Belgrade, Vojni muzej, 1991, p. 21.

71　Frantz Fanon, *The Wretched of the Earth*, Harmondsworth: Penguin, 1961, p. 240.

72　Miro Bajramović quoted in Zoran Dalasković, 'The Confessions begin', *War Report*, no. 55, October 1997, 9.

73　Ibid., p. 254.

74　Goldstein, op. cit., pp. 253–4.

75　James Gow, *Triumph of the Lack of Will: International Diplomacy and the Yugoslav War*, London: Hurst, 1997, p. 43.

76　Mirko Grmek, Marc Gjidara and Neven Šimac (eds), *Etničko Čišćenje. Povijesni dokumenti o jednoj srpskoj ideologiji*, Zagreb: Nakladni zavod Globus, 1993, p. 8.

77　John R. Lampe, *Yugoslavia as History. Twice There Was a Country*, Cambridge: Cambridge University Press, 2000, p. 204.

78　Stjepan Meštrović, Slaven Letica and Miroslav Goreta, *Habits of the Balkan Heart. Social Character and the Fall of Communism*, College Station: Texas A&M University Press, 1993, p. 142.

5 The death of the hero cult

1　Glenda Sluga, *Bonegilla: 'A Place of No Hope'*, Melbourne: Melbourne University Press, 1988, p. ix.

2　I have chosen the Serbian spelling for this region for historical reasons in the context of this chapter and because the word actually means something in that language (i.e. 'of blackbirds'). More recently Kosova or Kosovë, (the Albanian forms) have been used. In his book, *NATO kao lijeva ruka Boga?/NATO as the Left hand of God?* Ljubljana/Zagreb: Bastard Biblioteque, 1999, Slavoj Žižek adopts the spelling Kosov@ to retain both the a and the o.

3　Slobodan Milošević, *Naša Borba*, 14 June 1996, quoted in Edit Petrović, 'Ethnonationalism and the Dissolution of Yugoslavia', in Joel M. Halpern and David A. Kideckel (eds), *Neighbors at War. Anthropological Perspectives on Yugoslav Ethnicity, Culture and History*, Pennsylvania: Penn State Press, 2000, p. 170.

4　Leon Trotsky, *The Balkan Wars 1912–13*, New York: Monad Press, 1980, p. 62.

5　Ivo Banac, *The National Question in Yugoslavia: Origins, History, Politics*, Ithaca: Cornell University Press, 1984, p. 292.

6　I.e. Bakarno Guvno, the furthest limit of the medieval Serbian kingdom.

7　Trotsky, op. cit., (1980), p. 122.

8　Noel Malcolm, *Kosovo A Short History*, London: Macmillan, 1998, p. 67.

9　Michael Sells, *The Bridge Betrayed: Religion and Genocide in Bosnia*, 2nd edn, Berkeley: University of California Press, 1998, p. 31.

10　This betrayal complex is discussed in Florian Bieber, *Serbischer Nationalismus vom Tod Titos zum Sturz Miloševićs*, Unpublished Doctoral Dissertation, Vienna University, March 2001, p. 472.

11　Laura Silber and Allan Little, *The Death of Yugoslavia*, Harmondsworth: Penguin, 1995, pp. 215–16.

12　RS in an interview with the author, 15 March 1999.

13　Teofil Pančić, 'After U2', *Vreme*, 23 October 1997, reprinted at <http://www.bosnia.org.uk/bosrep/novdec97/afteru2.htm> on 15 October 2001.

14　Julie Mertus, *Kosovo: How Myths and Truths Started a War*, Berkeley: University of California Press, 1999, p. 184.

15　Mark Wheeler, 'One Nation or Many?', in Noll Scott and Derek Jones (eds), *Bloody Bosnia. A European Tragedy*, London, Broadcasting Support Services in association with Channel Four and *The Guardian*, 1994, p. 21.

16 Dragoljub Ojdanić quoted in *Vikend (Danas)*, 14 March 2001. Found at <http://www.danas/co.yu/20010317/vikend8.htm> on 5 September 2001.

17 This symbolism is discussed at some length in Sells, op. cit., pp. 86–92.

18 See for example, Ivan Čolović, 'Vreme i prostor u savremenoj političkoj mitologiji', in Mirjana Prošić-Dvornić (ed.), *Kulture u tranziciji*, Belgrade: Plato, 1994, p. 124.

19 Jovan Cvijić, *La péninsule balkanique. Geographie humaine*, Paris: A. Colin, 1918, p. 282.

20 Omer Ibrahimagić, *Srpsko osporavanje Bosne i Bošnjaka*, Sarajevo: Magistrat, 2001, p. 209.

21 Denis, quoted in Paul Garde, 'Les Balkans vus de France au XXe siécle', *Esprit*, December 2000, 22.

22 Both quotations from Bećković are from Robert Thomas, *Serbia under Milošević. Politics in the 1990s*, London: Hurst, 1999, p. 49.

23 Tone Bringa, *Being Muslim the Bosnian Way*, Princeton: Princeton University Press 1995, p. 167.

24 Noel Malcolm, *Kosovo: a Short History*, London: Macmillan, 1998, p. 10.

25 Lenard J. Cohen, *Serpent in the Bosom. The Rise and Fall of Slobodan Milosevic*, Boulder, Colorado: Westview, 2001, p. 224.

26 The phrase was popularized by Dimitrije Bogdanović, *Knjiga o Kosovu*, Belgrade: Srpska akademija nauka i umetnosti, 1985, p. 7.

27 Ervin Hladnik-Milharčič and Ivo Štandeker, 'Tako v nebesih kot na zemlji', *Mladina* 7 June 1989, 8.

28 International Commission on Kosovo, *The Kosovo Report: Conflict: International Response: Lessons Learned*, Oxford: Oxford University Press, 2000, p. 49.

29 Julie Mertus, 'Women in Kosovo: Contested Terrains. The Role of National Identity in Shaping and Challenging Gender Identity', in Sabrina P. Ramet (ed.), *Gender Politics in the Western Balkans: Women and Society in Yugoslavia and the Yugoslav Successor States*, Pennsylvania: Penn State University Press, 1999, p. 173.

30 Chris Bird, 'Living with the enemy next door', *Guardian Weekly*, 16–22 September 1999, 4.

31 See '"Memorandum" (grupa akademika Srpske akademije nauka i umetnosti o aktuelnim drustvenim pitanjima u našoj zemlji)', in Boze Čović (ed.), *Izvori velikosrpske agresije*, Zagreb: August Cesarec & Skolska knjiga, 1993, pp. 296–300.

32 Laura Silber and Allan Little, *The Death of Yugoslavia*, Harmondsworth: Penguin, 1995, p. 75–7.

33 Banac, op. cit., pp. 371–2.

34 Julie Mertus, *Kosovo: How Myths and Truths started a War*, Berkeley: University of California Press, 1999, p. 106.

35 This subject is discussed by Wendy Bracewell, 'Rape in Kosovo: Masculinity and Serbian Nationalism', *Nations and Nationalism*, vol. 6, no. 4, 2000, 570.

36 Sabrina P. Ramet (ed.), *Balkan Babel: The Disintegration of Yugoslavia From the Death of Tito to Ethnic War*, Boulder, Colorado: Westview, 1996, p. 185.

37 Homi K. Bhabha, 'The Other Question. Stereotype, Discrimination and the Discourse of Colonialism', in ibid., *The Location of Culture*, London: Routledge, 1994 p. 66.

38 Mertus, op. cit., p. 109.

39 A recent discussion with undergraduates on nationalism in the former Yugoslavia at Middlesex University brought home this point. One student who was doing an essay on Ivo Andrić recounted the famous and very vivid impalement scene in *Na Drini Ćuprija* (Bridge on the Drina) almost verbatim. The students remembered this part of the seminar more clearly than anything else that was discussed that day.

40 Wendy Bracewell, 'Women, Motherhood and Contemporary Serbian Nationalism', paper delivered at History Workshop Conference, Leeds, 1994, p. 14.

41 Jandranka Slatina published a report on the killings in Travnik in Bosnia in the Banja Luka newspaper *Nezavisne Novine* in September 1999, almost four years after the

signing of the Dayton Peace Treaty. 'Bosnian Serb Daily breaks Taboo' <http://www.iwpr.net/balkans/news> on 17 September 1999.

42 Roy Gutman, *A Witness to Genocide: The First Inside Account of the Horrors of Ethnic Cleansing in Bosnia*, Shaftesbury: Element, 1993, p. 41.

43 International Commission on Kosovo, op. cit., pp. 68–9.

44 Ibid., p. 74.

45 Ibid., p. 90.

46 Ibid., p. 91.

47 Bracewell, op. cit., pp. 563–90.

48 Caroline Kennedy-Pipe and Penny Stanley, 'Rape in War. Lesssons of the Balkan Conflicts in the 1990s', in Ken Booth (ed.), *The Kosovo Tragedy. The Human Rights Dimension*, London: Frank Cass, 2001, p. 69.

49 Justin McCarthy, *Death and Exile, The Ethnic Cleansing of Ottoman Muslims 1821–1922*, Princeton: Darwin Press, 1996, p. 72.

50 'Turkish Outrages', *The Times* 26 August 1903, cited in Ryan Gingeras, 'Macedonia in Crisis: British Press Coverage of the Ilinden Uprising of 1903 and the Conceptualization of the Balkans', Paper delivered at the 6th World Congress of the Association for the Study of Nationalities (ASN), Columbia University 5–7 April 2001.

51 George Kennan (ed.), *The Other Balkan Wars: a 1913 Carnegie Endowment Inquiry in Retrospect*, Washington DC: Carnegie Endowment for International Peace, 1993, p. 305.

52 Peter Maass, *Love the Neighbor. A Story of War*. New York: Vintage, 1996, p. 7.

53 Dubravka Ugrešić, *The Culture of Lies*, Pennsylvania: Penn State Press, 1998, p. 117.

54 Lydia Sklevicky, *Konji, Žene, Ratovi*, edited postumously by Dunja Rihtman-Auguštin, Zagreb: Druga, 1996.

55 Andrei Simić, 'Machismo and Cryptomatriachy: Power, Affect and Authority in the Traditional Yugoslav Family', in Ramet (ed.), op. cit., p. 25.

56 Maria Todorova, *Imagining the Balkans*, New York/Oxford: Oxford University Press 1997, p. 14.

57 P. B. Joanne, *États du Danube et des Balkans*. Première Partie, Paris: Librarie Hachette, 1895, p. 187. See also an earlier description in, *Die Türkische Nachbarländer an der Südostgrenze Österreichs: Serbien, Bosnien, Türkisch-Kroatien, Herzegovina und Montenegro*, Pest, Wien und Leipzig: Hartleben's Verlag-Expedition, 1854, pp. 57–8.

58 Brendan Simms, *Unfinest Hour: Britain and the Destruction of Bosnia*, London: Allen Lane, 2001, p. 284.

59 Stevan M. Weine, *When History is a Nightmare: Lives and Memories of Ethnic Cleansing in Bosnia-Herzegovina*, New Brunswick, New Jersey: Rutgers University Press, 1999, p. 48.

60 Norman M. Naimark, *Fires of Hatred. Ethnic Cleansing in Twentieth Century Europe*, Cambridge, Massachusetts: Harvard University Press, 2001, p. 168.

61 Iztok Durjava, 'Boris Kobe: Taboriščni Tarok, 1945', in Božidar Jezernik, *Spol in spolnost in extremis: antropološka študija o nemških koncentracijskih taboršćih Dachau, Buchenwald, Mauthausen, Ravensbrück, Auschwitz 1933–1945*, Ljubljana: Borec, 1993, p. 244.

62 Molly Moore, 'NATO Troops find Serbian Torture Cell', *Guardian Weekly*, 27 June 1999, 15.

63 Naimark, op. cit., 168.

64 Obrad Kesić, 'Women and Gender Imagery in Bosnia: Amazons, Sluts, Victims, Witches and Wombs', in Sabrina P. Ramet (ed.), *Gender Politics in the Western Balkans: Women and Society in Yugoslavia and the Yugoslav Successor States*, Pennsylvania: Penn State University Press, 1999, p. 187.

65 Kesić, op. cit., p. 192.

66 Ibid., pp. 192–3.

67 Omarska-Keraterm trial. Žigić's brutal quest for a family's 'pot of gold'. At <http://www.iwpr.net> on 3 October 2001.

68 Dušan Makavejev dir. *Montenegro – or Pearl and Pigs*, 1981.

69 Naimark, op. cit., p. 173.
70 Anastasia N. Karakasidou, *Fields of Wheat, Hills of Blood. Passages to Nationhood in Greek Macedonia 1870–1990*, Chicago: University of Chicago Press, 1997, pp. 151–2.
71 Dorothy Q. Thomas and Regan E. Ralph, 'Rape in War: The Case of Bosnia', in Ramet (ed.), op. cit., pp. 207.
72 This point was articulated originally by Susan Brownmiller in, *Against Our Will: Men, Women and Rape*, New York: Simon and Schuster, 1975.
73 Julie Mertus, Jasmina Tesanović, Habiba Metikos and Rada Borić, (eds), *The Suitcase. Refugee Voices from Bosnia and Croatia*, Berkeley: University of California Press, 1997, p. 138.
74 Marjorie Housepian, *Smyrna 1922: the Destruction of a City*, London: Faber, 1972, p. 150.
75 Rezak Hukanović, *The Tenth Circle of Hell. A Memoir of Life in the Death Camps of Bosnia*, London: Abacus, 1998, pp. 43–4.
76 Kennedy-Pipe and Stanley, in Booth (ed.), op. cit., p. 79.
77 Madeleine Rees and Sarah Maguire, 'Rape as a Crime against Humanity', *Tribunal*, November/December, 1996, 8.
78 'Tableau des Bouches du Cattaro suivi d'une Notice sur Montenegro', *Annales des Voyages*, Tome Quatrième, X–XII Paris, 1808, 223.
79 Cyprien Robert, *Les Slaves de Turquie*, Paris: L. Passard et Jules Labitte, 1844, p. 178.
80 Trotsky, op. cit., (1980), p. 121.
81 Anton Antonowicz, 'The Widow of a Warlord Who Believes She's a Star', *Mirror*, 28 July 2001, 26–7.
82 Bracewell, op. cit., (2000), p. 581.
83 Ivo Žanić, *Prevarena povijest. Guslarska estrada, kult Hajduka i rat u Hrvatskoj i Bosni i Hercegovini 1990–1995. Godine*, Zagreb: Durieux, 1998, p. 28.
84 Nebojsa Čagorović, 'Montenegrin Identity: Past, Present and Future', *Journal of Area Studies*, vol. 3, 1993, 135.
85 Haris Silajdžić, 'Human Rights in Bosnia and Hercegovina'. A document released by the foreign ministry in Sarajevo on 15 June 1993, in Gale Stokes (ed.) *From Stalinism to Pluralism: A Documentary History of Eastern Europe Since 1945*, Oxford: Oxford University Press, 2nd edn, 1996, p. 287.
86 Marlise Simons, 'France Examines Its Role in Run-up to Srebrenica', *International Herald Tribune*, 12 December 2000, 8.
87 Naimark, op. cit., p. 169 observes that Ratko Mladić told a reporter that his men never raped women: 'We Serbs . . . are too picky.'
88 For a recent account of conditions in Republika Srpska, see 'Nadnica za Grijeh. Sučeljavanje za Republikom Srpskom u Bosni', 8 October 2001 at <http://www.intl-crisis-group/projects.balkans/bosnia/reports/A400476š08102001.pdf> on 11 November 2001.
89 Tim Judah, *The Serbs. History, Myth and Destruction of Yugoslavia*, New Haven: Yale University Press, 1997, p. 3.

6 The destruction of community

1 The word in French for a mixed fruit or vegetable salad was coined from the word for Macedonia, meaning a mixture of complementary elements.
2 James Pettifer, 'The New Macedonian Question', in James Pettifer (ed.), *The New Macedonian Question*, Basingstoke, Palgrave, 2001, 2nd edn, p. 17.
3 Keith Brown, 'The Macedonian Question', in *Central and South-Eastern Europe*, London: Europa, 2000, p. 53.
4 Many of the wartime atrocities were recorded by a special Carnegie Endowment Enquiry. This important historical document was republished with a commentary and editorial comments by George Kennan as, *The Other Balkan Wars: a 1913 Carnegie Endowment Inquiry in Retrospect*, Washington DC: Carnegie Endowment for

International Peace, 1993, pp. 310–11. The original Carnegie Endowment Report was headed by a commission of seven men, one each from Austria-Hungary, Germany and Great Britain, Russia and the United States and two from France, who travelled in the region in August and September 1913 and returned to write the report in Paris. On this see, Richard C. Hall, *The Balkan Wars 1912–13. Prelude to the First World War*, London: Routledge, 2000, p. 138.

5 Elisabeth Barker, 'The Origin of the Macedonian Dispute', in J. Pettifer (ed.) op. cit., p. 13.

6 Nilüfer Mizanōglu Reddy, 'The Embroidered Jacket', *Turkish Area Studies*, no. 52, April 2001, 29.

7 Misha Glenny, *The Fall of Yugoslavia. The Third Balkan War*, Harmondsworth: Penguin 1992, p. 74.

8 Jane K. Cowan and K. S. Brown, 'Introduction: Macedonian Inflections', in Jane Cowan (ed.), *Macedonia. The Politics of Identity and Difference*, London: Pluto, 2000, 15.

9 George Prevelakis, 'The Return of the Macedonian Question', in F.W. Carter and H.T. Norris (eds), *The Changing Shape of the Balkans*, London: UCL Press, 1996, p. 140.

10 Peter Trudgill, 'Greece and European Turkey: From Religious to Linguistic Identity', in Stephen Barbour and Cathie Carmichael (eds), *Language and Nationalism in Europe*, Oxford: Oxford University Press, 2000, p. 244.

11 Trudgill, in Barbour and Carmichael, op. cit., p. 257.

12 Ibid., p. 251.

13 Radoslav Radenkov, 'The Turkish Minority in Bulgaria', *East European Reporter*, vol. 3, no. 4, 1989, p. 27.

14 Fran Barbalić, 'The Jugoslavs of Italy', *Slavonic Review*, vol. 15, no. 43, 1936, 177–90.

15 Anastasia N. Karakasidou, *Fields of Wheat, Hills of Blood. Passages to Nationhood in Greek Macedonia 1870–1990*, Chicago: University of Chicago Press, 1997, p. 187.

16 Stoyan Christowe, *Heroes and Assassins*, New York: McBride, 1935, p. 35. I am grateful to Professor Božidar Jezernik for suggesting this reference to me.

17 Jovan Cvijić, *La péninsule balkanique. Geographie humaine*, Paris: A. Colin, 1918.

18 Božidar Jezernik, *Dežela, kjer je vse narobe. Prispevki k etnologiji Balkana*. Ljubljana: Znanstveno in publicistično središče, 1998, pp. 174–5.

19 Jezernik, op. cit., p. 190.

20 Ivo Banac, *The National Question in Yugoslavia: Origins, History, Politics*, Ithaca: Cornell University Press, 1984, p. 316.

21 Jonathan Matthew Schwartz, *Pieces of Mosaic. An Essay on the Making of Makedonija*, Højbjerg, Denmark: Intervention Press, 1996, p. 24.

22 Schwartz, op. cit., (1996), p. 25.

23 Jonathan Matthew Schwartz, 'Civil Society and Ethnic Conflict in the Republic of Macedonia', in Joel M. Halpern and David A. Kideckel (eds), *Neighbors at War. Anthropological Perspectives on Yugoslav Ethnicity, Culture and History*, Pennsylvania: Penn State Press, 2000, p. 390.

24 *Clockwork Orange* aside, as a citizen of the United Kingdom, I would find it difficult to envisage the breakdown or even breakup of Britain, although there is theoretically no reason why this should not happen.

25 Carlo Ginzburg, 'Clues: Roots of an Evidential Paradigm', in ibid., *Myths, Emblems, Clues*, Hutchinson Radius, London: 1990, pp. 114–15.

26 I.I.B., interview with the author, 25 August 2001.

27 Xavier Bougarel, *Bosnie. Anatomie d'un conflit*, Paris: La Découverte, 1996, p. 87.

28 John B. Allcock, *Explaining Yugoslavia*, London: Hurst, 2000, p. 376.

29 One song had the chorus 'Slobo, daj salate, biće mesa, biće mesa klačemo Hrvate', (Slobodan Milošević, give us the salad – we're slaughtering the Croats so there will be meat, will be meat). Marcus Tanner, *Croatia. A Nation Forged in War*, New Haven: Yale University Press, 1997, p. 266.

30 Tanner, op. cit., (1997), pp. 266–7.

31 Ivana Maček, 'Predicament of War. Sarajevo Experience and the Ethics of War', in Bettina E. Schmidt and Ingo W. Schröder (eds), *Anthopology of Violence and Conflict*, London: Routledge, 2001, p. 199.

32 For a clear account of the war in Bosnia see James Gow, *The Triumph of the Lack of Will*, London: Hurst, 1997.

33 These observations are based in part on my own experience of staying with a black colleague in Zagreb in 1989 and from the recollections of a Sudanese student who studied architecture in Sarajevo in the late 1980s.

34 Tone Bringa, *Being Muslim the Bosnian Way*, Princeton: Princeton University Press, 1995, p. 118.

35 Bringa, op. cit., p. 150.

36 Kupreskić Judgement, VII–VIII, International Tribunal for the Prosecution of Persons Responsible for Serious Violations of International Humanitarian Law Committed in the Territory of the Former Yugoslavia Since 1991, 14 January 2000, at <http://www.pict-pcti.org/ . . . CTY.01.14.kupreskic.html> on 10 October 2001.

37 This term was used by the Montenegrin journalist Nebojša Čagorović, who wrote for the independent Montenegrin newspaper *Monitor* in the early 1990s.

38 Noel Malcolm, *Kosovo. A Short History*, London: Macmillan, 1998, p. xxviii.

39 Typical figures in these jokes were 'Mujo', 'Haso,' 'Fata,' and 'Huso'. All these are traditional Muslim names.

40 Andrei Simić, 'Nationalism as Folk Ideology. The Case of the Former Yugoslavia', in Joel M. Halpern and David A. Kideckel (eds), *Neighbors at War. Anthropological Perspectives on Yugoslav Ethnicity, Culture and History*. Pennsylvania: Penn State Press, 2000, p. 115. In his memoirs about a visit to a PEN conference in 1965 at lake Bled in Slovenia, Arthur Miller recalled that, 'When I asked an individual out of curiosity if he was Croatian or Slovenian or whatever, and the question caused a slight uneasiness, it seemed minimal enough to be dismissed as more or less irrelevant in this rapidly modernizing country,' *Echoes down the Corridor. Collected Essays, 1944–2000*, New York: Viking, 2000, pp. 249–50.

41 Julie Mertus, *Kosovo: How Myths and Truths started a War*, Berkeley: University of California Press, 1999, p. 1.

42 Chris Bird, 'Living With the Enemy Next Door', *Guardian Weekly*, 16–22 September 1999, 4.

43 Norman M. Naimark, *Fires of Hatred. Ethnic Cleansing in Twentieth Century Europe*, Cambridge, Massachusetts: Harvard University Press, 2001, p. 169.

44 Julius Strauss, 'Albanians Slaughtered in Macedonia', *The Daily Telegraph*, 15 August 2001, 2.

45 Roy Gutman, *A Witness to Genocide: The First Inside Account of the Horrors of Ethnic Cleansing in Bosnia*, Shaftesbury: Element, 1993, p. 88.

46 Peter Maass, *Love the Neighbor. A Story of War*, New York: Vintage, 1996, p. 7.

47 Julie Mertus, Jasmina Tesanović, Habiba Metikos and Rada Borić, (eds), *The Suitcase. Refugee Voices from Bosnia and Croatia*, Berkeley: University of California Press, 1997, p. 41.

48 Rezak Hukanović, *The Tenth Circle of Hell. A Memoir of Life in the Death Camps of Bosnia*, London: Abacus, 1998, p. 41.

49 Dunja Rihtman-Auguštin, 'O susjedima', in Božidar Jakšić (ed.), *Tolerancija – Tolerance*, Belgrade-Zemun: Republika – XX vek, 1999, pp. 151–64.

50 Chuck Sudetić, 'Piles of Bones in Yugoslavia Point to Partisan Massacres', *New York Times*, 9 July 1990, p. A6.

51 Rašković, cited in Stevan M. Weine, *When History is a Nightmare: Lives and Memories of Ethnic Cleansing in Bosnia-Herzegovina*, New Brunswick, New Jersey: Rutgers University Press, 1999, p. 95.

52 Tim Judah, *The Serbs. History, Myth and Destruction of Yugoslavia*, New Haven: Yale University Press, 1997, pp. 132–3.

53 Martin Bell, *In Harm's Way. Reflections of a War-Zone Thug*, Harmondsworth: Penguin, 1996, p. 123.
54 Gale Stokes, *Three Eras of Political Change in Eastern Europe*, Oxford: Oxford University Press, 1997, p. 120.
55 Matteo Milazzo, *The Chetnik Movement and Yugoslav Resistance*, Baltimore and London: Johns Hopkins University Press, 1975, p. 63.
56 Mango, op. cit., p. 346.
57 Mart Bax, 'Barbarization in a Bosnian Pilgrimage Center', in Joel M. Halpern and David A. Kideckel (eds), *Neighbors at War. Anthropological Perspectives on Yugoslav Ethnicity, Culture and History*, Pennsylvania: Penn State Press, 2000, p. 193.
58 Bax, in Halpern and Kideckel op. cit., pp. 187–8.
59 Ibid., p. 188.
60 Leon Trotsky, *The Balkan Wars 1912–13*, New York: Monad Press, 1980, p. 119.
61 Kennan (ed.), op. cit., pp. 310–11.
62 Branimir Anzulović, *Heavenly Serbia: From Myth to Genocide*, London: Hurst, 1999, p. 4.
63 Gutman, op. cit., p. 66.
64 International Commission of Inquiry appointed at the Request of the Greek Red Cross, *Treatment of Greek Prisoners in Turkey*, London: Anglo-Hellenic League, 1923, p. 27.
65 Tim Judah, *Kosovo. War and Revenge*, New Haven: Yale University Press, 2000, p. 247.
66 Frantz Fanon, *The Wretched of the Earth*, Harmondsworth: Penguin, 1961, p. 203.
67 Dona Kolar-Panov, *Video, War and the Diasporic Imagination*, London: Routledge, 1997, p. 153.
68 Carrie Booth Walling, 'The History and Politics of Ethnic Cleansing', in Ken Booth (ed.), *The Kosovo Tragedy. The Human Rights Dimension*, London: Frank Cass, 2001, p. 47.
69 Andrew Mango, *Atatürk*, London: John Murray, 1999, p. 115.
70 Walter Crawfurd Price, *The Balkan Cockpit, the Political and Military Story of the Balkan wars in Macedonia*, London: T. Werner Laurie, 1914, pp. 96–7.
71 Karakasidou, op. cit., p. 75.
72 Kolar-Panov, op. cit., p. 158.
73 Zlata Filipović, *Zlata's Diary. A Child's Life in Sarajevo*, Harmondsworth: Penguin, 1994, pp. 56–7.
74 Filipović, op. cit., pp. 96–7.
75 Jonathan Steele, 'Voters Defy Nationalists by Returning to Pre-war Home Towns', *The Guardian*, 15 September 1997, 12.
76 John Allcock, 'Rural *ressentiment* and the breakup of Yugoslavia', Workshop on 'Urban–Rural Dissonances in the Balkans', American Association for the Advancement of Slavic Studies, St Louis, Missouri, 18–21 November 1999.
77 Paul Theroux, *The Pillars of Hercules. A Grand Tour of the Mediterranean*, London: Hamish Hamilton, 1995, p. 243.
78 Veronica Horwell, 'A Kind of Peace', *The Guardian*, 12 October 1999, G2, 2.
79 Chris Bird, 'Living With the Enemy Next Door', *Guardian Weekly*, 16–22 September 1999, 4.
80 Judah, op. cit., (2000), p. 243.
81 The fate of both communities is described very movingly in Marjorie Housepian, *Smyrna 1922: the Destruction of a City*, London: Faber, 1972.
82 Anne Swardson and R. Jeffrey Smith, 'Hunger Adds to Kosovo's Perils', *Guardian Weekly*, 9 May 1999, 15.
83 Jon Swain, 'Days of Shame. Did the West Cynically Sacrifice Thousands of Muslim Lives in Srebrenica?', *The Sunday Times*, Review Section 3, 19 May, 1996, 1.
84 Swain, op. cit., p. 1.
85 Robert Fisk saw piles of skulls of Armenians in Eastern Turkey in 1993. 'Men had been lined up on bridges to have their throats cut and be thrown into rivers; in orchards and fields, women and children had been knifed. Armenians had been shot by the thousand, sometimes beaten to death with clubs,' 'Dead Reckoning: Holocausts

vs holocausts', *The Independent*, 5 August 2000, <http://www.pipeline.com/~rgibson/fisk.html> on 8 October 2001.

86 Peter Finn, 'Nato Losing the Battle for Kosovo Minds', *Guardian Weekly*, 12–18 August 1999, 31.

87 Slavenka Drakulić, *Balkan Express. Fragments from the Other Side of War*, London: Hutchinson, 1993, p. 63.

88 Drakulić, op. cit., p. 63.

89 C.M. Woodhouse, *The Greek War of Independence: its Historical Setting*, London: Hutchinson, 1952, p. 74.

90 'Bosnian Serb Daily Breaks Taboo', <http://www.iwpr.net/balkans/news> on 17 September 1999.

91 Jonathan Steele, 'They Tracked Us Day and Night. Then They Gunned Us Down', *Guardian Weekly*, 15–21 July 1999, 3.

92 Victor Turner, *The Forest of Symbols: Aspects of Ndembu Ritual*, Ithaca: Cornell University Press, 1967.

93 Bax, in Halpern and Kideckel op. cit., p. 194.

94 Allcock, op. cit., (2000), p. 339.

95 Simon Clements, *A Journal of My Travels . . . in the Year 1715*, British Library, Egerton Mss 2167.

96 Alenka Puhar, 'Childhood Nightmares and Dreams of Revenge', *Journal of Pyschohistory*, vol. 22, no. 2, Fall, 1994 at <http://www.psychohistory.com/yugoslav/yugoslav.htm> on 1 October 2001.

97 Chuck Sudetić, 'Piles of Bones in Yugoslavia Point to Partisan Massacres', *New York Times*, 9 July 1990, p. A6.

98 Cathie Carmichael, 'Locating Trieste in the Eighteenth and Nineteenth Centuries', in Borut Brumen and Zmago Smitek (eds), *Mediterranean Ethnological Summer School*, Ljubljana: Inštitut za multikulturne raziskave, 1995, pp. 11–12.

99 Glenda Sluga, *The Problem of Trieste and the Italo-Yugoslav Border. Difference, Identity and Sovereignty in Twentieth Century Europe*, New York: SUNY, 2000, p. 166.

100 Sluga, op. cit., p. 166.

101 Mary Douglas, *Purity and Danger: An Analysis of the Concepts of Pollution and Taboo*, London: Routledge and Kegan Paul, 1966, p. 69.

102 Simić, in Halpern and Kideckel (eds), op. cit., p. 112.

103 Justin McCarthy, *Death and Exile, The Ethnic Cleansing of Ottoman Muslims 1821–1922*, Princeton, NJ: Darwin Press, 1996, p. 74.

104 McCarthy, op. cit., p. 75.

105 Mark Mazower, *Inside Hitler's Greece*, New Haven: Yale University Press, new edn, 2001, p. 248.

106 Mazower, op. cit., (2001) p. 240.

107 On the history and demise of the old Turkish bridge at Mostar, see Božidar Jezernik, 'Qudret Kemeri: a Bridge Between Barbarity and Civilisation', *Slavonic and East European Review*, 73, 1995, 470–84.

108 Ivo Goldstein, *Croatia: A History*, London: Hurst, 1999, p. 24.

109 George F. Kennan, *The Other Balkan Wars. A 1913 Carnegie Endowment Inquiry in Retrospect with a New Introduction and Reflections on the Present Conflict*, Washington DC: Carnegie Endowment for International Peace, 1993, p. 325.

110 Radenkov, op. cit., p. 27.

111 Judah, op. cit., (2000), pp. 1–2.

112 Euan Cameron, *The European Reformation*, Oxford: Clarendon Press, 1991, pp. 249–50.

113 Gérard Prunier, *The Rwanda Crisis. History of a Genocide 1959–1994*, London: Hurst, 1995, p. 256.

114 Vladimir Dedijer (ed.), *The War Diaries of Vladimir Dedijer*, Ann Arbor: University of Michigan Press, vol. 1, 1990, p. 68.

115 Dedijer, op. cit., (1990), p. 70. During the Armenian genocide of 1915, there were

reports that Armenians were tortured by having horseshoes nailed to their feet and hands in what must have been an elaborate attempt to dehumanize them.

116 Traian Stoianovich, *Balkan Worlds: The First and Last Europe*, New York and London: Sharpe, 1994, p. 280.

117 Pieter Spierenburg, 'Masculinity, Violence and Honor: An Introduction', in ibid. (ed.), *Men and Violence. Gender, Honor and Rituals in Modern Europe and America*, Columbus, Ohio: Ohio Sate University Press, 1998 p. 4.

118 Figure 5 in Halpern and Kideckel (eds), op. cit., p. 179.

119 Maass, op. cit., p. 7.

120 Crawfurd Price, op. cit., p. 355.

121 Kennan, op. cit., p. 324.

122 Cornelia Sorabji, 'A Very Modern War: Terror and Territory in Bosnia-Hercegovina', in Robert A. Hinde and Helen E. Watson (eds), *War: A Cruel Necessity? The Bases of Institutionalized Violence*, London: I.B. Tauris, 1995, p. 83.

123 Charles Dobson, 'Appendix: The Smyrna Holocaust', in Lysimachos Oeconomos, *The Tragedy of the Christian Near East*, London: Anglo-Hellenic League, 1923, p. 28.

124 Robert Hayden, 'Muslims as "Others" in Serbian and Croatian Politics', in Halpern and Kideckel (eds), op. cit., p. 123.

125 Michael Sells, *The Bridge Betrayed: Religion and Genocide in Bosnia*, 2nd edn, Berkeley: University of California Press, 1998, p. 4.

126 Sells, op. cit., p. 4.

127 Kupreskić Judgement, VII–VIII, International Tribunal for the Prosecution of Persons Responsible for Serious Violations of International Humanitarian Law Committed in the Territory of the Former Yugoslavia Since 1991, 14 January 2000, at <http://www.pict-pcti.org/. . . CTY.01.14.kupreskic.html> on 10 October 2001.

128 Bringa, op. cit., p. 166.

129 Ibid., p. 74.

130 Robert Gary Minnich has written about the tremendous importance of gifts of pork in Slovenia and elsewhere in the former Yugoslavia, which were independent of the state and associated with acephalous (clan-based) societies in, 'The Gift of *Koline* and the Articulation of Identity in Slovene Peasant Society', *Ethnologia Slavica*, vol. 22, 1990, 151–61. The 'gift' of pork to Muslims might also be an inversion of this important ritual, again somewhat Bakhtinian in nature.

131 Norman Cigar, *Genocide in Bosnia. The Policy of Ethnic Cleansing*, College Station: Texas A&M University Press, 1995, p. 59.

132 Roy Gutman, *A Witness to Genocide: The First Inside Account of the Horrors of Ethnic Cleansing in Bosnia*, Shaftesbury: Element, 1993, p. 78.

133 As Ed Vulliamy reported, op. cit., p. 54, 'We stumbled upon a gathering of some eighty opprobrious Chetniks camped down at Prijedor police station in September 1992 . . . They had little enlightening to say, except to register that in the town of Kluj, "The Turks cannot eat pigs, but they run like pigs and squeal like pigs."'

134 J.A.R Marriott, *The Eastern Question: an Historical Study in European Diplomacy*, Oxford: Clarendon Press, 1940, 4th edn, p. 205.

135 International Commission of Inquiry appointed at the Request of the Greek Red Cross, *Treatment of Greek Prisoners in Turkey*, London: Anglo-Hellenic League, 1923, p. 27. The word courban or churban 'alludes to the destruction of the second Temple and the subsequent diaspora of the Jews'. Frangiski Abadzopolou, 'The Holocaust: Questions of Literary Representations', in Ioannes K. Chasiotes *et al.* (eds), *The Jewish Communities of Southeastern Europe: from the Fifteenth Century to the End of World War II*, Salonika: Institute for Balkan Studies, 1997, pp. 2–3.

136 Leon Trotsky, *The Balkan Wars 1912–13*, New York: Monad Press, 1980, p. 127.

137 Trotsky, op. cit., (1980), p. 120.

138 George Sava, *The Chetniks*, London: Regular Publication, 1955, p. 31.

139 Pam Ballinger, 'Remembering the Istrian Exodus: Memory in a Trans-State

Context', in Bojan Baskar and Borut Brumen (eds), *Mediterranean Ethnological Summer School*, vol. II, Ljubljana: Inštitut za multikulturne raziskave, 1998, p. 62.

140 Stanoje Jovanović and Dragan Jerković, *Zločin Hrvatske države '91*, Belgrade, Vojni muzej, 1991, p. 16.

141 Dona Kolar-Panov, *Video, War and the Diasporic Imagination*, London: Routledge, 1997, p. 146.

142 Djordje Stefanović, 'Michael Hechter's Rational Choice Theory of Nationalism v. the Post-Communist Experience', Paper delivered at the Association for the Study of Nationalities 6th Annual World Convention, New York, April 2001.

143 Sometimes spelt as odalism, from the Old High German word *uodal*, meaning a homestead. The concept is pre-feudal and refers to the notion of uninterrupted possession of land. Similar beliefs are found among rural dwellers until recent times from Ireland to Russia.

144 Mark Thompson in his, *A Paper House: The Ending of Yugoslavia*, London: Hutchinson Radius, 1992, p. 196, tells a witty story about a graffiti artist in Sarajevo who had sprayed 'this is Serbia' in 1991. Underneath someone else had sprayed, 'Wrong, dimwit, it's a post office'.

145 Vladimir Dedijer, *The Yugoslav Auschwitz and the Vatican*, Buffalo, New York: Prometheus Books, 1992, p. 131.

146 Sells, op. cit., p. 150.

147 Abadzopolou, op. cit., p. 6.

148 Allcock, op. cit., (2000), p. 398.

149 Jutta Lauth Bacas, 'The Constructions of National Identity in a Local Setting: the Case of Lésbos, an Island at the Greek-Turkish Border', *Anthropological Journal on European Cultures*, vol. 4, no. 2, 1995, 76.

150 Maček, op. cit., p. 201.

151 Radovan Haluzik, 'Rumours and Legends in the Present Ethnic Conflict in the Former Yugoslavia and the Caucasus', Paper presented at the Centre for South-East European Studies, School of Slavonic and East European Studies, University of London: 8 December 1999.

152 Colonel L.C. Vialla de Sommières, *Voyage historique et politique au Montenegro*, Paris: Alexis Eymery, 1820, vol. 1, pp. 144–5.

153 Sava, op. cit., p. 41.

154 Allcock, op. cit., (2000), p. 382.

155 R.S. in an interview with the author, 15 March 1999.

156 Joyce Cary, *Memoir of the Bobotes* London: Michael Joseph, 1964, cited in Richard C. Hall, *The Balkan Wars 1912–13. Prelude to the First World War*, London: Routledge, 2000, p. 136.

157 Hugh Poulton, 'Non-Albanian Muslim Minorities in Macedonia', in Pettifer, op. cit., p. 107.

7 Ethno-psychology

1 Robert D. Kaplan, *Balkan Ghosts. A Journey through History*, New York: St. Martin's Press, 1993, p. xxiii.

2 As Bojan Baskar points out, 'Cvijić was directly involved in the endeavour of putting Yugoslavia on the map. His voluminous work on the Balkan peninsula was thus to provide a human geographical ground for the new nation-state of the Southern Slavs or Yugoslavs. Consequently, he had to minimize the ethnic and cultural diversity of the populations of the territory.' Bojan Baskar, 'Made in Trieste. Geopolitical Fears of an Istrianist Discourse on the Mediterranean', *Narodna Umjetnost*, vol. 36, no. 1, 1999, 122.

3 That is not to say that the Dinarics do not exist in a physical sense as a mountain range, but any individual who wanted – for example – to create a strong state

spanning Central Europe might begin by arguing that the Alps constitute a distinctive region. While I agree with Pamela Ballinger, 'Definitional Dilemmas: Southeastern Europe as "Culture Area"', *Balkanologie*, vol. 3, no. 2, December 1999, 83 that 'notions like honour and shame have hindered the critical anthropological investigation of Mediterranean societies', I would disagree with her description of 'ethnographic concepts' of Jovan Cvijić as 'indigenous' since the anthropogeography of the latter was motivated by wider political concerns, chiefly linked to the Serbian nationalist project and its wider dissemination prior to 1918. His major works were written in French and German as well as Serbian. After the spread of nationalist discourse in the late eighteenth century, the dichotomy between 'indigenous' and 'foreign' is blurred because of ideological parallelisms.

4 Jovan Cvijić, *La péninsule balkanique. Geographie humaine*, Paris: A. Colin, 1918, pp. 281–379.

5 On the discursive construction of the Morlacchi as wild inhabitants of the Dinaric Hinterland of the Eastern Adriatic Littoral, see Valentina Gulin, 'Morlacchism Between Enlightenment and Romanticism (Identification and Self-identification of the European Other), *Narodna Umjetnost*, vol. 34, 1997, 77–100.

6 The subject of a recent monograph by Larry Wolff, *Venice and the Slavs: the Discovery of Dalmatia in the Age of Enlightenment*, Stanford: Stanford University Press, 2001.

7 Hugh Trevor Roper, 'Sir Thomas More and *Utopia*', in ibid., *Renaissance Essays*, London: Fontana, 1986, p. 47.

8 Trevor Roper, op. cit., p. 47.

9 Baskar, op. cit., (*Narodna Umjetnost*, 1999), 123.

10 Vesna Goldsworthy, *Inventing Ruritania: the Imperialism of the Imagination*, New Haven: Yale University Press, 1998, p. 31.

11 Dunja Rihtman Auguštin, *Ulice moga grada. Antropologija domaćeg terena*, Belgrade: Biblioteka XX vek, 2000, pp. 171–8.

12 Vasa Čubrilović, 'Iseljavanje Arnauta', in Bože Ćović (ed.), *Izvori velikosrpske agresije*, Zagreb: August Cesarec & Skolska knjiga, 1991, pp. 112–13. Here Čubrilović used a fairly established idea but turned it into an 'ideology of ethnic cleansing'. The Montenegrin military commander Marko Milijanov, writing in the later nineteenth century had thought that it would not be hard for the Albanians and Montenegrins to get along 'since they are not far from you (Montenegrins), or you from them'. Quoted in Ivo Banac, *The National Question in Yugoslavia: Origins, History, Politics*, Ithaca: Cornell University Press, 1984, p. 297.

13 Bojan Baskar 'Anthropologists Facing the Collapse of Yugoslavia', *Diogenes*, vol. 47, no. 188, 1999, 60.

14 Stephanie Schwandner-Sievers, 'The Enactment of "tradition". Albanian Constructions of Identity, Violence and Power in Times of Crisis', in Bettina E. Schmidt and Ingo W. Schröder (eds), *Anthopology of Violence and Conflict*, London: Routledge, 2001, p. 97.

15 Bora Kuzmanović and Mirjana Vasović, 'Tradicionalistička orientacija', in Zagorka Golubović (ed.), *Društveni karakter i društvene promene u svetlu nacionalnih sukoba*, Beograd: BIGZ, 1995, pp. 111–31.

16 Dinko Tomašić, *Personality and Culture in East European Politics*, New York: Stewart, 1948.

17 Tomašić, op. cit., p. 56.

18 Ibid., p. 41.

19 Ibid., p. 114.

20 Personal communication, American Association for the Advancement of Slavic Studies, St Louis, Missouri, November 1999.

21 Milovan Djilas, *Land without Justice*, New York: Harcourt Brace Jovanovich, 1958.

22 Ante Ciliga, *Sam kroz Europu u ratu*, Rome: Na pragu sutranšnjice, 1978, Part II, 'U balkanskom vrtlogu: tri godine u NDH', especially pp. 217–441.

23 Mary Edith Durham, *Some Tribal Origins, Laws and Customs of the Balkans*, London:

George Allen and Unwin, 1928, pp. 159–69.

24 Tomašić, op. cit., p. 38.

25 See for example, Rebecca West, *Black Lamb and Grey Falcon: the Record of a Journey Through Yugoslavia in 1937*, London: Macmillan, 1941. Representations of Albanians as violent have been discussed at some length by Stephanie Schwandner-Sievers, 'Evoking the Past: Albanian Identifications and Local Power', Unpublished Doctoral Dissertation, Berlin Free University, September 2001.

26 Alenka Puhar, 'Childhood Nightmares and Dreams of Revenge' *Journal of Pyschohistory*, vol. 22, no. 2 Fall, 1994 at <http://www.psychohistory.com/yugoslav/yugoslav.htm> on 1 October 2001.

27 This 'mountain men' stereotype is never used about the Slovenes, despite the fact that the mountains of the Eastern Alps are far higher than the Dinarics.

28 Traian Stoianovich, *Balkan Worlds: The First and Last Europe*, New York and London: Sharpe, 1994, p. 331.

29 Stevan M. Weine, *When History is a Nightmare: Lives and Memories of Ethnic Cleansing in Bosnia-Herzegovina*, New Brunswick, New Jersey: Rutgers University Press, 1999, p. 122.

30 John Kifner, quoted in Marko Živković, 'Violent Highlanders and Peaceful Lowlanders. Uses and Abuses of Ethno-Geography in the Balkans from Versailles to Dayton', *Replika*, Special Issue, 1997, 110.

31 David A. Norris, *In the Wake of the Balkan Myth: Questions of Identity and Modernity*, London: Macmillan, 1999, p. 38.

32 Norman Stone, 'Dubrovnik: The Case for a War Crime Trial', *The Guardian*, 13 November 1991, 1.

33 Misha Glenny, *The Rebirth of History. Eastern Europe in the Age of Democracy*, Harmondsworth: Penguin, 1990, p. 140.

34 John B. Allcock, *Explaining Yugoslavia*, London: Hurst, 2000, p. 389.

35 Stjepan Meštrović, Slaven Letica and Miroslav Goreta, *Habits of the Balkan Heart. Social Character and the Fall of Communism*, College Station: Texas A&M University Press, 1993.

36 Meštrović *et al.* (1993), op. cit., p. 61.

37 Florian Bieber, *Serbischer Nationalismus vom Tod Titos zum Sturz Miloševićs*, Unpublished Doctoral Dissertation, Vienna University, March 2001, p. 9.

38 Jill Irvine, 'Nationalism and the Extreme Right in the Former Yugoslavia', in Luciano Cheles *et al.* (eds) *The Far Right in Eastern and Western Europe*, London: Longman, 1995, p. 149.

39 Bojan Baskar, 'Anthropologists Facing the Collapse of Yugoslavia', *Diogenes*, vol. 47, no. 188, 1999, 61.

40 Mirjana Prošić-Dvornić, 'Serbia: the Inside Story', in Joel M. Halpern and David A. Kideckel (eds), *Neighbors at War. Anthropological Perspectives on Yugoslav Ethnicity, Culture and History*, Pennsylvania: Penn State Press, 2000, p. 332, fn. 29.

41 Stoianovich, op. cit., p. 330.

42 The ambivalence of Miroslav Krleža is discussed by Dunja Rihtman Auguštin in 'Zašto i otkad se grozimo Balkana', in ibid., op. cit., pp. 211–36.

43 Ivo Žanić, 'The Most Croat', *War Report*, no. 28, November/December 1995, 41–2.

44 Ivo Rendić-Miočević, *Zlo velike jetre: povijest i nepovijest Crnogoraca, Hrvata, Muslimana i Srba*, Split: Književni krug, 1996, pp. 51–131.

45 The term Vlasi or Vlahi is sometimes used by Dalmatians to refer to the inhabitants of the Dinarics, but its use by intellectuals is a deliberate form of denigration.

46 Ivan Crkvenčić, 'Promjene broja pučanstva Knina od druge polovice 19. stoljeća', in Stjepan Antoljak (ed.), *Kninski Zbornik*, Matica Hrvatska: Zagreb, 1993, 27. Furthermore, Crkvenčić argues (p. 34) that the Serbs only constituted a majority in the Knin area after 1953.

47 Rendić-Miočević, op. cit.

48 Vladimir Dedijer, *The Yugoslav Auschwitz and the Vatican*, Buffalo, New York: Prometheus Books, 1992, p. 357.

49 A critical view of Orthodoxy has also been resurrected as a kind of sub-thesis to the notion of a clash of civilizations between the Islamic and Christian worlds. '. . . in the Balkans, Catholics, Protestants and even Jews tend to exhibit values more similar if not identical to the ones shared by the Orthodox or Muslims they live with than by their fellow believers in the secularized western societies. This helps interpret for example the Croatian drift towards an undemocratic, intolerant society: it may have a Catholic majority but it had nevertheless developed until recently in an intolerant Orthodox-dominated Yugoslav world'. Panyote Elias Dimitras, 'Writing and Rewriting History in the Context of Balkan Nationalism', *Southeast European Politics*, October 2000, vol. 1, no. 1, 48–9. I would rather emphasize the fascistic elements in Croatian nationalist ideology and undemocratic practices, which are definitely 'Western' in their origins.

50 Susan Woodward, *Balkan Tragedy. Chaos and Dissolution After the Cold War*, Washington: Brookings Institute, 1995, p. 354.

51 Martin Bell, *In Harm's Way. Reflections of a War-Zone Thug*, Harmondsworth: Penguin, 1996.

52 Mirko Grmek, 'Predgovor', in Rendic-Miocević, op. cit., p. 8.

53 Ivo Žanić, *Prevarena povijest. Guslarska estrada, kult Hajduka i rat u Hrvatskoj i Bosni i Hercegovini 1990–1995. Godine*, Zagreb: Durieux, 1998, p. 22.

54 Slavoj Žižek, *NATO kao lijeva ruka Boga?/NATO as the Left hand of God?* Ljubljana/Zagreb: Bastard Biblioteque, 1999, p. 43.

55 Zlata Filipović, *Zlata's Diary. A Child's Life in Sarajevo*, Harmondsworth: Penguin, 1994. pp. 130–1.

56 'Slovenci in Srbi smo bratje', *Mladina*, 25 June 1989, 48.

57 Dubravka Ugrešić, *The Culture of Lies*, Pennsylvania: Penn State Press, 1998, pp. 205–6. Isaura the Slavegirl is a Brazilian soap opera.

58 Ivo Banac, 'Post-Communism as Post-Yugoslavism: the Yugoslav Non-Revolutions of 1989–1990', in Ivo Banac (ed.), *Eastern Europe in Revolution*, Ithaca: Cornell University Press, 1991, p. 178.

59 Jovan Teokarević, 'Neither War nor Peace: Serbia and Montenegro in the First Half of the 1990s', in David Dyker and Ivan Vejvoda (eds), *Yugoslavia and After. A Study in Fragmentation, Despair and Rebirth*, London: 1996, p. 193.

60 Djordje Stefanović, 'Michael Hechter's Rational Choice Theory of Nationalism v. the Post-Communist Experience', Paper delivered at the Association for the Study of Nationalities 6th Annual World Convention, New York: April 2001.

61 Svetlana Slapšak, 'What are Women Made of? Inventing Women in the Yugoslav Area', in G. Brinker-Gabler and S. Smith (eds), *Writing New Identities*, Minneapolis and London: University of Minnesota Press, 1997, p. 372.

62 Chuck Sudetić, 'Piles of Bones in Yugoslavia Point to Partisan Massacres', *New York Times*, 9 July 1990, p. A6.

63 Letica quoted in Lenard J. Cohen, *Broken Bonds: the Disintegration of Yugoslavia*, Boulder, Colorado: Westview, 1993, p. 223. Milovan Djilas is reported to have remarked in 1985 that Yugoslavia's break up would be '(l)ike Lebanon. Wait and see.' Kaplan, op. cit., 1993, p. 75.

64 Ivo Banac, op. cit., (1991), p. 174.

65 Stojan Cerović, 'Koga briga?', *Vreme* 547, 28 June 2001 at <http://www.vreme.com/cms/view.php?id=290987> on 30 June 2001.

66 Vera Stein Erlich, *Family in Transition: a Study of 300 Yugoslav Villages*, Princeton: Princeton University Press, 1966, p. 385.

67 Frantz Fanon, *The Wretched of the Earth*, Harmondsworth: Penguin, 1961, p. 250.

68 Maria Todorova, *Imagining the Balkans*, Oxford: Oxford University Press, 1997, p. 183.

69 Stoianovich, op. cit., p. 59.

70 Allcock, op. cit., p. 383.

71 Thanasis D. Sfikas, 'National Movements and Nation Building in the Balkans, 1804–1922: Historic Origins, Contemporary Misunderstandings', in Thanasis D. Sfikas and Christopher Williams (eds), *Ethnicity and Nationalism in East Central Europe and the Balkans*, Ashgate: Aldershot, 1999, p. 14.

72 Franklin Lindsay, *Beacons in the Night*, Cambridge: Cambridge University Press, 1993, p. 348. This recourse to history as an explanatory category was used by former British Foreign Secretary Lord Douglas Hurd when discussing the US and British bombing of Afghanistan (2001/2). He was asked: 'Are we reaping the rewards of supporting the mujahadeen against the Soviets?' To which he replied: 'No. Afghanistan has been a boiling pot for generations. We helped them stop the Russians from overrunning the place – I don't regret that. Since then, they went back to fighting each other and so they allowed terrorism to take root, along with heroin dealing. I think its become a total mess and we don't carry the blame.' James Ellis, Interview with Douglas Hurd, *Metro*, 9 October 2001, 10.

73 George Bush, quoted in Roy Gutman, *A Witness to Genocide: The First Inside Account of the Horrors of Ethnic Cleansing in Bosnia*, Shaftesbury: Element, 1993, p. xxxi.

74 Tim Allen and Jean Seaton, *The Media of Conflict: War Reporting and Representations of Ethnic Violence*, London and New York: Zed Books, 1999, p. 1.

75 John D. Treadway, 'Of Shatter Belts and Powder Kegs: A Brief Survey of Yugoslav History', in Constantine P. Danopoulos and Kostas G. Messas (eds), *Crises in the Balkans. Views From the Participants*, Boulder, Colorado: Westview 1997, pp. 40–1.

76 Christian Giordano, 'The Balkans: European Periphery, Epicentre of Ethnicity and Landscape of Feuds', *Anthropological Journal on European Cultures*, vol. 4, no. 2, 1995, 104–5.

77 Paula Franklin Lytle, 'U.S. policy Towards the Demise of Yugoslavia: the "Virus of Nationalism"', *East European Politics and Societies*, vol. 6, no. 3, 1992, 315.

78 Some of these barbarities are described in Joanna Bourke, *An Intimate History of Killing. Face to Face Killing in Twentieth Century Europe*, London: Granta, 1999.

79 Mark Thompson, *Forging War: The Media in Serbia, Croatia, Bosnia and Hercegovina*, Luton: University of Luton Press/Article 19. International Centre against Censorship, 1999, p. 298.

80 Mark Mazower, *The Balkans*, London: Weidenfeld and Nicolson, 2000, p. 129.

81 Durham, op. cit., (1928), p. 161.

82 Venetian reports of the cruelty of the Uscoks dwelt on their violent excesses, but were often exaggerated for literary purposes. One tale began as a simple murder of a servant. In time it changed and was 'followed by a tale of the servant's heart being roasted and eaten, culminating in the accusation that the uscoks responsible had made straps for their leather moccasins . . . from his skin'. Catherine Wendy Bracewell, *The Uscoks of Senj. Piracy, Banditry and Holy War in the Sixteenth Century Adriatic*, Ithaca: Cornell University Press, 1992, p. 168.

83 James Gow, *The Triumph of the Lack of Will. International Diplomacy and the Yugoslav War*, London: Hurst, 1997, p. 41.

84 Richard C. Hall, *The Balkan Wars 1912–13. Prelude to the First World War*, London: Routledge, 2000, p. 137.

85 Gow, op. cit., p. 43.

86 *The Daily Telegraph*, 7 May 1998, quoted in Allen and Seaton, op. cit., p. 1.

87 Tim Judah, *The Serbs. History, Myth and Destruction of Yugoslavia*, New Haven and London: Yale University Press, 1997, p. 74.

88 Glen Bowman, 'Xenophobia, Fantasy and the Nation: the Logic of Ethnic Violence in Former Yugoslavia', *Balkan Forum*, vol. 2, no. 2, 1994, 153.

89 Military recruitment for the draft was an utter failure in parts of Serbia, particularly in Vojvodina where less than 20 per cent of the young men eligible for service turned up, the others preferring to desert. Mirjana Prošić-Dvornić, '"Druga Srbija": mirovni i ženski pokret', in Mirjana Prošić-Dvornić (ed.), *Kulture u tranziciji*, Belgrade: Plato, 1994, p. 196, fn17.

90 Vladimir Arsenijević, *U potpaljublju. Saponska opera*, Beograd: Vreme, 1995.
91 Norman Cigar, 'The Serbo-Croatian War', in Stjepan Meštrović (ed.), *Genocide After Emotion. The Postemotional Balkan War*, London: Routledge, 1996, p. 67.
92 Ivana Maček, 'Predicament of War. Sarajevo Experience and the Ethics of War', in Bettina E. Schmidt and Ingo W. Schröder (eds), *Anthopology of Violence and Conflict*, London: Routledge, 2001, p. 200.
93 Lenard J. Cohen, *Serpent in the Bosom. The Rise and Fall of Slobodan Milosevic*, Boulder, Colorado: Westview, 2001, p. 278.
94 Mart Bax, 'Barbarization in a Bosnian Pilgrimage Center', in Joel M. Halpern and David A. Kideckel (eds), *Neighbors at War. Anthropological Perspectives on Yugoslav Ethnicity, Culture and History*, Pennsylvania: Penn State Press, 2000, p. 193.
95 For a discussion of the context of violence in Hercegovina see Mart Bax, 'Ruža's Problems: Gender Relations and Violence in a Bosnian Rural Community', in Sabrina P. Ramet (ed.), *Gender Politics in the Western Balkans: Women and Society in Yugoslavia and the Yugoslav Successor States*, Pennsylvania: Penn State Press, 1999, pp. 259–73.
96 Thompson, op. cit., (1999), p. 299.

8 Conclusion

1 Walter Benjamin, quoted in Carlo Ginzburg, *The Cheese and the Worms*, Harmondsworth: Penguin, 1992, p. xxvi.
2 Carlo Ginzburg, 'Just One Witness', in Saul Friedländer (ed.), *Probing the Limits of Representation. Nazism and the Final Solution*, Cambridge, Massachusetts: Harvard University Press, 1992b, p. 96.
3 See, for example, <http://iacenter.org/bosnia/deich.htm> and <http://www.flip-side.org/vol3/feb00/00fe266.htm> accessed on 15 December 2001. It may well be that Alić was of slender build before he was incarcerated, but I decided (somewhat reluctantly) after reading this discourse about Alić, not to include photographs of people in this book. Many of the relatives of individuals mentioned here, or the individuals themselves, are still alive. The further display of their suffering could be viewed as a kind of 'pornography', to paraphrase the Croatian writer Slavenka Drakulić when discussing the fact that night after night people from outside Bosnia watched television images of Sarajevo under fire, but many did little or nothing to prevent the war from continuing.
4 Norman Cigar, *Vojislav Koštunica and Serbia's Future*, London: Saqi Books, 2001, p. 32.
5 This term is used (ironically) by Slobodan Naumović, 'Romanticists or Double Insiders? An Essay on the Origins of Ideologised Discourses in Balkan Ethnology', *Ethnologia balkanica*, 2, 1998, 101–20.
6 Cathie Carmichael, 'Conclusions: Language and National Identity in Europe', in Stephen Barbour and Cathie Carmichael (eds), *Language and Nationalism in Europe*, Oxford: Oxford University Press, 2000, pp. 280–9.
7 The reference to Karl Marx' famous essay on the philosophy of history, *The Eighteenth Brumaire of Louis Napoleon*, in Lewis S. Feuer (ed.) *Marx and Engels. Basic Writings on Politics and Philosophy*, Glasgow: Collins, 1969, p. 360, in which he states that 'men make history, but not in the circumstances of their own choosing'. For Marx, tradition weighed like an 'nightmare (sometimes the German term for nightmare *Alptraum* is translated as 'alp' in English which is certainly more evocative) on the brain' and was a barrier to progression of better ideas. Here I have inverted the notion of tradition and suggest that it was the burden of nationalism as an ideology, rather than tradition that peoples in the Balkans had to carry 'on the brain'.
8 Mark Mazower, *Dark Continent: Europe's Twentieth Century*, Harmondsworth: Penguin, 1998, p. 40.
9 This may be one way of combating the 'problem' of nationalism that we have some-how collectively set ourselves as something to 'understand and eventually solve'.

Florian Bieber, 'The Challenge of Democracy in Divided Societies: Lessons from Bosnia – Challenges for Kosovo', in Džemal Sokolović and Florian Bieber (eds), *Reconstructing Multiethnic Societies. The Case of Bosnia-Herzegovina*, Aldershot: Ashgate, 2001, p. 112.

10 Florence Hartmann, *Milošević. La Diagonale du Fou*, Paris: Denoël, 1999, p. 244.

11 Dražena Peranić, 'A Journey Across Unexpected Borders', *War Report*, November/December 1995, 46.

12 Smiljan Simac, 'Croatie, Serbie: les fausses symétries', *Le Monde*, 25 May 1999, 13–14.

13 Mirko Klarin, 'The Case Against Karadžić', *Tribunal*, August/September, 1997, 3. These remarks were made in the context of Bosnia, but seem equally applicable here.

14 Peter Maass, *Love thy Neighbor. A Story of War*, New York: Vintage, 1996, p. 87.

15 Rorty's ideas are discussed in the context of Bosnia in Stevan M. Weine, *Redefining Merhamet after a Historical Nightmare*, in Joel M. Halpern and David. A. Kideckel (eds), op. cit., p. 412.

16 Jonathan Glover, *A Moral History of the 20th Century*, London: Jonathan Cape, 2000.

17 James Meek, 'From Ivory Towers to Killing Fields', *Guardian Weekly*, 18–24 November 1999, 23.

18 Weine, in Halpern and Kideckel (eds), op. cit., p. 408.

19 Dubravka Ugrešić, *The Culture of Lies*, Pennsylvania: Penn State Press, 1998, p.188.

20 Mark Mazower, *Inside Hitler's Greece*, New Haven: Yale University Press, new edn, 2001, p. 255.

21 Ivana Maček, 'Predicament of War. Sarajevo Experience and the Ethics of War', in Bettina E. Schmidt and Ingo W. Schröder (eds), *Anthopology of Violence and Conflict*, London: Routledge, 2001, p. 215.

22 This may be direct evidence of the kind of 'sentimental education' to which Rorty was referring.

23 Peter Maass, *Love thy Neighbor. A Story of War*, New York: Vintage 1996, p. 106.

24 Mirko Klarin, 'Defendant for the Prosecution', *Tribunal*, November/December 1996, 3.

25 Tim Judah, *Kosovo. War and Revenge*, New Haven: Yale University Press, 2000, p. 244.

26 On this subject, see Robert Greenberg, 'Dialects and Ethnicity in the Former Yugoslavia. The Case of Southern Baranja (Croatia)', *Slavic and East European Journal*, vol. 42, 1998, 710–22

27 Mark Mazower, *The Balkans*, London: Weidenfeld and Nicolson, 2000, p. 93.

28 Jonathan M. Schwartz, 'The Petrified Forest of Symbols: Deconstructing and Envisaging Macedonia', *Anthropological Journal on European Cultures*, vol. 4, no. 1, 1995, 15.

29 Balkan societies have suffered considerably both from the 'drain' of educated people and the deterioration of the educational systems as a result of war and ethnic cleansing. Daniel Daianu and Thanos Veremis, 'Introduction', in Thanos Veremis and Daniel Daianu (eds), *Balkan Reconstruction*, London: Frank Cass, 2001, p. 4.

30 In John Sturges' 1955 film *Bad Day at Black Rock*, a stranger (played by Spencer Tracey) arrives to deliver a posthumous Congressional Medal of Honour to a Japanese-American comrade who, four years earlier, has been murdered by a group of townspeople who were 'patriotic drunk'. The local doctor reflects: 'Four years ago, something terrible happened here. We did nothing about it. Nothing! The whole town fell into a sort of settled melancholy, and all the people in it closed their eyes, and held their tongues, and failed the test with a whimper. And now something terrible is going to happen again.'

31 International Commission on Kosovo, *The Kosovo Report: Conflict: International Response: Lessons Learned*, Oxford: Oxford University Press, 2000, p. 295.

32 Isaiah Berlin made a celebrated distinction between cultural and political nationalism, although I have preferred to use the term *Heimatliebe* as this term is dissociated from any notion of loyalty to the state or putative genetic association with other people. See, Nathan Gardels, 'Two Concepts of Nationalism: An Interview with Isaiah

Berlin', *New York Review of Books*, 21 November 1991, 19–23. This dichotomy has been criticized by more recent writers on nationalism, notably Anthony Smith in his *Nations and Nationalism in a Global Era*, Cambridge: Polity, 1996.

33 Maria Todorova, *Imagining the Balkans*, New York/Oxford: Oxford University Press, 1997, p. 189.

Bibliography

Frangiski Abadzopolou, 'The Holocaust: Questions of Literary Representations', in Ioannes K. Chasiotes *et al.* (eds), *The Jewish Communities of Southeastern Europe: from the Fifteenth Century to the End of World War II*, Salonika: Institute for Balkan Studies, 1997, pp. 2–21.

Ahmed Akbar, 'Ethnic Cleansing: a Metaphor for Our Time?', *Ethnic and Racial Studies*, vol. 18, no. 1, 1995, 2–25.

John B. Allcock, 'Constructing "The Balkans"', in John B. Allcock and A. Young (eds), *Black Lambs and Grey Falcons: Women Travellers in the Balkans*, Bradford: Bradford University Press, 1991, pp. 170–91.

John B. Allcock, 'Rural *ressentiment* and the breakup of Yugoslavia', Workshop on 'Urban-Rural Dissonances in the Balkans', American Association for the Advancement of Slavic Studies, St Louis, Missouri, 18–21 November 1999.

John B. Allcock, *Explaining Yugoslavia*, London: Hurst, 2000.

J.B. Allcock and A. Young (eds), *Black Lambs and Grey Falcons: Women Travellers in the Balcans*, Bradford: Bradford University Press, 1991.

Tim Allen and Jean Seaton, *The Media of Conflict: War Reporting and Representations of Ethnic Violence*, London and New York: Zed Books, 1999.

Benedict Anderson, *Imagined Communities*, London: Verso, 1991.

Anton Antonowicz, 'The Widow of a Warlord Who Believes She's a Star', *The Mirror*, 28 July 2001, 26–7.

Branimir Anzulović, *Heavenly Serbia: From Myth to Genocide*, London: Hurst, 1999.

Badredine Arfi, 'Ethnic Fear: The Social Construction of Insecurity', *Security Studies*, vol. 8, no. 1, 1998, 151–203.

Vladimir Arsenijević, *U potpaljublju. Saponska opera*, Belgrade: Vreme, 1995.

Milica Bakić Hayden, 'Nesting Orientalisms: The case of the Former Yugoslavia', *Slavic Review*, vol. 54, no. 4, 1995, 917–931.

Mikhail Bakhtin, *Rabelais and his world*, Bloomington, Indiana: Indiana University Press, 1984.

Pam Ballinger, 'Definitional Dilemmas: Southeastern Europe as "Culture Area"', *Balkanologie*, vol. 3, no. 2, December 1999, 73–91.

Pam Ballinger, 'Remembering the Istrian Exodus: Memory in a Trans-State Context', in Bojan Baskar and Borut Brumen (eds), *Mediterranean Ethnological Summer School*, vol. 2, Ljubljana: Inštitut za multikulturne raziskave, 1998.

Ivo Banac, *The National Question in Yugoslavia: Origins, History, Politics*, Ithaca: Cornell University Press, 1984.

Ivo Banac, 'Post-Communism as Post-Yugoslavism: the Yugoslav Non-Revolutions of

1989–1990', in Ivo Banac (ed.), *Eastern Europe in Revolution*, Ithaca: Cornell University Press, 1991.

Fran Barbalić, 'The Jugoslavs of Italy', *Slavonic Review*, vol. 15, no. 43, 1936, 177–90.

Tony Barber, 'A Call to Save Sarajevo', *The Independent*, 26 July 1993, 1.

Stephen Barbour and Cathie Carmichael (eds), *Language and Nationalism in Europe*, Oxford: Oxford University Press, 2000.

Roland Barthes, *New Critical Essays*, translated by Richard Howard, New York: Hill and Wang, 1980.

Elisabeth Barker, 'The Origin of the Macedonian Dispute', in James Pettifer (ed.) *The New Macedonian Question*, Basingstoke, Palgrave, 2001, 2nd edn, pp. 3–14.

Bojan Baskar, 'Made in Trieste. Geopolitical Fears of an Istrianist Discourse on the Mediterranean', *Narodna Umjetnost*, vol. 36, no. 1, 1999, pp. 121–34.

Bojan Baskar, 'Anthropologists Facing the Collapse of Yugoslavia', *Diogenes*, vol. 47, no. 188, 1999, 60.

Stephen Bates, 'Blood stained hands dabble in paint', *The Guardian*, 15 July 1997, 11.

Stephen Bates, 'Serb fury at jail for killer', *The Guardian*, July 15th, 1997, 11.

Mart Bax, 'Ruža's Problems: Gender Relations and Violence in a Bosnian Rural Community', in Sabrina P. Ramet (ed.), *Gender Politics in the Western Balkans: Women and Society in Yugoslavia and the Yugoslav Successor States*, Pennsylvania: Penn State Press, 1999, pp. 259–73.

Mart Bax, 'Barbarization in a Bosnian Pilgrimage Center', in Joel M. Halpern and David A. Kideckel (eds), *Neighbors at War. Anthropological Perspectives on Yugoslav Ethnicity, Culture and History*, Pennsylvania: Penn State Press, 2000, pp. 187–202.

Miron Krešimir Begić, *Ustaški Pokret 1929–1941: pregled njegove poviesti*, Buenos Aires: Naklada Smotre Ustaša, 1986.

Vitomir Belaj, 'Jokes about the Serbs, Autumn 1991', *Etnološka stičišča*, vols 5 and 7, 1997, 46–52.

Martin Bell, *In Harm's Way. Reflections of a War-Zone Thug*, Harmondsworth: Penguin, 1996.

Andrew Bell-Fialkoff, *Ethnic Cleansing*, New York and Oxford: St. Martin's Press, 1996.

Esther Benbassa, *Juifs des Balkans: espaces judéo-ibériques, XIVe–Xxe siècles*, Paris: La Découverte, 1993.

Chris Bennett, *Yugoslavia's Bloody Collapse. Causes, Course and Consequences*, London: Hurst, 1995.

Homi K. Bhabha, *The Location of Culture*, London: Routledge, 1994.

Florian Bieber, 'The Conflict in Former Yugoslavia as a "Fault Line War"? Testing the Validity of Samuel Huntington's "Clash of Civilizations"', *Balkanologie*, vol. 3, no. 1, 1999, 33–48.

Florian Bieber, 'Muslim National Identity in the Balkans before the Establishment of Nation States', *Nationalities Papers*, vol. 28, no. 1, March 2000, 13–28.

Florian Bieber, 'The Challenge of Democracy in Divided Societies: Lessons from Bosnia – Challenges for Kosovo', in Džemal Sokolović and Florian Bieber (eds), *Reconstructing Multiethnic Societies. The Case of Bosnia-Herzegovina*, Aldershot: Ashgate, 2001.

Florian Bieber, *Serbischer Nationalismus vom Tod Titos zum Sturz Miloševićs*, Unpublished Doctoral Dissertation, Vienna University, March 2001.

Marc Biondich, *Stjepan Radić, the Croat Peasant Party and the Politics of Mass Mobilization, 1904–1928*, Toronto: University of Toronto Press, 2000.

Chris Bird, 'Living With the Enemy Next Door', *Guardian Weekly*, 16–22 September 1999, 4.

Chris Bird, 'Chief of "Balkan Auschwitz" Gets 20 Years in Jail', *The Guardian*, 5 October 1999, 16.

Ljubo Boban, 'Jasenovac and the Manipulation of History', *East European Politics and Societies*, vol. 4, no. 3, 1990, 580–92.

Ljubo Boban, 'Still More Balance on Jasenovac and the Manipulation of History', *East European Politics and Societies*, vol. 6, no. 2, 1992, 207–17.

Christopher Boehm, *Montenegrin Social Organization and Values: Political Ethnography of a Refuge Area Tribal Adaptation*, New York: AMS Press, 1983.

Dimitrije Bogdanović, *Knjiga o Kosovu*, Belgrade, Srpska akademija nauka i umetnosti, 1985.

Sergio Bonazza, 'Austro-Slavism as the Motive of Kopitar's Work' *Slovene Studies*, vol. 5, 1993, 155–64.

Carrie Booth Walling, 'The History and Politics of Ethnic Cleansing', in Ken Booth (ed.), *The Kosovo Tragedy. The Human Rights Dimension*, London: Frank Cass, 2001, pp. 47–66.

'Bosnian Serb Daily Breaks Taboo' <http://www.iwpr.net/balkans/news> on 17 September 1999.

Xavier Bougarel, *Bosnie. Anatomie d'un conflit*, Paris: La Découverte, 1996.

Xavier Bougarel, in 'La "revanche des campagnes", entre réalité sociologique et mythe nationaliste', *Balkanologie*, vol. 2, no. 1, 1998, 17–36.

Joanna Bourke, *An Intimate History of Killing. Face to Face Killing in Twentieth Century Europe*, London: Granta, 1999.

Glen Bowman, 'Xenophobia, Fantasy and the Nation: the Logic of Ethnic Violence in Former Yugoslavia', *Balkan Forum*, vol. 2, no. 2, 1994, 135–64.

Catherine Wendy Bracewell, *The Uscoks of Senj. Piracy, Banditry and Holy War in the Sixteenth Century Adriatic*, Ithaca: Cornell University Press, 1992.

Wendy Bracewell, 'Women, Motherhood and Contemporary Serbian Nationalism', paper presented at History Workshop Conference, Leeds, 1994, pp. 1–16.

Wendy Bracewell, 'Rape in Kosovo: Masculinity and Serbian Nationalism', *Nations and Nationalism*, vol. 6, no. 4, 2000, 563–90.

Michael Branch and Celia Hawkesworth (eds), *The Uses of Tradition: A Comparative Enquiry into the Nature, Uses and Functions of Oral Poetry in the Balkans, the Baltic and Africa*, London: School of Slavonic and East European Studies Occasional Paper, no. 6, 1994.

Fernand Braudel, *The Mediterranean and the Mediterranean World in the Age of Philip II*, vol. 1, London: Fontana, 1982.

Tone Bringa, *Being Muslim the Bosnian Way*, Princeton: Princeton University Press, 1995.

V. Brodnjak, *Razlikovni rječnik srpskog i hrvatskog jezika*, Zagreb, Skolske novine, 1993.

Keith Brown, 'The Macedonian Question', in *Central and South-Eastern Europe*, London: Europa, 2000, pp. 53–7.

Susan Brownmiller, *Against Our Will: Men, Women and Rape*, New York: Simon and Schuster, 1975.

Rogers Brubaker, *Nationalism Reframed. Nationhood and the National Question in Europe*, Cambridge: Cambridge University Press, 1996.

Michael Burleigh and Wolfgang Wippermann, *The Racial State: Germany 1933–1945*, Cambridge: Cambridge University Press, 1991.

Nebojša Čagorović, 'Montenegrin Identity: Past, Present and Future', *Journal of Area Studies*, vol. 3, 1993, pp. 129–36.

Joško Caleta, 'Gusle moje, "nova" davorijo': Trends and Processes in the Music Making of Croatian Guslari at the Beginning of the 21st Century', Paper delivered at the Mediterranean Ethnology Conference, Piran, 20 September 2001.

Euan Cameron, *The European Reformation*, Oxford: Clarendon Press, 1991.

Elias Canetti, *Die gerettete Zunge: Geschichte einer Jugend*, Frankfurt am Main: Fischer, 1979.

Cathie Carmichael, 'Locating Trieste in the Eighteenth and Nineteenth Centuries', in

Borut Brumen and Zmago Smitek (eds), *Mediterranean Ethnological Summer School*, Ljubljana: Inštitut za multikulturne raziskave, 1995, pp. 2–11.

Cathie Carmichael, '"A People exists and that People has its language". Language and Nationalism in the Balkans', in Stephen Barbour and Cathie Carmichael (eds), *Language and Nationalism in Europe*, Oxford: Oxford University Press, 2000, 221–39.

Cathie Carmichael, 'Conclusions: Language and National Identity in Europe' in Stephen Barbour and Cathie Carmichael (eds), *Language and Nationalism in Europe*, Oxford: Oxford University Press, 2000, pp. 280–9.

Joyce Cary, *Memoir of the Bobotes*, London: Michael Joseph, 1964.

Stojan Cerović, 'Koga briga?', *Vreme* 547, 28 June, 2001 at <http://www.vreme.com/cms/view.php?id=290987> on 30 June 2001.

Stoyan Christowe, *Heroes and Assassins*, New York: McBride, 1935.

Norman Cigar, *Genocide in Bosnia: The Policy of 'Ethnic Cleansing'*, College Station: Texas A&M University, 1995.

Norman Cigar, 'The Serbo-Croatian War', in Stjepan Meštrović (ed.), *Genocide after Emotion. The Postemotional Balkan War*, London: Routledge, 1996, pp. 51–90.

Norman Cigar, *Vojislav Koštunica and Serbia's Future*, London: Saqi Books, 2001.

Ante Ciliga, *Sam kroz Europu u ratu*, Rome: Na pragu sutranšnjice, 1978.

G.D. Clayton, *Britain and the Eastern Question: Missolonghi to Gallipoli*, London: Lion Library, 1974.

Simon Clements, *A Journal of My Travels . . . in the Year 1715*, British Library, Egerton Mss 2167.

Lenard J. Cohen, *Broken Bonds: the Disintegration of Yugoslavia*, Boulder, Colorado: Westview, 1993.

Lenard J. Cohen, *Serpent in the Bosom. The Rise and Fall of Slobodan Milošević*, Boulder, Colorado: Westview, 2001.

Philip J. Cohen, with a foreword by David Riesman, *Serbia's Secret War: Propaganda and the Deceit of History*, College Station: Texas A & M Press, 1996.

Stanley Cohen, *States of Denial. Knowing about Atrocities and Suffering*, Cambridge: Polity Press, 2001.

Ivan Čolović, *Bordel ratnika. Folklor, politika i rat*, Belgrade: Biblioteka XX vek, 1993.

Ivan Čolović, 'Vreme i prostor u savremenoj političkoj mitologiji', in Mirjana Prošić-Dvornić (ed.), *Kulture u tranziciji*, Belgrade: Plato, 1994, pp. 121–8.

Fanny Copeland, 'Who are the Yugo-Slavs?', *Balkan Review*, vol. 1, 1919, 41.

Bože Čović (ed.), *Izvori velikosrpske agresije*, Zagreb: August Cesarec & Skolska knjiga, 1993.

Jane Cowan (ed.), *Macedonia. The Politics of Identity and Difference*, London: Pluto, 2000.

Walter Crawfurd Price, *The Balkan Cockpit, the Political and Military Story of the Balkan Wars in Macedonia*, London: T. Werner Laurie, 1914.

Ivan Crkvenčić, 'Promjene broja pučanstva Knina od druge polovice 19. stoljeća', in Stjepan Antoljak (ed.). *Kninski Zbornik*, Zagreb: Matica Hrvatska, 1993.

Zvane Crnja, *Cultural History of Croatia*, translated by Vladimir Ivir. Zagreb: Office of Information, 1962, p. 278.

Vasa Čubrilović, 'Iseljavanje Arnauta', in Bože Čović (ed.) *Izvori velikosrpske agresije*, Zagreb: August Cesarec and školska knjiga, 1991, pp. 106–24.

Jovan Cvijić, *La péninsule balkanique. Geographie humaine*, Paris: A. Colin, 1918.

Daniel Daianu and Thanos Veremis, 'Introduction', in Thanos Veremis and Daniel Daianu (eds), *Balkan Reconstruction*, London: Frank Cass, 2001, pp. 1–11.

Zoran Dalasković, 'The Confessions begin', *War Report*, no. 55, October 1997, 9.

Robert Darnton, *The Kiss of Lamourette: Reflections in French History*, New York: Norton, 1990.

Mitar Debelonogić, *Balije*, Jahorinksi potok, 1997.

Vladimir Dedjer, *Dnevnik*, Belgrade: Jugoslaven ska knjiga, 1951, 2 vols (in Serbo-Croat).

Vladimir Dedijer, *The War Diaries of Vladimir Dedijer*, Ann Arbor: University of Michigan Press, vol. 1, 1990.

Vladimir Dedijer, *Genocid na muslimana 1941–45, Zbornik documenta i svjedocenja*, Sarajevo: Svietlost, 1990.

Vladimir Dedijer, *The Yugoslav Auschwitz and the Vatican: the Croatian Massacre of Serbs during World War II*, Buffalo, NY: Prometheus Books, 1992.

Panyote Elias Dimitras, 'Writing and Rewriting History in the Context of Balkan Nationalism', *Southeast European Politics*, October 2000, vol. 1, no. 1, 41–59.

Aleksa Djilas, *The Contested Country: Yugoslav Unity and Communist Revolution, 1919–195*, Cambridge, Massachusetts: Harvard University Press, 1991.

Milovan Djilas, *Land without Justice*. New York: Harcourt Brace Jovanovich, 1958.

Nina Dobrković, 'Yugoslavia and Macedonia in the Years 1991–6: From Brotherhood to Neighbourhood', in James Pettifer (ed.), *The New Macedonian Question*, Basingstoke, Palgrave, 2001, 2nd edn, pp. 79–95.

Charles Dobson, 'Appendix: The Smyrna Holocaust', in Lysimachos Oeconomos, *The Tragedy of the Christian Near East*, London: Anglo-Hellenic League, 1923.

Dom i Svijet, Broj 291, 10, travanj, 2000 at <http://www.hic.hr/dom/291/dom22.htm> 10 October 2001.

Mary Douglas, *Purity and Danger: An Analysis of the Concepts of Pollution and Taboo*, London: Routledge and Kegan Paul, 1966.

Slavenka Drakulić, *Balkan Express. Fragments From the Other Side of War*, London: Hutchinson, 1993.

Adolf Dressler, *Kroatien*, Essen: Essenerverlagsanstalt, 1942.

Ger Duijzings, *Religion and the Politics of Identity in Kosovo*, London: Hurst, 2000.

Vladimir Dvorniković, *Karakterlogija Jugoslovena*, Belgrade: Kosmos, 1939.

Jovan Erdeljanović, *Stara Crna Gora*, Belgrade: Rodoljub, 1926.

Mary Edith Durham, *Some Tribal Origins, Laws and Customs of the Balkans*, London: George Allen and Unwin, 1928.

Mary Edith Durham, *The Struggle for Scutari*, London: Edward Arnold, 1914.

'Extract of a Letter from Orschowa, in Servia, dated January last', *The Times*, 25 August, 1815, 3.

Lovett Fielding Edwards, *A Wayfarer in Yugoslavia*, London: Methuen, 1939.

Daniel Elazar *et al.* (eds), *The Balkan Jewish Communities: Yugoslavia, Bulgaria, Greece and Turkey*, Lanham, Md: University Press of America, 1984.

Georg Elwert: 'Nationalismus und Ethnizität: Über die Bildung von WirGruppen', *Kölner Zeitschrift für Soziologie und Sozialpsychologie*, no. 3, 1989, 440–64.

James Ellis, Interview with Douglas Hurd, *Metro*, 9 October 2001, 10.

Jovan Erdeljanović, *Stara Crna Gora*, Belgrade: Rodoljub, 1926.

Frantz Fanon, *The Wretched of the Earth*, Harmondsworth: Penguin, 1961.

Lewis S. Feuer (ed.) *Marx and Engels. Basic Writings on Politics and Philosophy*, Glasgow: Collins, 1969.

Zlata Filipović, *Zlata's Diary. A Child's Life in Sarajevo*, Harmondsworth: Penguin, 1994.

Peter Finn and R. Jeffrey Smith, 'Kosovo's Hit-and-Run Ground War', *Guardian Weekly*, 2 May 1999, 15.

Peter Finn, 'Nato Losing the Battle for Kosovo Minds', *Guardian Weekly*, 12–18 August 1999, 31.

Robert Fisk, 'Dead Reckoning: Holocausts vs holocausts', *The Independent*, 5 August 2000, <http://www.pipeline.com/~rgibson/fisk.html> on 8 October 2001.

Paula Franklin Lytle, 'U.S. Policy Towards the Demise of Yugoslavia: the "Virus of Nationalism"', *East European Politics and Societies*, vol. 6, no. 3, 1992, 303–18.

Francine Friedman, *The Bosnian Muslims. Denial of a Nation*, Boulder, Colorado: Westview 1996.

'Frontiers of Servia', *The Times*, 27 February 1815, 2.

Paul Garde, 'Les Balkans vus de France au XXe siécle', *Esprit*, December 2000.

Nathan Gardels, 'Two Concepts of Nationalism: An Interview with Isaiah Berlin', *New York Review of Books*, 21 November 1991, 19–23.

Clifford Geertz, *Interpretation of Cultures*, New York: Basic Books, 1973.

Ernest Gellner, *Nations and Nationalism*, Oxford: Blackwell, 1983.

H.H. Gerth and C. Wright Mills, *From Max Weber. Essays in Sociology*, London: Routledge and Kegan Paul, 1985.

Ryan Gingeras, 'Macedonia in Crisis: British Press Coverage of the Illinden Uprising of 1903 and the Conceptualization of the Balkans', Paper delivered at the 6th World Congress of the Association for the Study of Nationalities (ASN), Columbia University 5–7 April 2001.

Carlo Ginzburg, *Myths, Emblems, Clues*, London: Hutchinson Radius, 1990.

Carlo Ginzburg, *The Cheese and the Worms*, Harmondsworth: Penguin, 1992a.

Carlo Ginzburg, 'Just One Witness', in Saul Friedländer (ed.), *Probing the Limits of Representation. Nazism and the Final Solution*, Cambridge, Massachusetts: Harvard University Press, 1992b, pp. 82– 96.

Christian Giordano, 'The Balkans: European Periphery, Epicentre of Ethnicity and Landscape of Feuds', *Anthropological Journal on European Cultures*, vol. 4, no. 2, 1995, 95–106.

Misha Glenny, *The Rebirth of History. Eastern Europe in the Age of Democracy*, Harmondsworth: Penguin, 1990.

Misha Glenny, *The Fall of Yugoslavia. The Third Balkan War*, Harmondsworth: Penguin 1992.

Misha Glenny, *The Balkans 1804–1999. Nationalism, War and the Great Powers*, London: Granta, 1999.

Jonathan Glover, *A Moral History of the 20ᵗʰ Century*, London: Jonathan Cape, 2000.

Ivo Goldstein, *Croatia: A History*, London: Hurst, 1999.

Vesna Goldsworthy, *Inventing Ruritania: the Imperialism of the Imagination*, New Haven: Yale University Press, 1998.

Philip Gourevitch, *We Wish to Inform You that Tomorrow We Will Be Killed with Our Families. Stories from Rwanda*, London: Picador, 1998.

James Gow, *The Triumph of the Lack of Will. International Diplomacy and the Yugoslav War*, London: Hurst, 1997.

James Gow and Cathie Carmichael, *Slovenia and the Slovenes. A Small State in the New Europe*, London: Hurst, 2000.

Anthony Grafton, 'Introduction', in Nicolo Machiavelli, *The Prince*, Harmondsworth: Penguin, 1999, p. xix.

Robert Greenberg, 'Dialects and Ethnicity in the Former Yugoslavia. The Case of Southern Baranja (Croatia)', *Slavic and East European Journal*, vol. 42, 1998, 710–22.

Mirko Grmek, Marc Gjidara and Neven Šimac (eds), *Etničko Čišćenje. Povijesni dokumenti o jednoj srpskoj ideologiji*, Zagreb: Nakladni zavod Globus, 1993.

Valentina Gulin, 'Morlacchism Between Enlightenment and Romanticism (Identification and Self-identification of the European Other), *Narodna Umjetnost*, vol. 34, 1997, 77–100.

Roy Gutman, *A Witness to Genocide: The First Inside Account of the Horrors of Ethnic Cleansing in Bosnia*, Shaftesbury: Element, 1993.

158   *Bibliography*

Richard C. Hall, *The Balkan Wars 1912–13. Prelude to the First World War*, London: Routledge, 2000.

Radovan Haluzik, 'Rumours and Legends in the Present Ethnic Conflict in the Former Yugoslavia and the Caucasus', Paper presented at the Centre of South-East European Studies, School of Slavonic and East European Studies, University of London, 8 December 1999.

Robert Hamilton Lang, *Roumelian Coup D'état, Servo-Bulgarian War, and the Latest Phase of the Eastern Question*, London: Harrison, 1886.

Florence Hartmann, *Milošević. La Diagonale du Fou*, Paris: Denoël, 1999.

Robert Hayden, 'Balancing Discussion of Jasenovac and the Manipulation of History', *East European Politics and Societies*, vol. 6, no. 2, 1992, 207–17.

Robert Hayden, 'Muslims as "Others" in Serbian and Croatian Politics', in Joel M. Halpern and David A. Kideckel (eds), *Neighbors at War. Anthropological Perspectives on Yugoslav Ethnicity, Culture and History*, Pennsylvania: Penn State Press, 2000, pp. 116–24.

Robert Hayden and Milica Bakić Hayden, 'Orientalist Variations of the Theme "Balkans": Symbolic Geography in Recent Yugoslav Cultural Politics' *Slavic Review*, vol. 51, no. 1, 1992, 1–15.

Michael Hechter, 'Nationalism and Group Solidarity', *Ethnic and Racial Studies*, vol. 10, no. 4, 1987, 414–26.

Hermann Hesse 'Wanderung', in Werner Heilman (ed.) *Heimatgeschichten*, Munich: Wilhelm Heyne Verlag, 1982, pp. 239–49.

Ervin Hladnik-Milharčič and Ivo Štandeker, 'Tako v nebesih kot na zemlji', *Mladina*, 7 June 1989, 8.

Eric Hobsbawm, *Bandits*, Harmondsworth: Penguin, 1985.

Eric Hobsbawm and Terence Ranger (eds), *The Invention of Tradition*, Cambridge: Cambridge University Press, 1992.

Michael Holquist (ed.), *The Dialogic Imagination. Four Essays by M.M. Bakhtin*, Austin: University of Texas Press, 1981.

Branko Horvat, *Kosovsko Pitanje*, Zagreb: Globus, 1989.

Veronica Horwell, 'A Kind of Peace', *The Guardian*, 12 October 1999, G2, 2.

Jan Willem Honig and Norbert Both, *Srebrenica. Record of a War Crime*, Harmondsworth: Penguin, 1996.

Marjorie Housepian, *Smyrna 1922: the Destruction of a City*, London: Faber, 1972.

Miroslav Hroch, 'Nationalism and National Movements: Comparing the Past and the Present of Central and Eastern Europe', *Nations and Nationalism*, vol. 2, no. 1, 1996, 35–44.

Rezak Hukanović, *The Tenth Circle of Hell. A Memoir of Life in the Death Camps of Bosnia*, London: Abacus, 1998.

Samuel P. Huntington, *The Clash of Civilizations and the Remaking of the New World Order*, New York: Simon and Schuster, 1996.

Omer Ibrahimagić, *Srpsko osporavanje Bosne i Bošnjaka*, Sarajevo: Magistrat, 2001.

Gordana Igrić, 'In Search of the Indicted', *Tribunal*, August/September, 1997, p. 4.

International Commission of Inquiry appointed at the Request of the Greek Red Cross, *Treatment of Greek Prisoners in Turkey*, London: Anglo-Hellenic League, 1923.

International Commission on Kosovo, *The Kosovo Report: Conflict: International Response: Lessons Learned*, Oxford: Oxford University Press, 2000.

Jill Irvine, 'Nationalism and the Extreme Right in the Former Yugoslavia', in Luciano Cheles *et al.* (eds), *The Far Right in Eastern and Western Europe*, London: Longman, 1995.

Alija Izetbegović, 'The Islamic Declaration: A Programme for the Islamicisation of Muslims and the Muslim Peoples', *South Slav Journal*, vol. 6, Spring 1983, pp. 56–89.

T.G. Jackson, *Dalmatia, the Quarnero and Istria with Cettigne in Montenegro and the Island of Grado*, Oxford: Clarendon Press, 1887.

Barbara Jelavich, *History of the Balkans*, Cambridge: Cambridge University Press, 1983, 2 vols.

Fikreta Jelić-Butić, *Četnici u Hrvatskoj 1941–1945*, Zagreb: Globus, 1986.

Miroljub Jevtić, *Savremeni džihad kao rat*, Belgrade: Nova knjiga, 1989.

Božidar Jezernik, *Spol in spolnost in extremis: antropološka študija o nemških koncentracijskih taborščih Dachau, Buchenwald, Mauthausen, Ravensbrück, Auschwitz 1933–1945*, Ljubljana: Borec, 1993.

Božidar Jezernik, 'Qudret Kemeri: a Bridge Between Barbarity and Civilisation', *Slavonic and East European Review*, vol. 73, 1995, 470–84.

Božidar Jezernik, '"Evropeizacija" Balkanskih mest kot vzrok za njihovo "Balkanizacijo"', *Glasnik slovenskega etnološkega društva*, no. 35, 1995, 2–13.

Božidar Jezernik, *Dežela, kjer je vse narobe. Prispevki k etnologiji Balkana*. Ljubljana: Znanstveno in publicistično središče, 1998.

P. B. Joanne, *États du Danube et des Balkans*, Part I, Paris: Librarie Hachette, 1895.

Stanoje Jovanović and Dragan Jerković, *Zločin Hrvatske države '91*, Belgrade: Vojni muzej, 1991.

Tim Judah, *The Serbs. History, Myth and Destruction of Yugoslavia*, New Haven: Yale University Press, 1997.

Tim Judah, *Kosovo. War and Revenge*, New Haven: Yale University Press, 2000.

Robert D. Kaplan, *Balkan Ghosts. A Journey through History*, New York: St. Martin's Press, 1993.

Anastasia N. Karakasidou, *Fields of Wheat, Hills of Blood. Passages to Nationhood in Greek Macedonia 1870–1990*, Chicago: University of Chicago Press, 1997.

Adolf Karger, 'Die serbischen Siedlungsräume in Kroatien', *Osteuropa*, vol. 42, no. 2, 1992, 141–6.

Caroline Kennedy-Pipe and Penny Stanley, 'Rape in War. Lesssons of the Balkan Conflicts in the 1990s', in Ken Booth (ed.), *The Kosovo Tragedy. The Human Rights Dimension*, London: Frank Cass, 2001, pp. 67–84.

George F. Kennan, *The Other Balkan Wars. A 1913 Carnegie Endowment Inquiry in Retrospect with a New Introduction and Reflections on the Present Conflict*, Washington DC: Carnegie Endowment for International Peace, 1993.

Obrad Kesić, 'Women and Gender Imagery in Bosnia: Amazons, Sluts, Victims, Witches and Wombs', in Sabrina Petra Ramet (ed.), *Gender Politics in the Western Balkans: Women and Society in Yugoslavia and the Yugoslav Successor States*, Pennsylvania: Penn State University Press, 1999, pp. 187–202.

Pascalis Kitromilides, '"Balkan mentality": History, Legend, Imagination', *Nations and Nationalism*, vol. 2, 1996, 163–91.

Mirko Klarin, 'Defendant for the Prosecution', *Tribunal*, November/December 1996, 3.

Mirko Klarin, 'The Case Against Karadžić', *Tribunal*, August/September, 1997, 2–3.

Jacques Klein, Press statement on the UNMIBH-UNESCO Sarajevo Haggadah Project, at <http://www.unmibh.org/news/srsgspe/2001/06apr01.htm> on 15 December 2001.

Dona Kolar-Panov, *Video, War and the Diasporic Imagination*, London: Routledge, 1997.

Radomir Konstantinović, *Filosofija palanke*, Belgrade: Nolit, 1981.

'Kordić and Cerkez trial: HVO tactics in central Bosnia', at <http://www.bosnet.org> on 10 October 2001.

Monica Krippner, 'British Medical Women in Serbia During and After the First World War', J.B. Allcock and A. Young (eds), *Black Lambs and Grey Falcons: Women Travellers in the Balkans*, Bradford: Bradford University Press, 1991, pp. 65–81.

Bogdan Križman, *Pavelić u bjekstvu*, Zagreb: Globus, 1986.

Nikita Krushchev, *Krushchev Remembers*, London: Andre Deutsch, 1971.

Kupreskić Judgement, VII–VIII, International Tribunal for the Prosecution of Persons Responsible for Serious Violations of International Humanitarian Law Committed in the Territory of the Former Yugoslavia Since 1991, 14 January 2000, at <http://www.pict-pcti.org/. . . CTY.01.14.kupreskic.html> on 10 October, 2001.

Emir Kusturica dir. *Underground*, 1995.

Bora Kuzmanović and Mirjana Vasović, 'Tradicionalistička orientacija', in Zagorka Golubović (ed.), *Društveni karakter i društvene promene u svetlu nacionalnih sukoba*, Belgrade: BIGZ, 1995, pp. 111–31.

John R. Lampe, *Yugoslavia as History. Twice There Was a Country*, Cambridge: Cambridge University Press, 2000.

Jutta Lauth Bacas, 'The Constructions of National Identity in a Local Setting: the Case of Lésbos, an Island at the Greek-Turkish Border', *Anthropological Journal on European Cultures*, vol. 4, no. 2, 1995, 75–86.

Franklin Lindsay, *Beacons in the Night*, Cambridge: Cambridge University Press, 1993.

William Lithgow, *Discourse of a Peregrination in Europe, Asia and Affricke*, Amersterdam: Theatrum Orbis Terrarum: Da Capo Press, 1971.

Raymond Lohne, 'The Experience of Ethnic Cleansing. The Case of the Danube Swabians of Yugoslavia'. Paper delivered at the conference 'Ethnic Cleansing in Twentieth Century Europe', Duquesne University, Pittsburgh, 16–18 November 2000.

Jelena Lovrić, 'Dario Kordić: the Croatian Karadžić', *Tribunal*, November/December, 1996, 5.

Peter Maass, *Love thy Neighbor. A Story of War*, New York: Vintage, 1996.

Justin McCarthy, *Death and Exile, The Ethnic Cleansing of Ottoman Muslims 1821–1922*, Princeton, NJ: Darwin Press, 1996.

Ivana Maček, 'Predicament of War. Sarajevo Experience and the Ethics of War', in Bettina E. Schmidt and Ingo W. Schröder (eds), *Anthopology of Violence and Conflict*, London: Routledge, 2001, pp. 197–224.

Dušan Makavejev dir. *Montenegro – or Pearl and Pigs*, 1981.

Noel Malcolm, *Bosnia: A Short History*, London: Macmillan, 1994.

Noel Malcolm, *Kosovo: A Short History*, London: Macmillan, 1998.

Andrew Mango, *Atatürk*, London: John Murray, 1999.

Xavier Marmier, *Lettres sur L'Adriatique et le Montenegro*, vol. 2, Paris: Imprimerie Ch. Lahure, Société de Geographie, 1853.

J.A.R Marriott, *The Eastern Question: an Historical Study in European Diplomacy*, Oxford: Clarendon Press, 1940, 4th edn.

Hrvoje Matković, *Povijest Nezavisne Države Hrvatske*, Zagreb: Nakalda Pavičić, 1994.

Mark Mazower, *Dark Continent: Europe's Twentieth Century*, Harmondsworth: Penguin, 1998.

Mark Mazower, *The Balkans*, London: Weidenfeld and Nicolson, 2000.

Mark Mazower, *Inside Hitler's Greece*, New Haven: Yale University Press, new edn, 2001.

Ivan Mazuranić, *Smrt Smail-age Čengijića*, Zagreb: Matica Hrvatska, 1952.

James Meek, 'From Ivory Towers to Killing Fields', *Guardian Weekly*, 18–24 Novemeber 1999, 23.

Julie Mertus, Jasmina Tesanović, Habiba Metikos and Rada Borić, (eds), *The Suitcase. Refugee Voices from Bosnia and Croatia*, Berkeley: University of California Press, 1997.

Julie Mertus, *Kosovo: How Myths and Truths Started a War*, Berkeley: University of California Press, 1999.

Julie Mertus, 'Women in Kosovo: Contested Terrains. The Role of National Identity in Shaping and Challenging Gender Identity', in Sabrina Petra Ramet (ed.), *Gender Politics* in the Western Balkans: Women and Society in Yugoslavia and the Yugoslav Successor States,* Pennsylvania: Penn State University Press, 1999, p. 171–86.

Stjepan Meštrović, (ed.), *Genocide After Emotion. The Postemotional Balkan War* London: Routledge, 1996.

Stjepan Meštrović, Slaven Letica and Miroslav Goreta, *Habits of the Balkan Heart. Social Character and the Fall of Communism,* College Station: Texas A&M University Press, 1993.

Matteo Milazzo, *The Chetnik Movement and Yugoslav Resistance,* Baltimore and London: Johns Hopkins University Press, 1975.

Zorka Milich, *A Stranger's Supper: an Oral History of Centegenarian Women in Montenegro,* New York/London: Twayne Publishers/Prentice Hall International, 1995.

'Military Court in Nis Raises Issues of "Cleaning up" in Kosovo, 6 November 2000 found at <http://groups.yahoo.com/group/balkanhr/message/1276> on 2 May 2001.

Arthur Miller, *Echoes down the Corridor. Collected Essays, 1944–2000,* New York: Viking, 2000.

Robert Gary Minnich, 'The Gift of *Koline* and the Articulation of Identity in Slovene Peasant Society', *Etnologia Slavica,* vol. 22, 1990, 151–61.

Josip Mirnić, *Nemci u Bačkoj u drugom svetskom ratu,* Novi Sad: Institut za izućavanje istorije Vojvodine, 1974.

Nilüfer Mizanùglu Reddy, 'The Embroidered Jacket', *Turkish Area Studies,* no. 52, April 2001, 28–37.

Rastko Močnik, 'Eden nov orientalizam: Crnata mitologija na Balkanot', *Naše pismo,* vol. 11, no. 2, 1996.

Rastko Močnik, 'Balkan Orientalisms', in Bojan Baskar and Borut Brumen (eds), *Mediterranean Ethnological Summer School,* vol. II, Inštitut za multikulturne raziskave, Ljubljana, 1998.

Molly Moore, 'NATO Troops find Serbian Torture Cell', *Guardian Weekly,* 27 June 1999, 15.

Vera Mutafchieva, 'The Notion of the "Other" in Bulgaria: The Turks. An Historical Study', in *Anthropological Journal on European Cultures,* vol. 4, no. 2, 1995, 53–74.

'Nadnica za Grijeh. Sučeljavanje za Republikom Srpskom u Bosni', 8 October 2001 at <http://www.intl-crisis-group/projects.balkans/bosnia/reports/A400476š08102001.pdf> on 11 November 2001.

Norman M. Naimark, *Fires of Hatred. Ethnic Cleansing in Twentieth Century Europe,* Cambridge, Massachusetts: Harvard University Press, 2001.

Slobodan Naumović, 'Upotreba tradicije. Politička tranzicija i promena odnosa prema nacionalnim vrednostima u Srbiji 1987–1990', in Mirjana Prošić-Dvornić (ed.), *Kulture u tranziciji,* Belgrade: Plato, 1994, pp. 95–119.

Slobodan Naumović, 'Romanticists or Double Insiders? An Essay on the Origins of Ideologised Discourses in Balkan Ethnology', *Ethnologia balkanica,* vol. 2, 1998, 101–20.

Petar Petrović Njegoš, *Gorski Vijenac,* Sarajevo: Svjetlost, 1990.

David A. Norris, *In the Wake of the Balkan Myth: Questions of Identity and Modernity,* London: Macmillan, 1999.

Richard Norton-Taylor, 'Croats Jailed for Ethnic Slaughter', *Guardian Weekly,* 20–26 January 2000.

Giorgio Nurigiani, *La Macedonia nel Pensiero Italiano,* Roma: Casa Editrice 'Ausonia', 1933.

Dragoljub Ojdanić quoted in *Vikend (Danas),* 14 March, 2001. Found at <http://www.danas/co.yu/20010317/vikend8.htm> on 5 September 2001.

Maggie O'Kane, 'One Family's Story of the Terror inside Kosovo. And of the Friendly Bus Driver Who Turned into a Mass Murderer', *Guardian Weekly,* 27 June 1999, 1.

Omarska- Keraterm trial. Žigić's Brutal Quest for a Family's 'Pot of Gold', <http://www.iwpr.net,> 3 October 2000.

Teofil Pančić, 'After U2', *Vreme*, 23 October, 1997, reprinted at <http://www.bosnia.org.uk/bosrep/novdec97/afteru2.htm> on 15th October 2001.

Ken Parker (ed.), *Early Modern Tales of Orient*, London: Routledge, 1999.

Gabriel Partos, 'Macedonia Rebels Fear Reprisals', BBC News, 4 September 2001, at <http://www.bbc.co.uk.>

Aleksandar Pavković, 'The Serb National Idea: a Revival 1986–92', *Slavonic and East European Review*, vol. 72, no. 3, 1994, 441–95.

Aleksandar Pavković, *The Fragmentation of Yugoslav Nationalism and War in the Balkans*, Basingstoke: Macmillan, 2nd edn, 2000.

Srdja Pavlović, 'Understanding Balkan Nationalism: the Wrong People, in the Wrong Place, at the Wrong Time', *Southeast European Politics*, vol. 1, no. 2, 2000, 115–24.

Stevan K. Pavlowitch, *A History of the Balkans 1804–1945*, London: Longman, 1999.

Pawel Pawlikowski, dir. *Serbian Epics*, BBC films, 1992.

Asim Peco, *Turcizmi u Vukovim Rječnicima*, Belgrade: Vuk Karadžić, 1987.

Borislav Pekić, *Godine koje su pojeli skakavci*, vol. II, BIGZ Jedinstvo: Belgrade, 1991.

Dražena Peranić, 'A journey Across Unexpected Borders', *War Report*, November/December 1995, 46–7.

Artan Peto, 'La communauté juive en Albanie avant et durant la seconde guerre mondiale', in Ioannes K. Chasiotes *et al.* (eds), *The Jewish Communities of Southeastern Europe: From the Fifteenth Century to the End of World War II*, Salonika: Institute for Balkan Studies, 1997, pp. 425–31.

James Pettifer, 'The New Macedonian Question', in James Pettifer (ed.), *The New Macedonian Question*, Basingstoke: Palgrave, 2001, 2nd edn, pp. 15–27.

Edit Petrović, 'Ethnonationalism and the Dissolution of Yugoslavia', in Joel M. Halpern and David A. Kideckel (eds), *Neighbors at War. Anthropological Perspectives on Yugoslav Ethnicity, Culture and History*. Pennsylvania: Penn State Press, 2000, pp. 164–76.

Vladeta Popović (ed.), *The Mountain Wreath of P. P. Nyegosh, Prince Bishop of Montenegro, 1830–1851*, translated by James William Wyles, London: G. Allen and Unwin Ltd, 1930.

Hugh Poulton, 'Non-Albanian Muslim Minorities in Macedonia', in James Pettifer (ed.), *The New Macedonian Question*, Basingstoke, Palgrave, 2001, 2nd edn, pp. 107–125.

Maja Povrzanović, 'Crossing the Borders: Croatian War Ethnographies', *Narodna umjetnost*, vol. 32, no. 1, 1995, 91–106.

George Prevelakis, 'The Return of the Macedonian Question' in F.W. Carter and H.T. Norris (eds), *The Changing Shape of the Balkans*, London: UCL Press, 1996.

Mirjana Prošić-Dvornić, '"Druga Srbija": mirovni i ženski pokret', in Mirjana Prošić-Dvornić (ed.), *Kulture u tranziciji*, Belgrade: Plato, 1994, pp. 179–99.

Mirjana Prošić-Dvornić, 'Serbia: the Inside Story', in in Joel M. Halpern and David A. Kideckel (eds), *Neighbors at War. Anthropological Perspectives on Yugoslav Ethnicity, Culture and History*. Pennsylvania: Penn State Press, 2000, pp. 316–38.

Gérard Prunier, *The Rwanda Crisis. History of a Genocide 1959–1994*, London: Hurst, 1995.

Alenka Puhar, 'Childhood Nightmares and Dreams of Revenge', *Journal of Psychohistory*, vol. 22, no. 2, Fall 1994 at <http://www.psychohistory.com/yugoslav/yugoslav.htm> on 1 October 2001.

Andrew Purvis, Dejan Anastasijević and Massimo Calabresi, 'The Bloody Red Berets', *Time*, 19 March 2001, 27–9.

Andrew Purvis, Dejan Anastasijević, James Graff and Massim. Calabresi, 'A Valley Full of Dangers', *Time*, 19 March 2001, 28.

Radoslav Radenkov, 'The Turkish Minority in Bulgaria', *East European Reporter*, vol. 3, no. 4, 1989, 27–9.

Vitomir Miles Raguz, 'International-brand Justice Earns Bad Marks in Zagreb', *The Wall Street Journal Europe*, 13–14 July 2001, 7.

Jovan Rajić, *Istoriya raznih slovenskih naradov*, Vienna: 1794.

Pedro Ramet, 'From Strossmayer to Stepinac: Croatian National Ideology and Catholicism', *Canadian Review of Studies in Nationalism*, vol. 12, no. 1, 1985, 123–39.

Pedro Ramet, 'The Rock Scene in Yugoslavia', *East European Politics and Societies*, vol. 2, no. 2, Spring 1988, 396–410.

Sabrina P. Ramet, *Nationalism and Federalism in Yugoslavia 1962–1991*, Bloomington: Indiana University Press, 2nd edn, 1994, pp. 98–135.

Sabrina P. Ramet, 'Nationalism and the "Idiocy" of the Countryside: The Case of Serbia', *Ethnic and Racial Studies*, vol. 19, no. 1, 1996, 70–87.

Sabrina P. Ramet (ed.), *Balkan Babel: The Disintegration of Yugoslavia From the Death of Tito to Ethnic War*, Boulder, Colorado: Westview, 1996.

Robert Redfield, *Peasant Culture and Society*, Chicago: University of Chicago Press, 1965.

Madeleine Rees and Sarah Maguire, 'Rape as a Crime against Humanity,' in *Tribunal*, November/December, 1996, 8.

John Reed, *War in Eastern Europe. Travels Through the Balkans in 1915*, London: Orion 1999.

Slobodan Reljić, 'Demagogue in waiting', *Transitions*, March, 1998, 70–5.

Ivo Rendić-Miocević, *Zlo velike jetre: povijest i nepovijest Crnogoraca, Hrvata, Muslimana i Srba*, Split: Književni krug, 1996.

Alex Renton, 'Chamber of Horrors Jails a real Villain of Bosnia at Last', *Evening Standard*, 3 March 2000, 17.

Dunja Rihtman-Augustin, '"We were proud to live with you and are now immensely sad to have lost you." A chronicle of the war through newspaper death notices', *Narodna Umjetnost*, vol. 30, 1993, 279–302.

Dunja Rihtman-Augustin, 'Ugledna etnologinja i antropologinja govori o instrumental-izaciji folklora i teroru mitologijom', *Feral Tribune*, 23 studenoga, 1998, 22–3.

Dunja Rihtman-Augustin, 'O susjedima', in Božidar Jakšić (ed.), Tolerancija-Tolerance, Belgrade-Zemun: Republika – XX vek, 1999, pp. 151–64.

Dunja Rihtman-Augustin, *Ulice moga grada. Antropologija domaćeg terena*, Belgrade, Biblioteka XX vek, 2000.

Cyprien Robert, *Les Slaves de Turquie*, Paris: Passard et Jules Labitte, 1844.

Georg Rosen, *Die Balkan-Haiduken*, Leipzig, F.A. Brockhaus, 1878.

Dennison Rusinow, *The Yugoslav Experiment, 1948–1974*, London: Hurst, 1977.

Edward Said, *Orientalism. Western Conceptions of the Orient*, Harmondsworth: Penguin, 2nd edn, 1995.

Marko Samardžija, *Jezični purizam u NDH*, Zagreb: Hrvatska Sveučilisna Naklada, 1993.

George Sava, *The Chetniks*, London: Regular Publication, 1955.

John Schindler, 'Yugoslavia's First Ethnic Cleansing. The Expulsion of Danubian Germans, 1944–46'. Paper delivered at the conference 'Ethnic Cleansing in Twentieth Century Europe'. Duquesne University, Pittsburgh, 16–18 November 2000.

Bettina E. Schmidt and Ingo W. Schröder (eds), *Anthropology of Violence and Conflict*, London: Routledge, 2001.

George Schöpflin, *Nation, Identity, Power. The New Politics of Europe* London: Hurst, 2000.

Stephanie Schwandner-Sievers, 'The Enactment of "tradition". Albanian Constructions of Identity, Violence and Power in Times of Crisis', in Bettina E. Schmidt and Ingo W. Schröder (eds), *Anthopology of Violence and Conflict*, London: Routledge, 2001, pp. 97–120.

Stephanie Schwandner-Sievers, 'Evoking the Past: Albanian Identifications and Local Power', Unpublished Doctoral Dissertation, Berlin: Free University, September 2001.

Jonathan M. Schwartz, 'The Petrified Forest of Symbols: Deconstructing and Envisaging Macedonia', *Anthropological Journal on European Cultures*, vol. 4, no. 1,1995, 9–23.

Jonathan M. Schwartz, *Pieces of Mosaic. An Essay on the Making of Makedonija*, Intervention Press, Højbjerg, Denmark, 1996.

Jonathan M. Schwartz, 'Civil Society and Ethnic Conflict in the Republic of Macedonia', in Joel M. Halpern and David A. Kideckel (eds), *Neighbors at War. Anthropological Perspectives on Yugoslav Ethnicity, Culture and History*. Pennsylvania: Penn State Press, 2000, pp. 382–400.

Jonathan M. Schwartz, '"Contested Identity" or "Ethnic War"? The Endurance Test in the Republic of Macedonia'. Workshop on 'Macedonian Knots', Mediterranean Ethnology Conference, Piran, 20 September 2001.

Nusret Šehić, *Četništvo u Bosni i Hercegovini (1918–1941). Politička uloga i oblici djelatnosti Četničkih udruženja*, Sarajevo: Akademija nauka i umjetnosti Bosne i Hercegovine, 1971.

Laslo Sekelj, 'Anti-Semitism in Yugoslavia, 1918–1945', *East European Quarterly*, vol. 22, no. 2, 1988, 159–72.

Michael Sells, *The Bridge Betrayed: Religion and Genocide in Bosnia*, 2nd edn, Berkeley: University of California Press, 1998.

Vojislav Šešelj, *Pravo na istinu*, Belgrade: Multiprint, 1988.

Robert W. Seton-Watson, *The Problem of Small Nations and the European Anarchy*, Nottingham: Nottingham University Montague Burton International Relations Series, 1939.

Thanasis D. Sfikas, 'National Movements and Nation Building in the Balkans, 1804–1922: Historic Origins, Contemporary Misunderstandings', in Thanasis D. Sfikas and Christopher Williams (eds) *Ethnicity and Nationalism in East Central Europe and the Balkans*, Ashgate: Aldershot, 1999, pp. 13–44.

Laura Silber and Allan Little, *The Death of Yugoslavia*, Harmondsworth: Penguin, 1995.

Smiljan Simac, 'Croatie, Serbie: les fausses symétries', *Le Monde*, 25 May 1999, 13–4.

Andrei Simić, 'Machismo and Cryptomatriarchy: Power, Affect and Authority in the Traditional Yugoslav Family', in Sabrina P. Ramet (ed.), *Gender Politics in the Western Balkans: Women and Society in Yugoslavia and the Yugoslav Successor States*, Pennsylvania: Penn State Press, 1999, pp. 11–29.

Andrei Simić, 'Nationalism as Folk Ideology. The Case of the Former Yugoslavia', in Joel M. Halpern and David A. Kideckel (eds), *Neighbors at War. Anthropological Perspectives on Yugoslav Ethnicity, Culture and History*, Pennsylvania: Penn State Press, 2000.

Marlise Simons, 'France Examines Its Role in Run-Up to Srebrenica', *International Herald Tribune*, 12 December 2000, 8.

Brendan Simms, *Unfinest Hour: Britain and the Destruction of Bosnia*, London: Allen Lane, 2001.

Lydia Sklevicky, *Konji, Žene, Ratovi*, edited postumously by Dunja Rihtman-Auguštin, Zagreb: Druga, 1996.

Svetlana Slapšak, 'What are Women Made of? Inventing Women in the Yugoslav Area', in G. Brinker-Gabler and S. Smith (eds) *Writing New Identities*, Minneapolis and London: University of Minnesota Press, 1997, pp. 358–73.

'Slovenci in Srbi smo bratje', *Mladina*, 25 June 1989, 48.

Glenda Sluga, *Bonegilla: 'A Place of No Hope'*, Melbourne: Melbourne University Press, 1988.

Glenda Sluga, *The Problem of Trieste and the Italo-Yugoslav Border. Difference, Identity and Sovereignty in Twentieth Century Europe*, New York: SUNY, 2000.

Anthony D. Smith, 'Chosen Peoples', in John Hutchinson and Anthony D. Smith (eds), *Ethnicity*, Oxford: Oxford University Press, 1996, pp. 189–197.

Anthony D. Smith, *Nations and Nationalism in a Global Era*, Cambridge: Polity, 1996.

Anthony D. Smith, *Nationalism and Modernism: a Critical Survey of Recent Theories of Nations and Natioanlism*, London: Routledge, 1998.

Cornelia Sorabje, 'A Very Modern War: Terror and Territory in Bosnia-Hercegovina', in Robert A. Hinde and Helen E. Watson (eds), *War: A Cruel Necessity? The Bases of Institutionalized Violence*, London: I.B. Tauris, 1995.

Cornelia Sorabje, 'Islam and Bosnia's Muslim Nation', in F.W. Carter and H.T. Norris (eds), *The Changing Shape of the Balcans*, London: University College Press, 1996.

Pieter Spierenburg, 'Masculinity, Violence and Honor: An Introduction', in ibid. (ed.), *Men and Violence. Gender, Honor and Rituals in Modern Europe and America*, Columbus, Ohio; Ohio Sate University Press, 1998, pp. 1–29.

Jonathan Steele, 'Voters Defy Nationalists by Returning to Pre-war Home Towns', *The Guardian*, 15 September 1997, 12.

Jonathan Steele, 'They Tracked Us Day and Night. Then They Gunned Us Down', *Guardian Weekly*, 15–21 July 1999, 3.

Djordje Stefanović, 'Michael Hechter's Rational Choice Theory of Nationalism v. the Post-Communist Experience', Paper delivered at the 6th World Congress of the Association for the Study of Nationalities (ASN), Columbia University, 5–7 April 2001.

Vera Stein Erlich, *Family in Transition: a Study of 300 Yugoslav Villages*, Princeton: Princeton University Press, 1966.

Traian Stoianovich, *Balkan Worlds: The First and Last Europe*, New York and London: Sharpe, 1994.

Gale Stokes, *Nationalism in the Balkans. An Annotated Bibliography*, New York: Garland, 1984.

Gale Stokes (ed.), *From Stalinism to Pluralism: A Documentary History of Eastern Europe Since 1945*, Oxford: Oxford University Press, 2nd edn, 1996.

Gale Stokes, *Three Eras of Political Change in Eastern Europe*, Oxford: Oxford University Press, 1997.

Norman Stone, 'Dubrovnik: The Case for a War Crime Trial', *The Guardian*, 13 November 1991, 1.

Julius Strauss, 'Albanians Slaughtered in Macedonia', *The Daily Telegraph*, 15 August 2001, 2.

Bernard Stulli, *Židovi u Dubrovniku*, Zagreb: Jevrejska Općina Zagreba, 1989.

John Sturges dir. *Bad Day at Black Rock*, 1955.

Chuck Sudetić, 'Piles of Bones in Yugoslavia Point to Partisan Massacres', *New York Times*, 9 July 1990, p. A6.

Jon Swain, 'Days of Shame. Did the West cynically Sacrifice Thousands of Muslim Lives in Srebrenica?', *The Sunday Times*, Review Section 3, 19 May 1996, 1.

Anne Swardson and R. Jeffrey Smith, 'Hunger Adds to Kosovo's Perils', *Guardian Weekly*, 9 May 1999, 15.

'Tableau des Bouches du Cattaro suivi d'une Notice sur Montenegro', *Annales des Voyages*, vol. 4, X–XII Paris, 1808.

Marcus Tanner, *Croatia. A Nation Forged in War*, New Haven: Yale University Press, 1997.

Mikulas Teich and Roy Porter (eds), *The National Question in Europe in Historic Context*, Cambridge: Cambridge University Press, 1993.

Alfred Lord Tennyson, *Poetical Works*, London: Macmillan, 1926.

Jovan Teokarević, 'Neither War nor Peace: Serbia and Montenegro in the First Half of the 1990s', in David Dyker and Ivan Vejvoda (eds), *Yugoslavia and After. A Study in Fragmentation, Despair and Rebirth*, London: 1996, pp. 179–95.

Paul Theroux, *The Pillars of Hercules. A Grand Tour of the Mediterranean*, London: Hamish Hamilton, 1995.

Dorothy Q. Thomas and Regan E. Ralph, 'Rape in War: The Case of Bosnia', in Sabrina P. Ramet (ed.), *Gender Politics in the Western Balkans: Women and Society in Yugoslavia and the Yugoslav Successor States*, Pennsylvania: Penn State Press, 1999, pp. 203–18.

Robert Thomas, *Serbia under Milošević. Politics in the 1990s*, London: Hurst, 1999.

Mark Thompson, *A Paper House: The Ending of Yugoslavia* London: Hutchinson Radius, 1992.

Mark Thompson, *Forging War: The Media in Serbia, Croatia, Bosnia and Hercegovina*, Luton: University of Luton Press/Article 19. International Centre Against Censorship, 1999.

Maria Todorova, *Imagining the Balkans*, New York/Oxford: Oxford University Press, 1997.

Nikolai Tolstoy, 'The Klagenfurt Conspiracy: War Crimes and Diplomatic Secrets, *Encounter*, vol. 60, no. 5, 1983, 24–37.

Jozo Tomasevich, *War and Revolution in Yugoslavia*, Stanford: Stanford University Press, 1975.

Jozo Tomasević, *Četnici u drugom svjetskom ratu 1941–1945,* translated Nikica Petrak, Zagreb: Sveučilisna Nakalda Liber, 1979, p. 234.

Dinko Tomašić, 'Croatia in European Politics', *Journal of Central European Affairs*, vol. 2, 1942, 64–86.

Dinko Tomašić, *Personality and Culture in East European Politics*, New York: Stewart, 1948.

Ian Traynor, 'In the Cause of Croatia. Obituary of Gojko Sušak', *The Guardian*, 5 May 1998, 16.

Ian Traynor, 'Obituary of Franjo Tudjman', *The Guardian*, 13 December 1999, 18.

John D. Treadway, 'Of Shatter Belts and Powder Kegs: A Brief Survey of Yugoslav History', in Constantine P. Danopoulos and Kostas G. Messas (eds), *Crises in the Balkans. Views From the Participants*, Boulder, Colorado: Westview, 1997, 17–45.

Hugh Trevor Roper, 'Sir Thomas More and Utopia', in ibid., *Renaissance Essays*, London: Fontana, 1986, pp. 24–58.

Srdja Trifković, 'Rivalry between Germany and Italy in Croatia', *Historical Journal*, vol. 36, 1993, 537–59.

Stefan Troebst, 'IMRO + 100 = FYROM? The Politics of Macedonian Historiography', in James Pettifer (ed.), *The New Macedonian Question*, Basingstoke: Palgrave, 2001, 2nd edn, pp. 60–78.

Leon Trotsky, *The Balkan Wars 1912–1913*, New York: Monad Press, 1980.

Leon Trotsky, *My Life*, Harmondsworth: Penguin, 1980.

Peter Trudgill, 'Greece and European Turkey: From Religious to Linguistic Identity', in Stephen Barbour and Cathie Carmichael (eds), *Language and Nationalism in Europe*, Oxford: Oxford University Press, 2000, pp. 240–63.

Franjo Tudjman, *Bespuća povijesne zbiljnosti: Razprava o povijesti i filozofiji*, Zagreb: Hrvatska Sveučilisna Naklada, 5 edn, 1994.

Die Türkische Nachbarländer an der Südostgrenze Österreichs: Serbien, Bosnien, Türkisch-Kroatien, Herzegovina und Montenegro, Pest, Wien und Leipzig: Hartleben's Verlag-Expedn, 1854, pp. 57–8.

Victor Turner, *The Forest of Symbols: Aspects of Ndembu Ritual*, Ithaca: Cornell University Press, 1967.

Dubravka Ugrešić, *The Culture of Lies*, Pennsylvania: Penn State Press, 1998.

David Urquhart, *The Spirit of the East, Illustrated in a Journal of Travels Through Roumeli During an Eventful Period*, Philadelphia, 1839, vol. II.

Margaret Vandiver, 'Reclaiming Kozarac. Accompanying returning refugees', in Dzemal Sokolović and Florian Bieber (eds), *Reconstructing Multiethnic Societies. The Case of Bosnia-Herzegovina*, Aldershot: Ashgate, 2001.

Colonel L.C. Vialla de Sommières, *Voyage historique et politique au Montenegro*, Paris: Alexis Eymery, 1820, 2 vols.

Ed Vulliamy, *Seasons in Hell. Understanding Bosnia's War*, London: Simon and Schuster, 1994.

Immanuel Wallerstein, 'Fernand Braudel, Historian, "homme de la conjoncture"', *Radical History Review*, vol. 26, 1982, 105–19.

Stevan M. Weine, *When History is a Nightmare: Lives and Memories of Ethnic Cleansing in Bosnia-Herzegovina*, New Brunswick, New Jersey: Rutgers University Press, 1999.

Stevan M. Weine, 'Redefining Merhamet after a Historical Nightmare', in Joel M. Halpern and David A. Kideckel (eds), *Neighbors at War. Anthropological Perspectives on Yugoslav Ethnicity, Culture and History*. Pennsylvania: Penn State Press, 2000, pp. 401–12.

Rebecca West, *Black Lamb and Grey Falcon. A Journey Through Yugoslavia*, New York, 1941.

Mark Wheeler, 'One Nation or Many?', in Noll Scott and Derek Jones (eds), *Bloody Bosnia. A European Tragedy*, London: Broadcasting Support Services in association with Channel Four and *The Guardian*, 1994, pp. 16–21.

Hayden White, *Tropics of Discourse. Essays in Cultural Criticism*, Baltimore: Johns Hopkins University Press, 1985.

Larry Wolff, *Venice and the Slavs: the Discovery of Dalmatia in the Age of Enlightenment*, Stanford: Stanford University Press, 2001.

C.M. Woodhouse, *The Greek War of Independence: its Historical Setting*, London: Hutchinson, 1952.

Susan Woodward, *Balkan Tragedy. Chaos and Dissolution After the Cold War*, Washington: Brookings Institute, 1995.

Ivo Žanić, 'The Curse of King Zvonimir and Political Discourse in Embattled Croatia', *East European Politics and Societies*, vol. 9, no. 1, 1995, 90–122.

Ivo Žanić, 'The Most Croat', *War Report*, no. 28, November/December 1995, 41–2.

Ivo Žanić, *Prevarena povijest. Guslarska estrada, kult Hajduka i rat u Hrvatskoj i Bosni i Hercegovini 1990–1995. Godine*, Zagreb: Durieux, 1998.

Marko Živković, 'Violent Highlanders and Peaceful Lowlanders. Uses and Abuses of Ethno-Geography in the Balkans from Versailles to Dayton', *Replika*, special edn, 1997, 107–120.

Marko Živković, 'Too Much Character, too Little *Kultur*. Serbian Jeremiads 1994–95', *Balkanologie*, vol. 2, no. 2, 1998, 77–98.

Marko Živković, 'Inverted Perspective and Serbian Peasants: the Byzantine Revival in Serbia', at <http://www.ac.wwu.edu/~kritika/Anthro.html.> at 1 June 2001.

Slavoj Žižek, 'Eastern Europe's Republics of Gilead', *New Left Review*, vol. 30, no. 183, 1990, 50–62.

Slavoj Žižek, *NATO kao lijeva ruka Boga?/NATO as the Left Hand of God?* Ljubljana/Zagreb: Bastard Biblioteque, 1999.

Index

Lightning Source UK Ltd.
Milton Keynes UK
22 January 2010

148929UK00001B/93/P